Social Enterprises

Also by Benjamin Gidron

POLICY INITIATIVES TOWARDS THE THIRD SECTOR IN INTERNATIONAL PERSPECTIVE (*edited with M. Bar-Almog*)

THE THIRD SECTOR IN ISRAEL: Between Civil Society and the Welfare State (*edited with M. Bar and H. Katz*)

MOBILIZING FOR PEACE: Peace/Conflict Resolution Organizations in South Africa, Northern Ireland and Israel/Palestine (*edited with S. Katz and Y. Hasenfeld*)

SELF-HELP AND MUTUAL AID GROUPS: International and Multicultural Perspectives (*edited with F. Lavoie and T. Borkman*)

GOVERNMENT AND THE THIRD SECTOR: Emerging Relationships in Welfare States (*edited with R. Kramer and L. Salamon*)

Also by Yeheskel Hasenfeld

WE THE POOR PEOPLE (*with J. Handler*)

BLAME WELFARE, IGNORE POVERTY AND INEQUALITY (*with J. Handler*)

HUMAN SERVICE ORGANIZATIONS AS COMPLEX ORGANIZATIONS

Social Enterprises

An Organizational Perspective

Edited by

Benjamin Gidron
Israeli Social Enterprise Research Center,
Beit Berl Academic College, Israel

and

Yeheskel Hasenfeld
UCLA Luskin School of Public Affairs, USA

First published 2012 by
PALGRAVE MACMILLAN

Palgrave Macmillan in the UK is an imprint of Macmillan Publishers Limited,
registered in England, company number 785998, of Houndmills, Basingstoke,
Hampshire RG21 6XS.

Palgrave Macmillan in the US is a division of St Martin's Press LLC,
175 Fifth Avenue, New York, NY 10010.

Palgrave Macmillan is the global academic imprint of the above companies
and has companies and representatives throughout the world.

Palgrave® and Macmillan® are registered trademarks in the United States,
the United Kingdom, Europe and other countries

ISBN: 978–0–230–35879–9

This book is printed on paper suitable for recycling and made from fully
managed and sustained forest sources. Logging, pulping and manufacturing
processes are expected to conform to the environmental regulations of the
country of origin.

A catalogue record for this book is available from the British Library.

A catalog record for this book is available from the Library of Congress.

10 9 8 7 6 5 4 3 2 1
21 20 19 18 17 16 15 14 13 12

Printed and bound in the United States of America

Contents

Figures

Tables

Foreword

In recent years, social enterprises have received widespread attention as more effective alternatives to traditional public and nonprofit organizations in addressing social problems. In general, social enterprises are organizations which combine a market-orientation with a social mission. Within this broad organizing concept, a wide variety of organizations have been classified as social enterprises: nonprofit organizations reliant on earned income and fees; for-profit organizations with a social mission; hybrid organizational models that include for-profit and nonprofit components including nonprofits with for-profit subsidiaries; and new legal entities such as the community interest company (CIC) and the low profit limited liability company (L3C) which is a social mission organization that can obtain funds from investors.

Government and foundations have devoted extensive resources to support the start-up and growth of social enterprises. The Obama administration has supported numerous social enterprises through the Social Innovation Fund and many leading philanthropic funders including the Skoll World Forum and Roberts Enterprise Development Foundation (REDF), the Acumen Fund and the Omidyar Network place social enterprises at the center of their funding priorities and programs. Further, social enterprises have been promoted by national and international nonprofits committed to more entrepreneurial approaches to solving social problems including Community Wealth Ventures, Ashoka, Social Venture Partners and Venture Philanthropy Partners.

The growth of social enterprises reflects several very important trends in organized philanthropy and public policy. First, the venture philanthropy movement has brought business models from the for-profit sector to nonprofit organizations including greater attention to outcomes, using the discipline of the market to enhance performance and encouraging more entrepreneurial behavior by nonprofit leaders (Letts *et al.*, 1999; Morino, 2010). Many younger philanthropists from the high-tech world have been especially attracted to this venture philanthropy approach. Second, the growth of the nonprofit sector in the US and abroad creates more competition among nonprofits and substantial pressure of revenues, especially given the financial crisis. Consequently, social enterprises can be viewed as an adaptive response to a rapidly changing fiscal and political environment for nonprofits. Third, a broad rethinking of social policy has occurred throughout the world which has entailed, in part, a new emphasis on individual responsibility and workforce participation as evident in public policy toward low-income and disadvantaged individuals. Reflective of this trend, many social enterprises offer training, education and workforce development opportunities for the disadvantaged. A diverse set of social enterprises embodies this major shift in thinking: the Grameen Bank, a micro-credit organization that emphasizes small loans; Greyston Bakery, a for-profit bakery training the disadvantaged and owned by Greyston foundation; and Farestart, a nonprofit in Seattle which operates a restaurant, staffed by the disadvantaged who receive training in the restaurant business. The emphasis on work by the disadvantaged is not entirely new: the Salvation Army and Goodwill Industries have operated thrift stores and encouraged self-reliance and work participation since their founding in the 19th century. Nonetheless, the current support for workforce participation by the disadvantaged represents a marked change from social policies of earlier eras which placed greater emphasis on income support. Similarly, micro-credit organizations represent, at least in part, an effort to overcome the problems of more traditional development strategies to address poverty in the developing world.

This restructuring of social policy has also been profoundly influenced by the advent of the New Public Management (NPM) as a strategy to improve the performance of government. A key component of NPM is an emphasis on a more market-oriented, entrepreneurial orientation by government as a strategy to increase efficiency and effectiveness. Social enterprises with their market orientation and entrepreneurial ethos fit very well with NPM as indicated by the growth of social enterprises even in countries with long-standing policies of public provision and broad-based funding of social programs.

A fourth contributing factor to the growth of social enterprises is the corporate social responsibility movement which promotes corporate–nonprofit partnerships and more philanthropic giving and behavior by corporations. Ben and Jerry's, with its social mission, extensive philanthropic giving and local partnerships with youth-oriented nonprofits, is a good example. Finally, broad interest and support for community service and voluntarism throughout the world has sparked the creation of many new social enterprises offering innovative services using a more entrepreneurial program model.

Given the diversity of social enterprises, scholars have offered important typologies to help with categorization and promote further research (Dees, 1998; Alter, 2007). The growth and development of many different types of social enterprises have also been profiled extensively (Bornstein, 2007; Crutchfield and Grant, 2008) and leading national and international organizations such as Ashoka, REDF, the Skoll World Forum and Community Wealth Ventures have publicized and supported social entrepreneurs throughout the world. Yet the current interest in social enterprises also highlights the gap between existing scholarship on nonprofit organizations and the research on social enterprise. Pioneering research on nonprofit organizations was undertaken in the 1970s and 1980s by several scholars including Weisbrod (1977), Hansmann (1980), James (1983) and Salamon (1987). Subsequently, scholars of the nonprofit sector conducted research on a wide variety of topics including governance, giving and volunteering issues, advocacy and government–nonprofit sector relationships. Sustained attention by social scientists specializing in the nonprofit sector to social enterprises, social entrepreneurship and social innovation has generally been lacking though with some notable exceptions (see, for example, Light, 2007). Consequently, this book, *Social Enterprises: An Organizational Perspective*, edited by Benjamin Gidron and Yeheskel Hasenfeld, is especially welcome for the field of nonprofit sector research as well as policymakers and practitioners concerned with program effectiveness and the wise use of public and private resources.

The excellent chapters offer important and valuable insights on social enterprises and, collectively, the book contains several key themes regarding research, theory and practice as it pertains to social enterprises. Many authors apply conceptual frameworks from social science disciplines to the study of social enterprises. Examples in the book include the application of organizational ecology theory to understand the circumstances under which social enterprises will be effective; the use of institutional theory to understand the competing institutional logics of social services and markets within the context of workforce integration social enterprises (WISEs) such as Goodwill Industries; and the use of institutional theory to understand differences in the prevalence and organization of social enterprises in different countries. A more general point that arises from these chapters is the enduring value of a disciplinary lens for understanding nonprofit organizations and social enterprises.

The research presented in the book also highlights the knotty problems of governance and accountability posed by the increasing role of social enterprises. Traditional nonprofit organizations offer accountability rooted in a volunteer board of directors and philanthropic donors. Yet social enterprises with their mixed organizational forms also have a market logic. The resulting complexity is captured in the reference to the "double-bottom line" that social enterprises face: an accountability to their social mission as well as the market. Several of the chapters directly address the tension between the market and social mission logics of social enterprises and the implications of this tension for governance and practice. For instance, one chapter on fair trade coffee businesses provides a very insightful analysis of the outcomes of this tension for fair trade businesses as well as a useful matrix that researchers and practitioners can apply to other organizations and contexts. In another chapter on a nonprofit technology organization, the author examines the challenges of competing in a complicated market for technology assistance services while sustaining a commitment to their social mission. This accountability is especially complicated in the new hybrid organizations such as CICs; these entities are non-traditional organizations with innovative governance structures that require new monitoring systems by government and a major shift in the role of the board. Conventional categories do not fit these organizations, nor do existing board governance models. Overall, the book provides a very solid research base to develop new governance models to fit with the varied types of social enterprises. As the chapters detail, innovative structures can be an advantage in the current fiscal and political environment. L3Cs and CICs have structures that can help to attract capital that might otherwise go to for-profit entities (or go unspent entirely by private funders).

The chapters in the book also underscore an overlooked aspect of many social enterprises: their complex interconnections with government. Government regulation and monitoring are central to the creation and emergence of these CICs and other new social enterprises. WISEs typically receive substantial government grants and contracts; indeed some WISEs are almost entirely dependent upon government funds. And, microcredit organizations throughout the world have benefited from direct and indirect public subsidies. Despite the reliance on government funding and/or policy among many social enterprises, the support for social enterprises is rooted in part on the idea that these organizations are market-oriented rather than public (or publicly funded) organizations – a point discussed in detail in different chapters of the book. More generally, the book highlights the interaction between the discourse on social enterprise and social entrepreneurship and the policies and philanthropic practices that have powerfully shaped the development of social enterprises.

The discourse on social enterprise is also quite different across countries. Like the US, Europe has experienced significant growth in social enterprises. Yet, European social enterprises tend to be based in a social cooperative model and tend to be narrowly targeted on work integration efforts. The European approach also emphasizes the participatory aspect of social enterprises – a characteristic that receives relatively little attention in the US.

Importantly, the book is a major advance in theorizing about the sector. One persistent challenge for research on social enterprise has been the lack of a set of testable propositions based upon a theory of social enterprise. This book offers researchers a conceptual approach that provides a base to investigate key dimensions of social enterprises including their effectiveness and sustainability. More than ever, social enterprises face an uncertain, challenging future. Many social enterprises are built upon a logic of market revenues and competition; yet, the relative scarcity of public and private resources and a weak economy raise questions on the capacity of many social enterprises to develop a sustainable business model and revenue stream. Moreover, political and philanthropic support for social enterprises rests on the linkage between entrepreneurship, market-oriented behavior and program innovation. These interconnections are supposed to lead to more effective and efficient solutions to social problems. Yet, these central assumptions of the social enterprise model have not been rigorously examined by social scientists, as the authors in the book observe.

This book with its rich and detailed research on social enterprises including from a comparative perspective offers scholars a compelling intellectual roadmap for future research and investigation. It is a particularly propitious moment to undertake this research, given the challenging fiscal and organizational environment facing social enterprises.

Steven Rathgeb Smith
American University and University of Washington

References

Alter, Kim Sutra. 2007. *Social Enterprise Typology.* www.4lenses.org/setypology/print

Bornstein, David. 2007. *How to Change the World: Social Entrepreneurs and the Power of New Ideas.* New York: Oxford University Press.

Crutchfield, Leslie R. and Heather McLeod Grant. 2008. *Forces for Good: The Six Practices of High-Impact Nonprofits.* San Francisco: Jossey-Bass.

Dees, J. Gregory. 1998. "Enterprising Nonprofits". *Harvard Business Review* January–February: 55–67.

Hansmann, Henry B. 1980. "The Role of Nonprofit Enterprise". *Yale Law Review* 89: 835–98.

James, Estelle. 1983. "How Nonprofits Grow: A Model". *Journal of Policy Analysis and Management* 2(3): 350–65.

Letts, Christine W., William P. Ryan and Allen Grossman. 1999. *High Performance Nonprofit Organizations: Managing Upstream for Greater Impact.* New York: John Wiley.

Light, Paul C. 2007. *The Search for Social Entrepreneurship.* Washington, DC: Brookings.

Morino, Mario. 2010. *Leap of Reason: Managing to Outcomes in an Era of Scarcity.* Washington, DC: Venture Philanthropy Partners.

Salamon, Lester M. 1987. "Partners in Public Service: The Scope and Theory of Government-Nonprofit Relations". In Walter W. Powell (ed.), *The Nonprofit Sector: A Research Handbook.* New Haven, CT: Yale University Press, pp. 99–117.

Weisbrod, Burton. 1978. *The Voluntary Sector: An Economic Analysis.* Lexington, MA: D. C. Heath.

Acknowledgments

The editors acknowledge the use of the following materials that have previously appeared in other publications and for which permission has been obtained. Chapter 4 was previously accepted for publication by *Nonprofit and Voluntary Sector Quarterly*. The Postscript was previously published by *Entrepreneurship Theory and Practice*, 34(4): 611–33 (2010). The lists on pp. 97–98 are based on figure 3 in N. Bosma and J. Levie, *Entrepreneurship Monitor 2009 Global Report*, Global Entrepreneurship Monitor (2010), p. 15; retrieved from www.gemconsortium.org/about.aspx?page=pub_gem_global_reports. Table 4.1 is an adaptation based on table 1 in J. Mahoney, "Path Dependence in Historical Sociology", *Theory and Society* 29(4), 507–48 (2000), p. 517. Table 4.2 is an adaptation based on table 2 in X. Sala-i-Martin, J. Blanke, M. Hanouz, T. Geiger and I. Mia, "The Global Competitiveness Index 2010–2011: Looking beyond the Global Economic Crisis". In K. Schwab (ed.), *The Global Competitiveness Report 2010–2011*, Geneva: World Economic Forum (2010), p. 10, retrieved from http://www.weforum.org/reports/global-competitiveness-report-2010-2011-0.

The editors, contributors and publishers have made every effort to contact all copyright-holders, but if any have been overlooked the publishers will be pleased to make the necessary arrangements at the first opportunity.

Contributors

Inbal Abbou is a PhD candidate at the Guilford Glazer School of Business Management at Ben Gurion University, Israel. Her dissertation deals with patterns of corporate social responsibility among different business enterprises in Israel. She also fills the role of Chief Researcher at the Israeli Social Enterprise Research Center at the Beit Berl Academic College. She is interested in the interface between the business sector and the third sector, social enterprises and mixed markets.

Sondra N. Barringer is a PhD candidate in the Department of Sociology at the University of Arizona. Her dissertation research examines the financial behaviors of higher education organizations, and how they are shaped by multifaceted competition and the influence of key stakeholder groups. Her other research interests include the patterns of resource allocation in organizations, the privatization of public colleges and universities, the role of wealth and endowments in higher education and the extent of interlocking directorates between universities and corporations.

Curtis Child is an assistant professor in the Department of Sociology at Brigham Young University. He received his PhD in Sociology at Indiana University in 2011, where he also earned a Master of Public Affairs degree. Using the fair trade and socially responsible investing industries as study sites, his recent research focuses on how organizations manage the challenge of being simultaneously profit- and mission-oriented. Other research looks at why entrepreneurs decide to establish nonprofit or for-profit organizations, historical trends in commercial revenue generation among nonprofit organizations and the interface between social movements and corporations.

Kate Cooney is Lecturer at the Yale University School of Management where she teaches courses on Nonprofit Management and Social Enterprise. Her research and scholarship focus on the sustainability of social enterprise in the nonprofit sector, management of mixed goal organizations that integrate business activities with social aims and the institutional and economic determinants of organizational behavior. Her scholarly articles have been published in *Administration & Society*, *Voluntas*, *Social Service Review*, *Nonprofit and Voluntary Sector Quarterly*, *Journal of Poverty* and the *Journal of Social Policy*, among other peer-reviewed journals.

Jacques Defourny is Full Professor of Economics at HEC Management School at the University of Liège, Belgium, where he also acts as a director of the Centre for Social Economy (www.ces.ulg.ac.be). He was a founding coordinator (1996–2001) and the first president (2002–10) of the EMES European Research Network, which gathers the research of 12 university research centers and individual scholars working on social enterprise and the third sector across Europe (www.emes.net). His work focuses on the emergence of social enterprise in various parts of the world and on conceptual and quantitative analyses of the third sector in developed and developing countries. In addition to numerous articles in academic journals, he has authored or edited 12 books, including *The Third Sector: Co-operative, Mutual and Non-profit Organizations* (1992, also published in Spanish and Japanese), *Tackling Social Exclusion in Europe: The Role of the Social Economy* (2001, also published in French and Spanish), *The Emergence of Social Enterprise* (2001 and 2004, also published in Italian, Japanese and Korean) and a special issue of the *Social Enterprise Journal*, "Social Enterprise in Eastern Asia" (vol. 7, no 1, 2011).

Joseph Galaskiewicz is Professor of Sociology and has a courtesy appointment in the School of Government and Public Policy at the University of Arizona. He has written several articles and books, including *The Social Organization of an Urban Grants Economy* (1985) and (with Wolfgang Bielefeld) *Nonprofits in an Age of Uncertainty* (1998). He is a senior editor of *Management and Organization Review*, past president of the Association for Research on Nonprofit Organizations and Voluntary Action and a past chair of the OOW Section of the ASA. With funding from NSF he is currently studying the distribution of organizational resources in the Phoenix metropolitan area and its consequences for children's health and well-being.

Eve Garrow is an assistant professor at the University of Michigan School of Social Work. Her research seeks to understand how human service organizations respond to, manage and influence diverse and contradictory demands from their environments, and the consequences for policy implementation, human service delivery and client outcomes. Her work examines how characteristics of nonprofit human service organizations determine their receipt of government funding, how nonprofit social enterprises balance mission and market, and the factors that enable nonprofit advocacy groups to advocate and mobilize on behalf of social rights.

Benjamin Gidron is the founding director of the Israeli Social Enterprise Research Center (ISERC) at the Beit Berl Academic College. He has founded and directed the Israeli Center for Third-Sector Research (ICTR) at Ben Gurion University (BGU) of the Negev in Beer-Sheva, Israel for 12 years (1997–2009). He has been researching issues pertaining to the Third Sector and related topics for the past 25 years. He has also founded and directed the Graduate Nonprofit Organization Management Program in the Glazer Faculty of Management at BGU, where he was appointed. His book *Mobilizing for Peace: Conflict Resolution in South Africa, Northern Ireland and*

Israel/Palestine (with S. Katz and Y. Hasenfeld, 2002) was the recipient of the Virginia A Hodgkinson first Prize for the Best Research Publication in Nonprofit Organizations and Philanthropy in 2003. He was the founding president of the International Society for Third-Sector Research (ISTR) from 1992 to 1996.

Yeheskel Hasenfeld is Distinguished Professor of Social Welfare in the Luskin School of Public Affairs at the University of California, Los Angeles. He has published extensively on the attributes of human-service organizations and, with Joel Handler, on poverty and welfare reform. He is studying the role of nonprofit organizations, including social enterprises, in the provision of social services.

Janelle A. Kerlin is an assistant professor in the Department of Public Management and Policy at Georgia State University. She conducts research on politics and policy related to nonprofit development and operation from domestic and international perspectives. Her areas of interest include nonprofit commercial revenue trends, comparative social enterprise and international nonprofit organizations. She has published articles in the *Nonprofit and Voluntary Sector Quarterly, Voluntas, Nonprofit Management and Leadership* and the *American Review of Public Administration*. She has also authored several book chapters on social enterprise and international nonprofits. She is the author of *Social Service Reform in the Postcommunist State: Decentralization in Poland* (2005) and editor of *Social Enterprise: A Global Comparison* (2009). She holds a Master's in Social Work from Columbia University and a PhD in Political Science from the Maxwell School at Syracuse University.

Paul-Brian McInerney is an assistant professor in the Department of Sociology at the University of Illinois at Chicago. He graduated in 2006 with a PhD in Sociology from Columbia University. His research areas include economic and organizational sociology, social movements and social studies of technology. McInerney's research examines how agency and collective action shape organizational fields, markets and ultimately institutions. He has published articles and book chapters about the politics of open source software, institutional entrepreneurship, social enterprise and social movement mobilization. He has recently completed a book-length manuscript about how social movements shape markets. He is conducting research on values and valuation in farmers' markets throughout Chicago.

Alex Nicholls is the first tenured lecturer in Social Entrepreneurship appointed at the University of Oxford and was the first staff member of the Skoll Centre for Social Entrepreneurship in 2004. His research interests range across several key areas within social entrepreneurship and social innovation, including the nexus of relationships between accounting, accountability and governance, public and social policy contexts, social investment and Fair Trade. To date Nicholls has published more than 40 papers, chapters and articles and five books. Most appear in a wide range of peer-reviewed journals and books, including four sole-authored papers in the *Financial Times* top 30 journals (with another under review). His 2009 paper on social investment won the Best Paper Award (Entrepreneurship) at the British Academy of Management. In 2010, he edited a special edition of *Entrepreneurship, Theory and Practice* on social entrepreneurship – the first time a top-tier management journal has recognized the topic in this way. He is the general editor of the *Skoll Working Papers* series and editor of the *Journal of Social Entrepreneurship*. Nicholls is also the co-editor of *Fair Trade: Market Driven Ethical Consumption* (with Charlotte Opal, 2005) and the editor of a collection of key papers on social entrepreneurship: *Social Entrepreneurship: New Models of Sustainable Social Change* (2006) and *Social Entrepreneurship: New Models of Sustainable Social Change* (paperback edn with new preface, 2008). Both represent the best selling and most cited academic books on their subjects globally. In 2011, Nicholls published a co-edited volume on social innovation. In 2012, he will publish two co-edited volumes on social investment and a monograph on the politics of social entrepreneurship: *Social Investment* (with R. Patton and J. Emerson), *Measuring Social Impact* (with A. Somers and J. Nicholls) and *The Politics of Social Entrepreneurship*. He has held lectureships at a wide variety of academic institutions including the University of Toronto, Leeds Metropolitan University, the University of Surrey, Aston Business School and the University of Oxford. He has been a fellow of the Academy of Marketing Science and a member of the Institute of Learning and Teaching. Nicholls also sat on the regional social enterprise expert group for the south-east of England and is a member of the Advisory Group for the ESRC Social Enterprise Capacity Building Cluster. He is an honorary fellow at the Third Sector Research Centre at the University of Birmingham. Prior to returning to academic life, Nicholls held senior management positions at the John Lewis Partnership, the largest mutual retailer in Europe. He also acts as a non-executive director for a major fair trade company.

Marthe Nyssens is a full professor in the Department of Economics at the Catholic University of Louvain, Belgium, where she is the coordinator of a research team at the Centre for Interdisciplinary Research on Work–State–Society. Her research involves conceptual approaches to the third sector, in developed and developing countries, and links between third sector organizations and public policy. She teaches nonprofit organizations, social policies and development theories. She is a founding member of the EMES (www.emes.net), the European Research Network of established university research centers and individual researchers whose goal is to gradually build up a European corpus of theoretical and empirical knowledge, pluralistic in disciplines and methodology, around third sector issues. She conducts various research and studies for national, regional and European government units. She was the coordinator of the project 'The Socio-Economic Performance of Social Enterprises in the Field of Integration by Work' in the fifth program of research.

Steven Rathgeb Smith is currently the Nancy Bell Evans Professor of Public Affairs at the Evans School of Public Affairs at the University of Washington. He is a visiting professor for public affairs at the American University for the spring semester 2012. Between 2009 and 2011, he was the Waldemar A. Nielsen Chair in Philanthropy at Georgetown University. Smith was the editor from 1998 to 2004 of *Nonprofit and Voluntary Sector Quarterly*, the journal of the Association for Research on Nonprofit Organizations and Voluntary Action (ARNOVA). He was also president of ARNOVA from 2006 to 2008. He recently co-edited the book, *Governance and Regulation in the Third Sector: International Perspectives* (with Susan Phillips, 2010). His research projects include an investigation of advocacy by nonprofit organizations and a comparative analysis of nonprofit social services in Europe and the US. He has a PhD in Political Science from MIT.

Dennis R. Young is the Bernard B. and Eugenia A. Ramsey Professor of Private Enterprise in the Andrew Young School of Policy Studies at Georgia State University where he directs the school's Nonprofit Studies Program. He is the founding editor of the journal *Nonprofit Management and Leadership* and the new electronic journal *Nonprofit Policy Forum*, and is past president of the Association for Research on Nonprofit Organizations and Voluntary Action. He is the author of many scholarly articles and books, including *Financing Nonprofits* (2007) and the *Handbook of Research on Nonprofit Economics and Management* (with Bruce Seaman, 2010). Young received ARNOVA's 2004 Award for Distinguished Achievement and Leadership in Nonprofit and Voluntary Action Research and an honorary doctorate from the University of Liège in Belgium in 2010.

Abbreviations

ACD	Americans for Community Development
ARNOVA	Association for Research on Nonprofit Organizations and Voluntary Action
CAN	Community Action Network
CIC	community interest company
CIC ASS	CIC Association
GCR	Global Competitiveness Report
GEM	Global Entrepreneurship Monitor
EMES	Emergence des Entreprises Sociales en Europe [Social Enterprise in Europe]
IRS	Internal Revenue Service
L3C	low profit limited liability company
LINC	Low Income Networking and Communications
NPM	New Public Management
NPO	nonprofit organization
NTAPs	Nonprofit Technology Assistance Providers
PRI	program related investment
REDF	Roberts Enterprise Development Foundations
SEC	Social Enterprise Coalition
SEI	Social Enterprise Initiative
SPB	social purpose business
TSC	Technology Service Corps
WEF	World Economic Forum
WISEs	workforce integration social enterprises

Introduction

Benjamin Gidron and Yeheskel Hasenfeld

An important development of the past decade, especially since the economic crisis of 2008, has been the increased interest and proliferation of variegated forms of social enterprises. While social enterprises have a long history they have gained currency in the changing political and economic environment. Very broadly, social enterprises are organizations that are driven by a social mission and apply market-based strategies to achieve a social (or environmental) purpose. These vary from organizations or enterprises that find new creative ways to integrate marginalized populations (the homeless, ex-convicts, persons with handicaps, etc.) into society by creating suitable employment opportunities for them to others that focus on environmental issues, such as cooperatives that invest in wind turbines in order to protect the environment and save on energy cost. The spread of social enterprises has been global, and it received a big boost after Muhammad Yunus won the Nobel Peace Prize in 2006 for his innovative work on micro-financing. The idea of combining social (or environmental) purposes with a business orientation and creating an organization to carry out a social mission coupled with successful business ventures is intriguing and attractive to social entrepreneurs, investors, researchers and policymakers alike. Indeed, in several countries, such as the UK, the US, Belgium, Finland and Italy there are policy initiatives to promote such organizations (see Chapter 9).

The social enterprise concept undoubtedly resonates well with stakeholders interested in bridging the two fields, but at the same time it raises questions and concerns on its applicability and the specific conditions under which it can and should be applied. To the clients of welfare and marginalized populations it brings the hope of being able to find a 'real' place of employment, which puts demands on its workers but also treats them as equals, pays them a fair salary, provides them with opportunities for promotion and advancement on the job, and creates an environment where social capital is developed. Yet, it also raises the risk that such clients might become commodified and that their distinct social needs will be ignored (see Chapter 5). For business entrepreneurs it provides a new platform on which they can be

1

active as social investors, using their skills and knowledge of markets and business processes in the promotion of solutions to social or environmental problems, which, to an extent, can replace their philanthropic portfolio. At the same time, there are concerns that they might exploit the new form for narrow and hidden business interests. For the public policymakers they provide a new source of funding social programs so that they rely less on public sector or philanthropy, though it also raises difficult questions about their survivability and legitimacy (see Chapter 2). Policymakers struggle to define 'social enterprises' and how to regulate them so they do not abuse their status. Professionals who seek a balance between the social mission of the enterprise and its business ventures face a major dilemma. Is a business framework (as opposed to a social mission framework), which stresses competition and demands market-based performance standards, actually helpful for the social mission? Or is it potentially harmful, such that a less market oriented framework would be more fitting? If it is helpful, then which populations can benefit most from it and under what conditions? For example, there are major debates on the most appropriate ways to integrate poor and vulnerable populations in the labor market through such policies as labor activation currently in vogue in Europe (Eichhorst *et al.*, 2008). Exemplifying labor activation policies, work integration social enterprises (WISEs) have a mission of assisting persons unconnected to the labor market to gain work experience and training. They do so through a combination of social and employment-related services with actual work experience in a business enterprise (Nyssens *et al.*, 2006). Yet, WISEs have come under criticism that they contribute to the erosion of social rights by making them contingent on participation as workers in the business enterprise (Handler, 2005).

Despite the proliferation of studies on social enterprises, a critical perspective that examines these and other issues is generally lacking. Much of the literature tends to be normative and descriptive (for a review see Chapters 1 and 3). We propose that in order to advance theory and research on social enterprises, we need to study them from an organizational perspective. Recognizing that they are hybrid forms of organizations which combine logics, practices and structures from competing fields, an organizational approach to understand them is essential if we are to study some of the following questions. Does the concept of 'social enterprise' present a new organizational form? What are the forces that give rise to a variety of such organizations? How do they resolve the inherent contradictions in their operations? How do they survive and attain sustainability? How do they avoid mission drift? What impact do they have on those they claim to serve? To answer these and related questions, we need to theorize and do research about them that is anchored in an organizational perspective. That is, the unit of analysis is the organization itself and the organizational fields within which it is located. Such a perspective looks at environmental conditions and forces that give rise to social enterprises and shape their missions. It focuses on the different organizational fields in which such organizations situate themselves and how they negotiate their different logics. It problematizes the ways such organizations attain legitimacy and the dynamics by which they reconcile and manage competing logics. It explores the power relations among stakeholders and how these affect the governance of the organization. It pays attention to the internal processes within the organization and how they shape its daily practices. It looks at the discrepancies between what the organizations claim to be doing and what their actual practices are. The purpose of this volume is to lay the foundations and contribute to the study of social enterprises as organizations.

We begin this chapter by recognizing that a key characteristic of social enterprises is their hybridity. By this we mean that the various forms they take may combine features from public, nonprofit and for-profit organizations. While the particular mixture may vary, what is distinctive about these organizations is the inclusion in their operations of a business logic coupled with either a social service logic or a public service logic. These logics are expressed in 'material practices, assumptions values, beliefs and rules by which individuals produce and reproduce their material subsistence, organize time and space, and provide meaning to their social reality' (Thornton and Ocassio 2008, 101). Ideally, the business logic is harnessed to promote the social mission of the organization. Consequently, social enterprises struggle with ways to balance between these competing logics. These struggles, the solutions that emerge and their consequences on the operation and services are the central themes of this book. These themes are addressed through the lenses of three major organizational theories that frame much of the theory and research on the organizational dilemmas, attributes, governance and processes of social enterprises – population ecology, institutional logics and political economy.

Population ecology looks at social enterprises as hybrid forms that evolve from the dynamic relations between multiple populations within a community ecology. According to Minkoff (2002, 382) a community ecology perspective 'emphasizes the interdependence and co-evolution of organizational populations. An organizational community is composed of multiple populations that are at once distinctive with respect to their dominant features and interdependent with respect to resource flows'. A population is defined as all organizations that have a unitary character, which means that they (a) share a common dependence on the material and social environment; (b) have a similar structure; and (c) their structure and other characteristics are quite stable over time (Hannan and Freeman, 1989). In the case of hybrid organizations, they are formed in response to developments and changes in the populations from which they draw their form. Therefore, 'they must negotiate a niche that blends population boundaries, finding ways to articulate a multidimensional identity and clarify what are the form's boundaries and sources of accountability' (Minkoff, 2002, 383). As a blended population there is a need to delineate the boundaries of the community ecology that gives rise to its form (Ruef, 2000). In other words, the emergence of specific hybrid forms can be understood only when the community ecology and its co-evolving populations are identified. For example, understanding the emergence of WISEs requires exploring the dynamic relations between the population of the business organizations and social services from which WISEs arise. In particular, economic and political developments and changes in the respective fields will inevitably influence the birth, survival and mortality of the hybrid form.

What may explain the founding of social enterprises? An ecological perspective asks us to examine local political, social and economic conditions that affect the community ecology which gives rise to different forms of social enterprises. It explores the effects of such factors as the crisis in philanthropic giving in prompting search for new sources of revenues like business enterprises. It explores the challenges to the legitimacy of financial institutions and their search for new sources of moral support through social enterprises. It pays attention to the incentives that the state generates through the creation of new legal entities such as the Community Interest Company (CIC) in the UK and the Low Profit Limited Liability Company (L3C) in the US. As noted by Cooney (Chapter 9), these new legal entities are set up to provide an incentive structure to blend business with social purpose. In general, social enterprises are more like to arise and survive when they have institutional linkages to government agencies that provide them with both legitimacy and resources (Baum and Oliver, 1991).

The ecological perspective pays particular attention to the role of entrepreneurs and their ability to exploit opportunities in the environment and mobilize resources to found new organizational forms such as social enterprises (Aldrich, 2006). Entrepreneurs bring variations among forms of social enterprises, experimenting with different hybrid combinations. The niche in which they are located will select those forms that are more likely to survive because they fit the resources available in the niche, they garner greater legitimation, they respond more effectively to consumers of their services, and they are able to stand up to the competition in the niche.

The ecological perspective is useful to the study of organizational failure or disbanding of social enterprises. It recognizes that the field of social enterprises is shaped not only by rates of founding but also by rates of failure. The theory proposes that as the rate of founding increases, signaling success of such an organizational form, other entrepreneurs are attracted to the field and increase the rate of founding. However, over time, the density of social enterprises increases. At some critical point the carrying capacity of the environment can no longer support higher density leading to a greater rate of failure (Ruef, 2000; Hannan, 2005). A case in point is micro-financing which has seen a rapid entry of new enterprises, leading to market saturation, cut throat and beggar-thy-neighbor hyper-competition, and consequently a high rate of failure (Chowdhury, 2011).

The ecological perspective is also enriched by the institutional logics framework (Thornton and Ocassio, 2008). The emergence of social enterprises is often coupled with the density of existing organizational forms in the community ecology from which the enterprises borrow rules and practices (Ruef, 2000). For example, in a community ecology with high densities of corporations and foundations the so called 'hero entrepreneurs' are more likely to flourish (see the Postscript). Similarly, as noted above, social enterprises are more like to arise when government regulations, initiatives and incentives encourage their formation. In the same vein, when the enterprise can develop an identity that appeals to a particular audience (e.g. government, donors, investors) that will grant it legitimacy and resources, it is more likely to survive (Hsu and Hannan, 2005).

From an institutional perspective, social enterprises arise out of the intersection of at least two competing logics. By combining social goals with a business orientation, both critical for their mission and survival, they attempt to bridge between two kinds of logics that are not often incorporated into the same organizational form. The business logic, with its focus on competition and private ownership, is generally not perceived as a fitting context to deal with social issues or problems. These are traditionally dealt with by a service logic that emphasizes a charitable, empathetic orientation. Putting these two orientations together calls for creative organizational solutions, especially if these organizations are to be stable and sustainable. Indeed, entrepreneurs that form social enterprises tend to exploit institutional contradictions in this heterogeneous and contested environment to further their interests. They do so by arranging and rearranging the discursive building blocks of institutional life to create new meanings (Friedland and Alford, 1991; Hardy and Maguire, 2008). If their organization becomes successful they actually reshape the cultural field to endorse and legitimize the new organizational form.

It is important to emphasize that the ability of entrepreneurs to exploit the institutional environment is made possible when broader cultural schemas from which they can borrow become available. In particular, the rise of neoliberal welfare regimes encourages the formation of social enterprises because they resonate well with the value assumptions of such regimes. According to Harvey (2005, 2) 'neoliberalism is in the first instance a theory of political economic practices that proposes that human well-being can best be advanced by liberating individual entrepreneurial freedom and skills within an institutional framework characterized by strong private property rights, free markets, and free trade'. Its moral underpinnings are individual liberty, the virtue of competition, individual responsibility and work ethic. Second, the neoliberal welfare regime is characterized by devolution and privatization and the celebration of business management of public and nonprofit organizations. As noted by Jurik (2004), proponents of neoliberalism argue that privatizing government services will save money and improve quality of services. Social enterprises epitomize these neoliberal assumptions (Cook *et al.*, 2003; Eikenberry, 2009; Kinderman, 2012). They celebrate market solutions to social problems, they shift state responsibilities to the private sector and they make social rights contingent on the successful market performance of the social enterprises. It is within this historical and political context that we need to situate social enterprises in order to understand their social locations and functions.

The institutional logics perspective addresses one of the most profound issues facing social enterprises, namely, how to balance between competing logics of social mission and business enterprise. The social mission logic is constituted by moral assumptions about the construction of social problems, desired solutions and the practices needed to attain them. The organizational field within which a social mission logic is dominant consists of other organizations and stakeholders that share the definition of the problem that coalesce around a set of desired solutions and the practices to respond to them. In contrast, the business logic is constituted by rules and practices that are dominant in the market place. Its organizational field is composed of producers and consumers that engage in exchange relations driven by cost and profit calculations. Mobilizing and maintaining legitimacy under competing logics becomes a central issue for the social enterprise. As noted by Kraatz and Block (2008, 249) 'when an organization is situated in a pluralistic context, its internal and external constituencies are likely recognize its capacity to abruptly change direction and reprioritize its identities and values'. Related to this is the fact that such organizations face the problem of governance – how to give voice to competing stakeholders – within the organization. Kraatz and Block propose four ways in which organizations such as social enterprises can cope with competing logics. First, in the political struggle they may drift toward the business logic justifying it as critical to the survival of the organization. The social mission becomes co-opted and subservient to the demands of the business enterprise (see Chapter 5). A second strategy is to compartmentalize the two logics in fairly autonomous organizational units. Institutional theory refers to it as loose coupling (Orton and Weick, 1990). The difficulty with such a strategy is that major failures in either organizational unit inevitably affect the other. Third, the organization may attempt to develop a governance structure that reinforces the mutuality of interests between the two units and foster cooperation between them. Still, such governance cannot mask the underlying tensions between the two units which may erupt at times of crisis for each unit. Finally, the organization may forge a new identity that comes to embrace both logics in a novel way which gains legitimacy in the institutional environment. An example might be Goodwill industries, which is broadly recognized as fulfilling a social mission of providing employment opportunities for persons with disabilities in a sheltered work setting, while successfully operating retail stores that provide the organization with most of its revenues.

Related to this, institutional theory also pays attention to the micro-processes by which social entrepreneurs attempt to mobilize legitimacy. Recognizing that the formation of many social enterprises is driven by entre-preneurship, there is a need to understand how social entrepreneurs can champion new practices in an organization field that is generally subject to regulative, normative and cognitive isomorphic pressures. Several studies have shown that entrepreneurs located in power positions in the field can use their position in their struggle to mobilize resources (Hardy and Maguire, 2008). Nicholls (in the Postscript) points to what he terms 'para-digm-building actors' such as government, foundations, fellowship organi-zations and network builders. In many instances such actors are embedded in multiple fields, as is the case for social enterprises, and can draw ideas, practices, legitimacy and resources through their boundary bridging posi-tions (Maguire *et al.*, 2004). Social entrepreneurs face not only the challenge of mobilizing resources, but they must struggle to gain currency of their new ideas and rationale or what is termed 'legitimating accounts' (Creed *et al.*, 2002). Nicholls refers to various discourses that social entrepreneurs use to enhance their legitimacy.

A political economy perspective brings the issue of power and how it is mobilized and exercised to the forefront in the analysis of social enter-prises. In particular, it addresses the issue of governance. Given the fact that social enterprises must respond to multiple and conflicting stakeholders, a political economy perspective would propose that the emerging govern-ance will be a reflection of the power relations among the various stake-holders. Recognizing that the social enterprise depends on its environment for resources and legitimacy, it must situate itself and interact with various stakeholders and interest groups that control needed resources. These stake-holders make their commitment of resources and legitimacy contingent on the ability of the social enterprise to incorporate their interests and values in its mission, structure and practices (Pfeffer and Salancik, 1978; Cress and Snow, 1996). From a resource dependency perspective, the greater the dependence of the organization on resources controlled by a stakeholder, the greater the influence of the stakeholder on the organization. Therefore, the governance of the social enterprise will reflect the power dynamics and constellations among the stakeholders on whom the enterprise depends. It further implies that certain stakeholders such as clients or consumers may be effectively shut out of the governance of the enterprise if they lack power or effective political representation.

The external power relations manifest themselves not only in the govern-ance of social enterprises but also internally in their actual practices. That is, within the organization, those units governed by the business logic compete for power with the units that embody the social mission of the enterprise. Units will gain a power advantage to the extent to which they control a greater share of the organization's resources (Salancik and Pfeffer, 1974; Chapter 5 in this volume). When they do so, they are more capable of influencing the practices of the social enterprise to buttress their power advantage.

By paying close attention to the mobilization and use of power the political economy perspective problematizes who benefits from the social enterprise. Ostensibly, the *raison d'être* of the social enterprise is to benefit disenfranchised and vulnerable populations. These are also populations generally deprived of voice and political resources. To ensure that the enterprise responds to their needs, they have to have a strong political representation in the enterprise, be able to coalesce with other stakeholders that share their interests, and wield sufficient power to influence the practices of the organization. A major area of research is to explore and explain the mechanisms by which social enterprises do represent the interests of their most vulnerable stakeholders.

Chapters in this book

The focus of this book – an organizational analysis of social enterprise – is presented in the following chapters, which are divided into two parts – theoretical approaches and empirical studies – and a Postscript.

Part I: theoretical approaches. This part is divided into two sections. In the first two chapters, by Dennis Young and by Joseph Galaskiewicz and Sondra Barringer, the authors are struggling with the hybridity of the organizational form of social enterprise and point out its precariousness and therefore its vulnerability and instability. Chapters 3 and 4, by Jacques Defourny and Marthe Nyssens and by Janelle Kerlin, present different aspects of the social enterprise concept as it expresses itself in different parts of the world – its intellectual and political foundations and antecedents (Chapter 3) and the institutional forces behind it (Chapter 4).

Dennis Young starts his chapter by citing a long list of recent studies on social enterprise but points out that as long as there is no agreed upon definition there can be no systematic data collection on the phenomenon, which hampers serious research. His chapter then moves on to discuss the problematic of the dual focus of the social enterprise organizational form, with direct impact on its stability. The discussion is on bases for equilibrium, which is necessary for organizational forms to survive. In the case of the for-profit and nonprofit organizational forms, such bases have developed over time, which can ensure the survivability of the *form*. He then presents a metaphor of two valleys, each representing one of the two organizational forms separated by a hill, which represents the organizational form of social enterprise. The nature of the hill is unknown – is there a plateau or a sharp peak on top? At any rate, as these organizations need stability, the tendency over time is to drift down the hill in either one or the other direction. Young goes on to discuss this problematic and the need to find a unique base for equilibrium, and he presents different conceptualizations and typologies of the social enterprise form, leading to a discussion on two critical aspects, namely governance and finance, which need to be strategically addressed in order to create stability. The rest of the chapter is devoted to analyzing different types of social enterprises, such as cooperatives, business ventures within nonprofit organizations, etc., and how this tension and the need for equilibrium is expressed there. The chapter ends with an important observation: 'while variations are manifold, the number of essentially distinct organizational arrangements for social enterprise is finite, and since some of those arrangements will tend towards instability, the aim of social enterprise designers should be to find those combinations of finance, governance and legal status that will last. The literature on this subject is very thin'.

In Chapter 2 Galaskiewicz and Barringer also deal with the vulnerability of the social enterprise form as a hybrid entity and add the dimension of people's perceptions and expectations, especially the fact that people are used to thinking in distinct categories and have difficulties in categorizing hybrids. They also suggest that being a social enterprise is risky because people often challenge their legitimacy, though, on the other hand, it does open opportunities not awarded to businesses and nonprofits. They review the literature on organizational identities and stress the importance of categories in this process that helps stakeholders to place the organization in its proper place in their perception. Regarding social enterprises they argue that 'when evaluating any type of organization, audiences will categorize it based on two sets of traits: organizational inputs and who benefits. On the input side, we are interested in the modality of exchange, e.g. a gift versus an exchange or market transaction (which we label "sales"). On the output side, we are interested in who benefits, e.g. the public, principals and agents'. A series of examples demonstrate different hybrid forms that mix funding sources and benefit different audiences. The authors further recognize the difficulties in evaluating the outputs of such entities. In general they portray an organizational entity that, because of its 'deviation' from known and familiar organizational forms, seems to be full of contradictions and therefore difficult to understand. Yet the fact that it exists puts the onus on researchers to figure out ways to understand it.

In Chapter 3 Defourny and Nyssens introduce an international and cultural angle to the discourse on social enterprise. They point out the different schools of thought, both in Europe and North America, that are at the base of the concept. They stress the differences between the European and the US traditions, whereby in Europe the social economy tradition does not exclude organizations that distribute profits, such as cooperatives (as is the case in the US for the nonprofit sector), provided these organizations develop social capital and create a framework for participation and involvement of members or users of services. They base their work on the EMES – The European Research Network's definition of social enterprise, with its well-known dual focus on the *economic and entrepreneurial dimension* on the one hand and the *social dimension* on the other., They introduce a third dimension, that of *participatory governance*, thus placing major importance on the way the entity is governed and managed, stressing the role of social enterprise as promoting democratically run institutions in society. The idea of a strong civil society base for social enterprises is also accentuated by other attributes, such as their governance bodies, their autonomy, their participative dynamic, the limitations on the rights of shareholders and the constraints on profit distribution. The authors conclude the chapter by pointing out the context within which social enterprises develop, which obviously varies in time and place, and they state that 'the perspective we have adopted in this chapter suggests that the various conceptions of social enterprise and social entrepreneurship are deeply rooted in the social, economic, political and cultural contexts in which such dynamics take place'.

Kerlin in Chapter 4 also uses a global approach in discussing the contextual forces in the background, which shape the social enterprise concept. Her study draws on the theory of historical institutionalism, which is based on the premise that 'existing institutional processes and patterns constrain the options available to actors in the innovation of institutions across time'. It also draws on national-level empirical data and country descriptions of social enterprise to construct a conceptual framework that informs models of social enterprise that exist internationally. The models are preliminarily checked against empirically based case studies of five countries' current institutional patterns and how these relate to the types of social enterprises found there. The study uses a very broad definition of 'social enterprise' to enable such a comparison. Based on the macrolevel data and comparative studies the chapter develops different models of social enterprise and links those to data on socioeconomic institutions The findings are in line with the theory of historical institutionalism, which suggests that as socioeconomic institutions will change over time due to shifts in power relations social enterprise models for different countries will change as well.

Part II: empirical studies. This consists of five chapters, each presenting data on various aspects of social enterprises. In Chapter 5 Eve Garrow and Yeheskel Hasenfeld focus on their study of WISEs and their conflicting orientations toward the marginalized populations they employ. In Chapter 6 Benjamin Gidron and Inbal Abbou report on their study of social enterprises in Israel; they discuss in particular the social business form. In Chapter 7 Paul-Brian McInerney reports on a case study of a social enterprise and its approach to its need to legitimate itself vis-à-vis different organizations in its task environment. In Chapter 8 Curtis Child discusses the pressures on business firms to support a double bottom-line and forces that may influence them to do so. Finally, in Chapter 9 Kate Cooney analyzes the new legal frameworks developed in the US (L3C and B Corporation) and the UK (CIC) in the past decade to allow a platform for social enterprise activity.

Garrow and Hasenfeld in Chapter 5 report on their study of WISEs, which are defined as human service organizations that provide job opportunities and job training for people with employment barriers – mostly people with handicaps, ex-convicts, etc. They raise the important question as to whether these types of organizations, often hailed as pursuing a double-bottom-line, are in reality placed in the market or the human service domain. The issue expresses itself especially in relation to their treatment of participants in those schemes – are they primarily clients or workers, resulting in processes of their commodification? Basing themselves on institutional theory, they suggest that organizations behave on the basis of the logic that governs them. Thus, they found that the greater the exposure of the particular WISE to the market logic, the more likely it will be to commodify its clients. In their analysis they introduce concepts such as embeddedness in the market to differentiate between business fields which may or may not be sensitive to the social mission of the entity, as well as the moderating role of the organizational form with similar consequences. They then build a causal model, which is tested in an empirical study. Their findings suggest that such enterprises based on a social mission, when adopting a market logic, can easily drift into a position of commodifying their clients and exploiting them, using therapeutic language to conceal this practice.

Gidron and Abbou in Chapter 6 focus on a specific form of social enterprise – the social business. In the absence of a legal framework to allow for a specific organizational form of social enterprise, some business entrepreneurs in Israel have pioneered the establishment of such entities. The authors discuss that particular (new) form, which is run as a regular business that needs to be self-sufficient and base itself on sales only while employing members of a marginalized population such as youths in distress or persons with handicaps. Several short case studies illustrate that practice. They report on a study of social enterprise that compares such social businesses with business ventures within NPOs that employ similar populations but have other sources of income at their disposal in the case of losses. The findings indicate clear differences between the two types of social enterprise, which are explained by the different orientations and predominant logics governing each. This leads to a discussion of the distinct roles of social businesses in the overall context of social enterprise.

McInerney in Chapter 7 'examines the case of a social enterprise as it attempts to establish moral legitimacy by justifying its organizational form and practices in the field of nonprofit providers of technology assistance'. He views social enterprises as having the ability 'to recombine practices and forms considered legitimate across multiple institutional domains'.

This makes them innovative but also vulnerable when faced with issues of legitimacy – they may be seen as business-like by NPOs, but not sufficiently business-like by commercial enterprises. His study is an ethnography of NPower – a nonprofit provider of technology assistance in New York City. Although legally registered as a nonprofit, the author defines them as a social enterprise since they combine values and practices from both the nonprofit and for-profit worlds. Their organizational domain consists of clients, donors and other similar providers of technology assistance and they operate in a 'mixed-form market, which is subject to multiple and contradictory institutional demands'. Their revenue model was highly influenced by the fact that they collaborated with for-profit consulting firms and venture capitalists, yet they also established a charitable program to benefit youths from low-income communities, which was funded by donations. The author concludes that on the basis of its practices the organization did not have difficulties in receiving moral legitimacy from the business institutional domain, which risks undermining moral legitimacy from the nonprofit institutional domain. The story of the organization is the need to deal with these contradictions and 'to be held accountable to different evaluative principles'.

Child in Chapter 8 encounters the issue of how social enterprises pursue financial and social returns, without one being a by-product of the other, or put differently – how do social enterprises balance their dual commitments to prosocial and financial goals? Taking the fair trade industry as the empirical background he conceptualizes four ideal-typical outcomes for social enterprise decisions. The most desired one is the 'win–win' option that increases the likelihood of maximizing both social and financial returns; opposite to this is a situation where a decision leads the company to diminish the likelihood of maximizing social and economic returns. Two other options have to do with pursuing one goal at the expense of the other, such as pursuing social goals at the expense of economic ones, with the risk of becoming insolvent. The author suggests that 'although social enterprises aspire to accomplish two goals, in practice market pressures and prosocial ones pull organizations in different directions'. A case study is presented on an independent family-owned company that imports coffee and also operates multiple coffee-shops. It needs to balance its decisions regarding the coffee it buys and offers to its clients between its commitment to the fair trade label and its economic imperative. Given a certain level of public consciousness, sometimes this means a win–win situation when increasing fair trade coffee also provides better financial returns. In analyzing the decision process the author introduces an additional variable: the business owners' personal commitments to the farmers growing the coffee used by the company, which was moved on to the next generation. That commitment was strengthened by a visit and a meeting with the coffee growers, which led to a decision to stick with the social mission against market pressures. The author asserts that the case 'add[s] flesh to the idea that meaningful encounters with others who are impacted on by a business's decisions can cause members of that business to alter conventional market-oriented activity'.

Cooney in Chapter 9 examines three efforts to create new platforms for social business: the CIC in the UK, the L3C and the B Corporation in the US. Using stakeholder theory, her analysis focuses on the attempts to protect via these new legal forms the social goals in socially oriented businesses; specifically she is interested in the degree to which they achieve the three key components of stakeholder salience, namely power, legitimacy and urgency. The next part is an analysis, based on social movement theory, of efforts to institutionalize those forms as social movements in their own right, facilitated by mobilizing structures, political opportunities and framing processes. The author first reviews the three new legal structures in the UK and the US and compares them in terms of the theoretical dimensions. Regarding the salience of stakeholders, the author finds that the CIC legal form 'provides the strongest platform for secondary stakeholders (such as community) to exert control over the direction of the firm'. As to the second analysis, the author recognizes the more developed infrastructure for social enterprise in the UK as compared to the US, which results in more meaningful institutionalization efforts by different mobilizing structures and a large number of political opportunities to support the new social enterprise entity.

The postscript by Alex Nicholls is in a sense an analysis of the state of research on the new field of social entrepreneurship/social enterprise. Using approaches from neo-institutional theory and focusing on frameworks for legitimation that characterize processes of knowledge-building of new fields, he observes that dominant discourses on social entrepreneurship represent legitimating materials from resource-rich actors in a process of what he terms 'reflexive isomorphism'. He further suggests that 'this process is prioritizing two discourses: narratives based on hero entrepreneur success stories and organizational models reflecting ideal-types from commercial business... The former supports internal logics that legitimate new venture philanthropic practices while the latter endorses internal logics that legitimate efficiency and the marketization of the state'. The author claims that in a pre-paradigmatic field such ideas were able to dominate the discourse on the concept. Such frameworks clearly lack a critical approach. The chapter then presents the role of scholarship in paradigm-building of social entrepreneurship as developed since the 1990s in several leading universities, which was precisely that of adding such a critical approach. As an alternative to the hero entrepreneur model and the marketization of social goods discourse the paradigm developed by scholarship stressed the logic of social innovation as *promoting social change*. It also recognizes social innovation as being episodic and dynamic. The chapter concludes by stressing that such a new paradigm needs to be further theorized and empirically tested.

References

Aldrich, Howard. 2006. *Organizational Evolution and Entrepreneurship*. Thousand Oaks, CA: Sage Publications.

Baum, Joel A., and Christine Oliver. 1991. 'Institutional Linkages and Organizational Mortality'. *Administrative Science Quarterly* 36: 187–218.

Chowdhury, Anis. 2011. 'How Effective is Microfinance as a Poverty Reduction'. In Anis Chowdhury and Jomo Kwame Sundaram (eds), *Poor Poverty: The Impoverishment of Analysis, Measurement and Policies*. London: A&C Black: 165–184.

Cook, Beth, Chris Dodds, and William Mitchell. 2003. 'Social Entrepreneurship-False Premises and Dangerous Forebodings'. *Australian Journal of Social Issues* 38: 57–72.

Creed, W.E. Douglas, Maureen A. Scully, and John R. Austin. 2002. 'Clothes Make the Person? The Tailoring of Legitimating Accounts and the Social Construction of Identity'. *Organization Science* 13(5): 475–496.

Cress, Daniel, and David A. Snow. 1996. 'Mobilizing at the Margins: Resources, Benefactors, and the Viability of Homeless Social Movement Organizations'. *American Sociological Review* 61: 1089–1109.

Eichhorst, Werner, Otto Kaufmann, and Regina Konle-Seidl (eds). 2008. *Bringing the Jobless into Work?: Experiences with Activation Schemes in Europe and the US*. Berlin: Springer-Verlag.

Eikenberry, Angela M. 2009. 'Refusing the Market'. *Nonprofit and Voluntary Sector Quarterly* 38(4): 582–596.

Friedland, Roger and Robert R. Alford. 1991 'Bringing Society Back in: Symbols, Practices and Institutional Contradictions'. In Walter W. Powell and Paul J. DiMaggio (eds) *The New Institutionalism in Organizational Analysis*. Chicago: The University of Chicago Press: 232–263.

Handler, Joel F. 2005. 'Myth and Ceremony in Workfare: Rights, Contracts, and Client Satisfaction'. *The Journal of Socio-Economics* 34: 101–124.

Hannan, Michael T. 2005. 'Ecologies of Organizations: Diversity and Identity' *Journal of Economic Perspectives* 19(1): 51–70.

Hannan, Michael T., and John Freeman. 1989. *Organizational Ecology*. Cambridge, MA: Harvard University Press.

Hardy, Cynthia, and Steve Maguire. 2008. 'Institutional Entrepreneurship'. In Royston Greenwood, Christine Oliver, Roy Suddaby and Kestin Sahlin (eds). *Organizational Institutionalism*. Los Angeles: Sage: 198–217.

Harvey, David. 2005. *A Brief History of Neoliberalism*. Oxford and New York: Oxford University Press.

Hsu, Greta, and Michael T. Hannan. 2005. 'Identities, Genres, and Organizational Forms'. *Organization Science* 16(5): 474–490.

Jurik, Nancy C. 2004. 'Imagining Justice: Challenging the Privatization of Public Life'. *Social Problems* 51(1): 1–15.

Kinderman, Daniel. 2012. '"Free Us Up so We Can Be Responsible!" The Co-evolution of Corporate Social Responsibility and Neo-liberalism in the UK, 1977–2010'. *Socio-Economic Review* 10(1): 29–57.

Kraatz, Matthew S., and Emily S. Block. 2008. 'Organizational Implications of Institutional Pluralism'. In Royston Greenwood, Christine Oliver, Kerstin Sahlin and Roy Suddaby (eds). *The SAGE Handbook of Organizational Institutionalism*. Thousand Oaks, CA: Sage Publications: 243–275.

Maguire, S., C. Hardy, and T.B. Lawrence. 2004. 'Institutional Entrepreneurship in Emerging Fields: HIV/AIDS Treatment Advocacy in Canada'. *Academy of Management Journal* 47(5): 657–680.

Minkoff, Debra C. 2002. 'The Emergence of Hybrid Organizational Forms: Combining Identity-Based Service Provision and Political Action'. *Nonprofit and Voluntary Sector Quarterly* 31: 377–401.

Nyssens, Marthe, Sophie Adam, and Toby Johnson. 2006. Social Enterprise: At the Crossroads of Market, Public Policies and Civil Society. New York, NY: Routledge.

Orton, J. Douglas, and Karl E. Weick. 1990. 'Loosely Coupled Systems: A Reconceptionalization'. *Academy of Management Review* 15(2): 203–222

Pfeffer, Jeffrey, and Gerald R. Salancik. 1978 *The External Control of Organizations: A Resource Dependence Perspective*. New York: Harper & Row.

Ruef, Martin. 2000. 'The Emergence of Organizational Forms: A Community Ecology Approach'. *American Journal of Sociology* 106(3): 658–714.

Salancik, Gerald R, and Jeffrey Pfeffer. 1974. 'The Bases and Use of Power in Organizational Decision Making: The Case of a University'. *Administrative Science Quarterly* 19(4): 453–473.

Thornton, Patricia, and William Ocassio. 2008. 'Institutional Logics' In Royston Greenwood, Christine Oliver, Roy Suddaby and Kestin Sahlin (eds). *The SAGE Handbook of Organizational Institutionalism*. Los Angeles: Sage: 99–129.

Part I
Theoretical Approaches

1
The State of Theory and Research on Social Enterprises

Dennis R. Young

Although "social enterprise" is a relatively new subject for study, there is quite a lot of literature that could be reviewed here.* Substantial papers have now been written on such aspects as comparative forms of social enterprise around the world (Borzaga and Defourny, 2001; Kerlin, 2010a, 2009, 2006), the various organizational and legal structures that ventures called social enterprise can assume (e.g. Brody, 2009), the relationship between venture philanthropy and social enterprise (Van Slyke and Newman, 2006), the multiple values and sources of income on which social enterprises are based (Herranz *et al.*, 2010), performance measurement for social enterprise (Bagnoli and Megali, 2009), strategies for balancing of social and commercial goals in social enterprises (Cooney, 2010; Mozier and Tracey, 2010), and of course many case studies of the experiences of particular social enterprises (e.g. Cooney, 2006; Cordes and Steuerle, 2009; Mannan, 2009; Squazzoni, 2009; Aiken, 2010; Teasdale, 2010; Harranz *et al.*, 2010). Scholars have also developed the rudiments of theory for social enterprise, trying to explain its emergence in a market economy and democratic society from various disciplinary viewpoints (Young 2008, 2009), the dangers associated with commercialization of nonprofit or philanthropic organizations (Weisbrod, 1998, 2004; Eikenberry, 2009), the different forms social enterprise assumes in alternative national contexts (Kerlin, 2009), the development of new (commercial) ventures within conventional nonprofit organizations (Oster, 2010), the circumstances under which social enterprises survive (Yitshaki *et al.*, 2008), how they contribute to the goals of the welfare state (Borzaga and Defourney, 2001) and related topics, especially the emergence and performance of hybrid organizations (Tuckman, 2009; Billis, 2010).

Amidst this blossoming of literature and interest in social enterprise, certain gaps in the knowledge base on the area have become painfully clear. First is the lack of systematic data on social enterprise from which valid comparisons can be made and hypotheses tested. The second is a lack of understanding of the dynamics. The importance of the first of these lacunae is obvious. Good data is the life blood of good research, and as Anderson and Dees (2006) point out, scholarship on social enterprise needs to move beyond rhetoric and advocacy to solid, objective empirical studies. The second is more subtle, having to do with the motley array of legal and economic forms that social enterprise assumes, some of which we have little experience with and even less research (Billitteri, 2007). One important question is the stability of these forms – not only whether they will last but whether they will remain true to their original intent or decay (in essence or explicitly) into more conventional forms, given the pressures of the economic and social environment – and whether there are solutions that can be expected to bolster the capacity of social enterprises to adhere to their original goals over time.

Definitions and data

One may liken the current state of empirical research on social enterprise to the early days of research on nonprofit organizations before 1990. An initial and most valuable thrust of pioneer scholars such as Gabriel Rudney (1987), Virginia Hodgkinson and Murray Weitzman (1993) and Lester Salamon and his colleagues in the Comparative Nonprofit Sector Project (Salamon *et al.*, 1999) was to create some standard definitions and databases with which nonprofits could be classified, described and counted. Despite the poor state of extant data these researchers largely succeeded because it was possible to specify a common definition of nonprofit organizations and to associate these definitions with particular legal entities that appeared in governmental tax-related and other databases. In fact, these efforts worked much better within the context of a single country such as the United States where there was some consensus around the nature of a nonprofit or third sector organization. The problems were much greater for extending these efforts internationally because countries had different viewpoints about what constituted a third sector organization and whether indeed the nonprofit form as defined in the United States was really the essential component of the broader social economy or third sector of other countries. Despite Salamon and colleagues' prodigious efforts to apply a common definition of a nonprofit organization across national boundaries, the results were subject to many caveats, and comparisons essentially had to rely mostly on employment figures rather than the richer array of descriptors that could be fashioned within the US or other countries individually.

Social enterprise researchers such as Anderson and Dees (2006) argue that database development needs to move beyond the "sector bias" of nonprofit research in order to embrace the full spectrum of social purpose initiatives. (Note, however, that even within the confines of the nonprofit sector, it is not trivial to define a subuniverse which according to one criterion – namely some level of dependence on earned revenues – qualifies organizations or their subunits as social enterprises (see Garrow, 2010).) While Anderson and Dees's position is entirely defensible, it makes the problems of measuring the universe of social enterprise much worse than those involving measurement of the nonprofit (or third) sector per se. First, there is no commonly accepted definition of a social enterprise, and although such a definition can be fashioned, it is unlikely to be specified in a way that would directly correspond to particular legal forms. The multipart specification developed by the EMES European research network is one valiant attempt at such a definition (Borzaga and Defourny, 2009). But social enterprise is really a mishmash of old and new legal forms, projects within organizations and partnerships and alliances among organizations that it requires a definition much more vague and generic if it is to be all-encompassing. (I will put forward my own broad definition below.) Inevitably, however, such a definition makes it difficult to demarcate what is in and what is out in terms of observed entities that are candidates for the social enterprise label. Nor is there any official comprehensive database that would ensure that many social enterprises aren't just missed by census takers or survey researchers. (How, for example, can we count for-profit variants of social enterprise or determine what portions of business activity are devoted to social purposes, despite having good statistics on business sector income and employment?) Even among the commonly cited European examples of social enterprise, the variety extends from social cooperatives in Italy, to community interest companies in the UK, to so-called BBBs (neighborhood development schemes) in the Netherlands (Kerlin, 2009; Borzaga and Defourny, 2001), with no common census or measurement indicators across these categories.

One approach to directly identifying the universe of social enterprises is through processes of self-reporting via websites such as that of Community Wealth Ventures or social or nonprofit business plan competitions such as the erstwhile Yale/Goldman Sachs program (Oster *et al.*, 2004). In addition, there are purposive surveys carried out by researchers seeking to study limited selections or varieties of social enterprise (e.g. Foster and Bradach, 2005; Cooney, 2010). But there is nothing that can be considered a comprehensive or unbiased census or sample.

An indirect method for identifying the universe of social enterprises is to survey populations of so-called social entrepreneurs. For example, the Global Entrepreneurship Monitor (GEM) surveys the adult population of numerous countries to identify entrepreneurs and the ventures with which they are associated (Bosma and Levie, 2009). This study distinguishes between traditional and social entrepreneurship activity and provides a useful perspective on the prevalence of such activity in developed and developing countries. However, the definition of these categories varies from country to country. Moreover, it is not clear that social entrepreneurship and social enterprise are entirely congruent concepts. Many manifestations of social enterprise may not be precisely associated with particular

entrepreneurs, e.g. partnerships initiated through government programs
or commercial activities undertaken within the umbrella of an existing
organization. Hence, a general population survey may fail to identify social
enterprises associated with people who do not think of themselves as entrepreneurs. Finally, surveying general populations to identify entrepreneurs
is necessarily an inexact undertaking. The GEM study requires surveying
at least 2,000 adults in each country, an effort that is likely to be affected
by response bias and which has little chance of documenting the entire
universe of social enterprises in a given national context. Without such a
census, future studies of social enterprises per se have no populations from
which to draw their own representative samples.

The construction of a universal database of social enterprises, either at the
national or international levels, may not be impossible. Indeed the necessity
of better data to improve social enterprise research is clear (Anderson and
Dees, 2006). Certainly, the efforts in Europe using the common EMES definition provide a beacon of light here. Such a project would require refinement
of definitions, careful crafting of taxonomies and massive surveying to
obtain original data. It would be expensive, but the rewards to research and
ultimately to social innovation and better ways of solving social problems,
as well as knowing what works and what doesn't, could be substantial.

Social enterprise dynamics and stability

Let me now turn to the issue of social enterprise dynamics and the problems
of stability of social enterprise forms. "Stability" of social enterprises is a
dual concept because of the melding of social and financial goals. Hence we
define the stability of social enterprises along two dimensions:

1. Whether such enterprises survive (as organizations or projects within
   organizations) in the long run, and
2. Whether they maintain their intended balance of social purpose impact
   and market success over time.

As noted, social enterprise takes many forms some of which we understand
fairly well and others with which we have little experience. For example, we
know a lot about conventional for-profit business, large business corporations, classical nonprofit organizations, traditional worker or consumer cooperatives and government agencies, all of which can be home to, or vehicles
of, social enterprise. We know something less about for-profit organizations
that formally take on social responsibilities and nonprofits that undertake
commercial ventures, and less still about so-called hybrid organizations
that purport to balance dual goals of market success and social purpose
or business-nonprofit-government partnerships that enlist diverse organizations that bring very different aspirations to social enterprise initiatives.

The gaps in our knowledge of various forms of social enterprise are particularly severe with respect to long term behaviors. For familiar forms such as business corporations we have well developed theory and empirical research that tells us how markets of profit-seeking entities function and what kinds of patterns they are likely to settle into over time. The theory of long term behavior of government agencies or nonprofit organizations is less precisely developed but here too we have an understanding of the forces at play and how they are likely to come to rest in particular circumstances. Presumably, democratic governments track median voter preferences over time, subject to the interplay of the political agendas of various rent-seeking special interests and bureaucratic forces. Nonprofits, by comparison, can be viewed as responding to market and government failures within the constraints of available resources and behavioral incentives (Steinberg, 2006). These aren't necessarily elegant or comprehensive theories but they do give us a sense of how these various economic entities settle into the larger economy and polity over the long haul. We don't have equivalent theory to understand the longer term roles and status of new forms of social enterprise including whether they are stable or transient.

Nature of the long run and the notion of equilibrium

The theory of markets postulates a long-run stable state based on a dynamic equilibration of supply and demand. In competitive markets (many sellers and buyers) prices and quantities adjust so that exactly the right amount of a good is produced and sold at a price that "clears the market" leaving no unfilled (excess) demand or unsold supply. In this "equilibrium", inefficient firms are weeded out or taken over and surviving firms settle into a stable state, selling all they can at the market price. Similarly, in markets for products or services with large economies of scale compared to the level of overall demand, all but a few firms may survive the competition, and the stable end game may feature firms that exhibit certain undesirable collusive or monopolistic behaviors such as restriction of output and pricing above marginal cost and production inefficiencies that may require governmental regulation.

In each of these cases, however, the essential nature of the firms involved is unchanged over time. Those that survive remain profit seeking with the same goals and objectives and basic characteristics with which they started. Hence, the for-profit firm is stable over time. There are interesting exceptions, such as failing firms (e.g. banks, automobile companies) deemed essential and taken over by government and so-called regained companies where bankrupt firms are taken over by workers in order to preserve their employment by transforming them into worker-owned enterprises (Kerlin, 2009). Even in those cases, however, the basic character of the firm may ultimately be returned to its original nature.

Classical charitable nonprofit organizations can be thought of in a similar manner, as they try to find stability in their markets with other organizations pursuing similar missions, possibly in competition with for-profit firms. Ultimately a nonprofit, if it survives, will settle into a combination of services and sources of support that allow it to continue to operate as a not-for-profit with a given (broadly defined) mission over a long period of time (Oster, 2010). Exceptions do occur – e.g. if nonprofits face heavy for-profit competition they are likely to emulate the behavior of their competitors in order to survive (Young and Steinberg, 1995). And, nonprofit organizations can be bought out by for-profit firms (sometimes creating new nonprofit foundations in the process) or be taken over by government, and they sometimes do decide to change their missions and start life over (for example, the famous case of the March of Dimes turning its focus from polio to birth defects). The latter possibility is related to the "mission drift" phenomenon wherein forces in the environment induce nonprofits to change direction, often giving more emphasis to commercial or other lucrative strategies in order to survive and grow (Jones, 2007). Alternatively, mission drift can stem from changes in the nature of social problems (e.g. demographic shifts or economic conditions), organizational personnel and philanthropic and governmental funding sources. But generally speaking nonprofit organizations are stable entities that settle into niches pursuing the general long term missions for which they were established, even if those missions tend to adapt to the times and to a changing economic and social environment.

Here we are interested in a particular kind of long term stability – not only whether particular organizations survive or how the resulting market of surviving organizations performs but rather whether the form itself is maintained over time or can be expected to evolve (essentially or literally) into another, more stable form, much as a radioactive element decays into a more stable element over time. Think of a hill top with valleys on either side (see Figure 1.1). For a round boulder there are three possible stable end states – resting at the top of the hill or at the bottom of one of the valleys. For-profit firms occupy one valley and are stable at the bottom of it, being pushed up and out of that valley only under extraordinary circumstances. Similarly, conventional nonprofit firms occupy another valley, stable around the bottom of the valley and rarely rolling out of that valley except under unusual circumstances. Social enterprises can be of either of these varieties, even if they mix profit making and social objectives. It would take a relatively strong force to tip a conventional nonprofit over the hill into the commercial valley, just as it would take such a force to move a for-profit firm into the valley of social purpose. Thus, the valley bottoms represent stable long run states for these two kinds of enterprises. However, some social enterprises such as social purpose businesses (see pp. 37–38) are conceived as true hybrids belonging to both valleys.

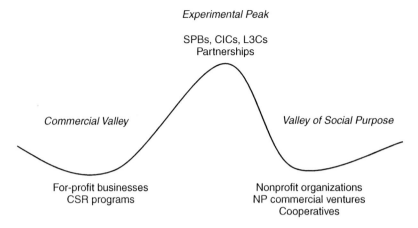

Figure 1.1 The topography of social enterprise

They sit at the top of the hill, in a more tenuous equilibrium such that relatively weak forces may potentially push them down into one of the valleys. The questions thus become – what does the top of the hill look like (is it relatively flat like a plateau or steep and round like a mountain peak)? and what does it take to stay at the top? Note that these social enterprises on the hill top test the popular notion of the "double-bottom line" by which such entities claim to govern themselves. As Anderson and Dees (2006) point out, most social enterprise ventures in studies they examined judged themselves by a social or a commercial standard and not both, suggesting the tenuousness of such a balance.

Before we can analyze this question we need to identify both the various generic forms of social enterprise and also the factors that pull them toward or away from their desired combinations of market success and social purpose achievement.

Varieties of social enterprise

As noted earlier, a comprehensive definition of "social enterprise" is necessarily vague. For my purposes here, I will subscribe to the following: "Social enterprise is activity intended to address social goals through the operation of private organizations in the marketplace". (Young, 2009, 23)

This definition is somewhat broader than others that focus more specifically on entrepreneurship and earned income strategies (Chertok *et al.*, 2008) or put more heavy emphasis on democratic governance and limits to profit making (Borzaga and Defourny, 2001). It accommodates a wide variety of forms, both conventional and new, including: small, privately held businesses whose owners intentionally address social as well as financial objectives; philanthropic and social responsibility programs of large publicly traded profit-making corporations; social purpose businesses with formal mandates to pursue a balance of profitable and social-purpose activities; partnerships consisting of for-profit, nonprofit and governmental organizations brought together around a public purpose; cooperatives of workers, consumers or other parties, governed by members who share both socially defined organizational goals and private benefits; nonprofit organizations established to address a social mission that entails services provided in a marketplace; and commercial initiatives of host nonprofit organizations designed to achieve some combination of financial return and social goal achievement.

There is no definitive typology of social enterprises, though there have been some thoughtful ones proposed. For example, the aforementioned GEM study (Bosma and Levie, 2009) specifies a four-category taxonomy of nonprofit, for-profit and hybrid forms with different types of social and commercial goals. An impressive effort by Alter (2007) offers a spectrum of possibilities ranging from traditional nonprofits to traditional for-profits, with various hybrid forms in-between (such as nonprofit commercial ventures and socially responsible businesses) and "social enterprise" occupying the midpoint of the spectrum. Alter further distinguishes various business models and social/commercial orientations by which social enterprises can operate. Nash (2010) also depicts a social enterprise spectrum spanning multiple dimensions of motives and key stakeholders, while Helm (2010) lays out various legal/organizational options for social enterprise activity. Galaskiewicz and Barringer (Chapter 2) develop categories of social enterprise based on organizational identities involving alternative stakeholders, institutional logics and performance criteria.

Another interesting typology, based on a four-way classification of decision-making structures, is offered by Teasdale (2010). With control (governance) and primary purpose (commercial vs. social) as his two basic dimensions, Teasdale identifies four generic categories of social enterprise: *social businesses* featuring corporate-type governance and commercial purpose; *nonprofit enterprises* featuring corporate governance and social purpose; *community businesses* featuring democratic governance and commercial purpose; and *community enterprises* featuring democratic governance and social purpose. This typology works fairly well for many varieties of enterprise mentioned above, but some are hard to classify. For example, cooperatives are democratically governed but can be commercial as well as social purpose in nature. Similarly, social businesses can generate and distribute profit while operating primarily for a social purpose. And partnerships can be an explicit mix of commercial and social purpose components.

Teasdale's construct illustrates that tensions can arise along both the governance and purpose dimensions. For example, experience with cooperatives and associations demonstrates that sharing of authority in a collective governance arrangement can be treacherous and may call for strong leadership, hierarchy and delegation of authority to overcome factionalism and free riding. However, our primary concern here is the organizational purpose dimension. Because all of the forms of social enterprise entail tension between the goals of social purpose and commercial success, they can all be subject to long run instability, despite various possible management strategies to ameliorate these tensions (Oster *et al.*, 2004; Mozier and Tracey, 2010). The first question is which of these forms occupy the stable valleys where they may oscillate around the bottoms but remain essentially unchanged, and which are positioned on the hill top and at risk of rolling down one way or another? The second question is what factors determine whether enterprises at the top of the hill stay there or roll down? A third question is what forces can sometimes jar an enterprise out of one of the valleys and up to the top of the hill or over into another valley?

Teasdale's (2010) construct suggests that the two principal mechanisms for maintaining or disturbing a social enterprise's long term equilibrium are external resource opportunities and pressures that appeal to social vs. commercial goals and the nature of internal governance. We will consider each of these, relative to the various forms of social enterprise. Of course the most interesting cases are those perched at the top of the hill – where the impacts of the external environment and the dynamics of governance are most critical. These are also the cases about which our knowledge is still quite rudimentary.

Equilibrium and governance

All forms of social enterprise have some governing body that sets long term policy and direction and is responsible for the integrity and success of the enterprise. However, the complex, multifaceted nature of many social enterprises, especially explicitly hybrid structures, challenges the effectiveness of conventional governing mechanisms (Cornforth and Spear, 2010).

In the case of corporate entities, such as nonprofit organizations and for-profit firms, a board of trustees or directors will have governance responsibility. For projects such as commercial ventures (undertaken by host nonprofit organizations) or philanthropy programs (undertaken by for-profit corporations), there may be an advisory body specific to the project, but control ultimately lies in the hands of the governing board of the host entity. Consider the case of corporate philanthropy. An internal corporate giving program is simply one part of the larger corporation's operations and strategy, subject to the same governance as any other part. However, if the program is separately incorporated as a foundation, it will have its own governing board, albeit one that is likely to include representation of the leadership of the parent corporation.

Similarly, an internal commercial venture of a nonprofit organization is directly subject to the governance of the host nonprofit, but if it is incorporated as a separate profit-making subsidiary it will have its own governing board reflecting its ownership. That ownership can be the nonprofit itself, in which case its board will be appointed by the board of the nonprofit, or it can be shared ownership with other investors, in which case the governing board will be more complex, consisting of some combination of directors appointed in relation to ownership shares. More than likely, the interests of the (nonprofit) host organization will dominate in this case, just as the interests of the parent corporation are likely to dominate the governance of a corporate foundation.

Social enterprise projects within host organizations may either already occupy one of the stable valleys – as part of a long-run profit-making strategy of the corporate host or as a sustaining, revenue producing project of a nonprofit host – but in some instances may be tenuously perched on the top of the hill. (Note, Kerlin's (2010b) analysis of the long term growth of earned income of nonprofit organizations suggests considerable stability to this form of social enterprise.) In this case, the governance body of the host organization may exert pressure to roll down into one of the valleys – in the case of the corporation to become more integrated into long term corporate commercial strategy or in the case of the nonprofit to adhere more closely to its social mission, perhaps by shedding aggressive commercial tactics or including some explicit loss-making but socially important features such as pricing structures or hiring strategies to accommodate needy clients. This is not an easy thing to predict, however. It probably serves the purpose of the corporation to have a good face to the community, and it serves the nonprofit to have a reliable source of earned revenue. These compensating considerations may be enough to keep the social enterprise project balanced at the top of the hill for a long time.

Finally, some social enterprises consist of partnership arrangements which are essentially business agreements between separate corporate entities such as government agencies, nonprofit organizations and for-profit businesses, formalized through a legal contract. Such partnerships may have their own staff and they may be immediately supervised by an advisory board consisting of representatives of the partners. Or indeed, the partnership may itself be incorporated with its governance in the hands of its partners. In such cases, the partnership board serves as a "secretariat", governing the partnership in a manner that reflects the pull and tug of self-interests among the partners, within the parameters of the formal agreement. Depending on the strengths of the partners within the governing body, the net effect may be to pull the venture in one direction or another, possibly down one of the slopes or toward dissolution or renegotiation of the agreement.

The stability of social enterprise partnerships is probably the most difficult to predict over the long haul as it depends on the balance of forces among the partners. At any given point in time, corporate or governmental interests could dominate, a strong internal socially focused nonprofit constituency could strengthen the nonprofit partner, or a dynamic tension among the partners could be maintained for a long time. Alternatively, partnerships can easily fall apart if the minimal requirements of each partner are not maintained.

Governing arrangements can be stabilizing or destabilizing forces on the social enterprises they guide. Much depends on the particulars of the design. Moreover, governance is not independent of the underlying economics of a social enterprise, as considered next.

Equilibrium and finance

Survival and growth are strong motivators for any organization, for-profit, non-profit and mixtures thereof. Thus, the focus and character of social enterprise will be influenced over time by the financial opportunities and pressures of its environment. Indeed, Herranz *et al.* (2010), building on Moore (2000), argue that sources of finance strongly affect the character of a nonprofit organization because of the different "value propositions" associated with transacting business in the commercial marketplace, with philanthropic sources and with government. The potentially corrupting influence of sources of financial support has long been an issue for nonprofit organizations. From the beginnings of the Great Society programs in the US in the 1960s and 1970s, "vendorism" has been a serious concern, i.e. that nonprofits were becoming mere service delivery appendages to government, no matter what their form of governing arrangements (Smith and Lipsky, 1993). More recently, concerns have focused on the commercialization of nonprofits because of their increasing reliance on earned income (Weisbrod, 1998). The attractions of governmental or commercial funding lie at the root of "mission drift" anxieties that some see as destabilizing the intrinsic nature and character of nonprofit organizations. Combining these historical concerns, Herranz *et al.* (2010) argue that contemporary social enterprises are commonly funded by all three sources of revenue – commerce, philanthropy and government – and that many ought to be understood as "tri-value organizations" subject as much to mission-corruption by government as any other source. (This idea raises the question of whether there is another valley of "government-capture" into which tenuously balanced social enterprises can fall.)

Certainly a myth associated with social enterprise is that it is all about generating earned market revenues to support social purposes. Some forms of social enterprise fit this description better than others. A museum or hospital gift shop, or a thrift store associated with a social service agency, are intended to be self-supporting and to generate financial surpluses for the host organization. The social purposes of these enterprises tend to be incidental; they would not be sponsored by their host organizations unless they made money. Still one cannot generalize this point. The Greyston Bakery is a commercial success but might continue to be supported by its sponsor, the Greyston Foundation, even if it lost money, because it generates substantial social benefits by employing marginalized community residents involved with the criminal justice system. So while financial reward can be a powerful force affecting enterprise stability it is not, as per the above discussion of governance, the sole determinant.

Many of the forms of social enterprise of course depend on combinations of market and nonmarket revenues. A social enterprise incorporated as a nonprofit organization will likely depend on a mix of charitable contributions and grants, government funds and earnings in the marketplace. A social purpose business in the form of a profit making entity might benefit from "program related investments" made by charitable foundations, or it might receive government grants or contracts. Certainly new social ventures of any type are likely to get started with foundation, corporate or governmental funding, as well as volunteer "sweat equity", and they will probably depend on such sources for considerable periods of time. Partnerships also bring the financial sources of the various types of partners together into some combination of government, corporate and charitable support. Clearly the form of a social enterprise will influence its ability to attract resources from different places. Philanthropic sources are more likely to favor nonprofit structures while commercial sources are likely to favor for-profit structures. Indeed, as Chertok *et al.* (2008, 47) observe: "one of the primary reasons entrepreneurs create hybrid organizations is that it allows them to approach philanthropic and commercial capital providers in ways that are familiar to each type of funder. The nonprofit can approach individual donors and foundations for a grant, and the for-profit can approach debt and equity investors on commercial terms".

The danger in all of these cases is that social enterprises will simply "follow the money", making organizational or project survival or growth subordinate to purpose and even co-opting governance since governing boards can be preoccupied with finances if the organization is in a financially precarious position or if highly lucrative opportunities present themselves. The best case scenario is where the sources of funding align well with the purpose of the enterprise over the long term, such as where a nonprofit has found a lucrative and benign market for an activity explicitly designed to generate funding for the organization (e.g. a thrift store selling upscale donated items), or where a nonprofit is funded by a government program with the same mission objectives (such as a work integration program for physically challenged workers). Trouble can occur when the money and the social enterprise goals pull in different directions, such as when a social enterprise is so successful commercially that it becomes a valuable asset for sale to a private party or leads its management to neglect the social purpose for commercial reasons. For example, a shop selling handicraft of challenged workers in a supported work environment needs to be careful not to exploit the workers just to increase sales and profits.

Since the correlation between finances and the form of social enterprise is not perfect, it is difficult to assess the stability issues in any simplistic way. The discussions of vendorism and mission drift in the nonprofit literature suggest that the nonprofit form of social enterprise can potentially be corrupted and destabilized in the long run by a commercial financial environment that is dissonant with the organization's social objectives. Alternatively, financially successful internal projects in nonprofit host organizations can also be derailed by forces that are in tension with an enterprise's goals. For example, a commercially successful project of a nonprofit might lose its competitive edge if a reliable source of charitable support insists on more emphasis on social considerations, e.g. a thrift shop that misses commercial opportunities because it is preoccupied with accommodating the needs of the volunteers that run it. The cases of social purpose businesses undertaken in for-profit form suffer from the fact that their commercial success might be exploited by subsequent owners (e.g. Ben and Jerry's Ice Cream sale to Unilever; see Page and Katz, 2011) who are not as committed to the original goals. Or a philanthropic initiative of a business corporation might be diverted from its social goals if other more lucrative uses of its resources are identified within the business strategy of the corporation, e.g. a new investment in a "public service" advertisement campaign that better highlights the merits of the corporate brand. Finally, social enterprises set up as partnerships will likely defer to those partners who bring the most to the table in terms of supportive resources. In many cases, as Herranz *et al.* (2010) describe, that party is likely to be government, through both direct and indirect flows of resources. Thus a partnership that combines philanthropic commitments, government funding and corporate investments may wobble in different directions, depending on how these sources change over time.

The hills and valleys of social enterprise

> I think you really have to make a choice and be a business or a nonprofit. It's hard to be both. (Will Rosensweig, founder of Republic of Tea; Strom, 2010, B8)

With governance and finance in mind, we can at least speculate on which forms of social enterprise will find themselves in the stable valleys of social purpose or commercial success, and which ones reside and may teeter on the hill tops. As previously observed, several forms of social enterprise employ fairly well understood forms of organization which tend to be stable over time. These include traditional for-profit businesses, corporate social responsibility and philanthropy programs within public corporations, traditional nonprofit organizations, commercial ventures undertaken by nonprofit organizations, and cooperatives of various types. These forms tend to operate in the valleys where limited perturbations around the stable bottom are the norm (again see Figure 1.1). But there are numerous variations on the theme. Consider each of these following cases and how finance and governance arrangements exert their influence.

A small, privately held for-profit business may be led by entrepreneurs who wish to balance profitability against selected social goals. This model can work very well for a period of time because the for-profit form offers substantial flexibility for private owners to follow their passions without heavy government oversight or extreme market pressures to maximize profits, so long as they are motivated to do so. Thus, the owner of a for-profit art gallery in New York can serve as a promoter of local artists so long as reasonable economic returns enable her to maintain the business (Young and Legorreta, 1986); a for-profit radio station can maintain its devotion to promoting classical music in a shrinking market as WCLV did in Cleveland for many years; and Newman's Own (www.newmansown.com/ourstory.aspx) can devote all of its profits to charitable causes. The problem with these for-profit social enterprises is their fragility as businesses with a social purpose. They are basically for-profit firms and once they are sold as businesses they are likely to gravitate toward conventional operation under new owners. This is actually why WCLV converted to nonprofit status when the long time owners decided to retire from actively managing the business after many years (see www.wclv.com). Selling the business would likely have assured the loss of the social goals by which the station operated. Such examples suggest that the financial exigencies of the market place will govern socially oriented small businesses in the long run, moving them deeper into the commercial valley, unless an explicit arrangement is eventually made to maintain the original orientation. And, indeed, that may not work if the mechanism for doing so is simply a hard to enforce contract with new owners.

The problem is obviously made worse if the corporation is publicly held as in the famous case of the Ben & Jerry ice cream company. In this case, the directors of the company need to protect themselves from hostile takeovers or legal suits by shareholders who object to pursuing social objectives at the expense of profit. As Page and Katz (2011) argue, protections can be built into the structure of the company, such as poison pills and different classes of shares associated with differential governing rights. Nonetheless, this requires substantial attention to defensive strategies as well as continued dedication to purpose on the part of the directors, and as the Ben & Jerry case appears to demonstrate, there are no guarantees that such strategies will be effective over the long term.

More generally, social responsibility or philanthropy programs of public corporations are likely to be stable occupants of the profit making valley, essentially serving as elements of overall corporate strategy for long run profitability. Certainly, the internal corporate culture can influence the status and respect with which these programs are treated by the company, but the pressures of the competitive product and equity markets and governance by external stockholders (who can sell their shares or even litigate if they feel that the corporation is sacrificing profits) will keep these programs within modest bounds. Even if such programs are established as separately incorporated foundations, they are likely to be governed by the leadership of the corporation and financed by company stock or annual flow-through allocations. In these cases, the fortunes of the foundation and the corporation are usually joined at the hip, even to the point of inhibiting the foundation from diversifying its holdings in order to achieve its own best risk/return positioning. Moreover, corporate foundations are likely to feel extra pressure from their corporate sponsors when they venture too far into controversial social causes (e.g. AT&T Foundation's support of Planned Parenthood) or when the corporation needs help in marketing its product. Volatility may also occur when corporate ownership or top management changes, but perturbations will most likely be in the direction of closer alignment to market success of the corporation. Only when the corporate philanthropy program is spun-off as a completely autonomous entity truly independent of its industry founder, can the program be assured of long term stability as a social purpose enterprise.

For social enterprises that take the form of a nonprofit organization as a whole (even one with a substantial level of dependence on earned revenue), the governance mechanism is likely to reflect explicitly interests of constituents and proponents of the mission, and the selection of members of the governing boards, whether by appointment of a self-perpetuating board or election by members of an association, will continue to reflect a mission orientation insulated from direct market pressures, subject to fiscal constraints. Thus, a social mission in principle becomes the touchstone for all strategic decisions. This is not to dispute that nonprofits are sometimes exploited by nefarious agents (for-profits in disguise, to use Weisbrod's term) or to argue that nonprofits do not have strong survival instincts or that they are not tempted by financial pressures to shift their activities toward goals favored by various sources of income, whatever they may be – governmental programs, foundation initiatives, major individual donors or related commercial product markets (Jones, 2007). "Mission drift" and vendorism are real possibilities in the short term and even for the duration if the nonprofit becomes captured by its funding source, for example a government organization that supplies a very large portion of its income. However, it seems the rare case where such a situation would actually dislodge the organization from its social purpose valley, and indeed with changing circumstances in the economic environment over time it is possible that the governance mechanism would help return the agency to the valley bottom where it can pursue its social mission with greater autonomy. For example, many government-funded social-service enterprises have faced this situation in the recent economic downturn, having to be innovative and independent in finding new sources of support as their government funding dried up. The inclination of nonprofit organizations, through their governance decisions, to diversify their revenue portfolios over time reflects this notion (Young, 2007).

For social enterprise in the form of ventures undertaken within the context of a host nonprofit organization and intended explicitly to be self-sustaining or a cash cow, the governing mechanism reflects that of the host organization, helping to maintain the enterprise within its boundaries as a social purpose undertaking. Here for example, it will be important for the project to keep the host organization's mission in mind as it pursues profitable options, for example avoiding damaging relationships such as cause-marketing ventures with companies selling harmful products. Exceptions to the mission stability of social enterprise ventures of nonprofit organizations can occur. For one thing, there is the risk of the tail wagging the dog, wherein the successful commercial venture causes mission drift in the host organization. Furthermore, the venture itself can be destabilized if it is organized as a separately incorporated subsidiary such as an entity to promote products commercialized from the nonprofit's mission-related work – for example companies designed to bring to market discoveries of university research programs or firms intended to sell the nonprofit's intellectual property, such as Sesame street characters or images of art from a museum. While a nonprofit can wholly own such ventures and certainly control its activities in the short term, the market opportunities may grow beyond the nonprofit's capacity to provide oversight or growth capital, leading to decisions to open up the venture to external investors and steering the venture out into the open marketplace, beyond the nonprofit's control and into the valley of commerce where it takes on a life of its own.

Cooperative forms of social enterprise are less common in the United States but very prominent in Europe and other parts of the world. Scholars including Borzaga and Defourny (2001) and Aiken (2010) describe several varieties of social enterprises in cooperative form including worker cooperatives, consumer cooperatives and so-called social cooperatives designed to involve client and worker groups in the provision of various kinds of social services. The cooperative form has a long history, even in the United States, though not all cooperative structures would be considered social enterprises in today's terms. For example, "mutual" companies have been important in the development of such industries as banking and insurance (Hansmann, 1996).

It is interesting to juxtapose the stability characteristics of cooperatives with those of nonprofit corporations. A critical feature of the latter is the non-distribution of profit constraint which, if effectively policed, is presumed to build trust, discourage consumer exploitation in circumstances of information asymmetry and help maintain social mission focus. The nonprofit form puts much more emphasis on this feature than on the particulars of organizational governance or even the sources of an enterprise's income. The cooperative form, by contrast, puts its main emphasis on governance by those constituents who are most directly affected by the enterprise's success and little on the level or distribution of financial surplus per se. Indeed, cooperatives are not precluded from generating or distributing financial surpluses, either in the form of dividends or in the value of services they provide to the cooperators. Rather cooperatives depend for maintaining their social focus on the interests of the cooperators and the directions they provide to the enterprise through the democratic process. Thus, as long as the social purpose of the organization is consonant with those of its members, and its members' social preferences are stable, the social enterprise should remain in its social purpose valley over time. Paradoxically, however, the social goal could indeed be the economic welfare of the members. In the case of worker cooperatives, for example, commercial success of the enterprise would be sought so long as the surpluses were equitably shared and consistent with other collective goals of the participants. So it is possible, that over time the members of a cooperative could lose their passion for the original social purpose, e.g. producing and sharing healthy food, and operate more in their more narrowly defined economic self-interest.

Tensions can arise, however, if the sources of a cooperative enterprise's finances pull in different directions than its social purpose. For example, cooperatives of displaced workers may have different goals than a government agency that funds them. Or, competitive success in a particular product market may require increases in productivity that require reductions in the workforce, or it may require greater specialization, less work-sharing or more growth and expansion than the cooperators may prefer. In these instances, stability of the enterprise may be threatened, forcing either dissolution or conversion to a conventional commercial form. Interestingly, this is the mirror-image of the phenomenon of "regained companies" wherein workers take over a failed commercial firm in order to preserve their livelihoods (Kerlin, 2009). The nature of the changing market place and whether it will tolerate or reward cooperative management structures thus seems likely to determine if the cooperative form of social enterprise remains stable, dissolves or eventually moves to the commercial valley.

In short, there can be a lot of wobbling even for the forms of social enterprise that inhabit stable valleys of social purpose or commerce, but we can expect these forms of social enterprise generally to endure because their underlying purposes are fairly well aligned with their governance mechanisms and their sources of finance, and perturbations from a mission are likely to be met with corrections toward their valley norms rather than with forces to accelerate them away from their original intent. However, other forms of social enterprise, including the newest social enterprise experiments with new legal forms and inter-organizational arrangements, seem less predictable and may very well decay into more stable but perhaps less innovative and socially impactful manifestations if their governance structures prove inadequate or their financial environments are volatile. In particular, so-called social purpose businesses and nonprofit-business partnerships seem to sit on the top of the hill looking down with some degree of vertigo (again see Figure 1.1). Several varieties of these arrangements are worthy of further examination in this regard:

So-called L3C organizations in the United States are an innovation designed to attract private capital to social causes and to leverage the endowments of charitable foundations (Billitteri, 2007). L3Cs are essentially limited liability for-profit corporations specifically designated to address social projects, paying profits to private investors and attracting "program-related investments" from foundations. The idea behind L3Cs is that the special legal form would allow charitable foundations to leverage their resources by investing part of their endowments in projects that have a high risk and a low financial but potentially high social return while still being considered prudent stewards of charitable resources under US tax law. At the same time this vehicle would presumably make it attractive for private parties to invest in social projects as well. Proponents believe that this structure would help to attract higher levels of philanthropic and private investment resources into projects with significant social returns.

> The L3C concept is contentious if only because it remains unclear whether it would indeed free charitable foundations to invest in them without jeopardizing their own charitable status (Kleinberger, 2010). Moreover, it is argued by some that this special form is unnecessary and that all it purports to accomplish can be undertaken by ordinary limited liability companies.
>
> The stability of L3Cs is also questionable. Poised specifically as a kind of hybrid organization balancing social and commercial goals on the hill top, it seems clear that both its governance and financial arrangements tend to push L3Cs into the commercial valley below. Private investors expect market returns and even foundation (PRI) investors want assurance of commercial success in order to protect their investments. Together these groups would govern the L3C with no real restraint short of some new governmental oversight mechanism, since these organizations would indeed be essentially private-profit making firms with perhaps good intentions but subject to long run forces all pointing in the direction of commercial success. Various governance arrangements (allocation

of different levels of governance rights to alternative investment groups) have been proposed to try to ensure that the LC3 maintains its blended mission, though it remains unclear as to what kind of scheme would be effective, stable or mandatory (Reiser, 2011).

Another interesting variation is the so-called B Corporation which is essentially an ordinary for-profit business that includes in its bylaws a provision requiring its directors to account for social benefits and environmental concerns. B Corporations may seek to use the trademark of the private, nonprofit B Lab which grants license to its trademark to business corporations that meet its standards for social and environmental practices and policies. It is up to shareholders in B Corporations to include social goals in their fiduciary oversight. As Reiser (2011) indicates, B Lab accreditation could potentially become a strong factor in keeping a B Corporation to a balanced path of social goals and market success if B Lab can become an important market player over time, gaining influence on consumer decision-making in the marketplace. The jury is out, however, as to whether B Corporations can remain stable on the mountain top or will inevitably fall into the commercial valley. Several elements point in the latter direction, including the challenges for the B trademark to gain visibility and influence and the incentives for B Corporations to neglect social goals or forgo their accreditation in the face of powerful profit-making opportunities.

A similar pioneering innovation is the community interest company (CIC) in the UK. Established under law in 2005, more than 1,400 such organizations now operate in that country. CICs are legally required to operate for the benefit of the community but may also pay (limited) profits to shareholders and financially compensate their board members (Chertok *et al.*, 2008). CICs may be publicly owned (by government) or privately owned. And if dissolved, its assets may only be distributed to a charity or another CIC. (The latter provision is called an "asset lock".) Clearly CICs are also perched on the hilltop with some pressures to roll down into the commercial valley, depending on ownership, board composition and the vitality of external regulation to push back. However, this hilltop may be fairly flat and indeed might even lean toward the social purpose valley, depending on shareholder composition and the vigor of the regulatory regime. According to Reiser (2011, 113, 114): "in a CIC, the community benefit requirement, asset lock, and dividend caps all structurally enforce a commitment to social goals", hence "the CIC may be evidence that a statute can go too far in enforcing blended mission ... to the detriment of the original goal of getting more funding for social purposes".

A related construct discussed by Gidron (2010) is the so-called social purpose business (SPBs). The SPB differs from the L3C, the CIC and the B Corp in that an SPB's profits are explicitly retained within the business and private investors are "rewarded" solely by the knowledge of the profitability and social returns on their investments. Essentially SPBs observe a non-distribution of profits constraint much like conventional nonprofit organizations. Presumably, successful SPBs would attract greater investments by socially minded investor/philanthropists while less successful ones would lose such support. SPBs could also be the beneficiaries of supportive tax policies such as investor tax credits or limited taxes on profits.

The question in this case is whether the SPB is really any different from a conventional nonprofit organization which must adhere to a non-distribution of profits constraint. One difference would be its governance which would be controlled by its investors rather than an otherwise appointed or elected nonprofit board. But given that these investors would essentially be philanthropists rather than profit-seekers, it is unclear whether the SPB wouldn't just be a particular version of a "stakeholder-driven" nonprofit organization where the stakeholders are the donor/investors (Krashinsky, 2003; Young, 2011). It seems likely that SPBs would essentially roll down into the social purpose valley without much pull back from commercial forces.

Social enterprise in the form of sometimes very complex partnership arrangements among private, public and nonprofit entities need to be examined on an individual basis for their particular governance and financing arrangements and the forces they create for stability, transformation or dissolution. A common form is the nonprofit holding company that owns business enterprises for the purpose of both generating revenue and providing training, employment and other supportive services. Tuckman (2009) documents that nonprofits frequently operate for-profit subsidies and he discusses some of the strategic and economic advantages of this strategy for the parent nonprofit. These include exploitation of economies of scale and scope, diversification of revenues and the strategic advantages of separate accounting for nonprofit and for-profit activities. Cordes *et al.* (2009) document some interesting variations of this form.

One set of examples is fairly straightforward. The Delancey Street Foundation owns a moving company, restaurant and catering service, print and copy shop, and an automotive service center. Pioneer Human Services is a nonprofit that owns manufacturing and water jet cutting, aerospace machining, silk screening, food buying, construction, institutional catering, property management and construction companies, along with a cafe, delicatessen, hotel and a business incubator for socially responsible businesses. Juma Ventures is a nonprofit that owns a series of Ben & Jerry franchises, and Juma also partners with financial institutions such as Citibank to provide financial literacy educational programs for high school students. In these cases, the stability of the overall enterprise seems assured as long as governance lies clearly in the hands of a nonprofit board focused on its social mission and the businesses are wholly owned by the nonprofit. Dangers of mission drift, however, derive from the heavy reliance of these nonprofit enterprises on sales revenues and the temptations to promote commercial successes at the expense of social goals. Moreover, it is possible that some of these businesses become merely cash cows for the enterprise as a whole, although this is not necessarily at odds with the social mission so long as the profitable businesses are strategically positioned within the larger mission-oriented program portfolio (Oster, 2010). In all, the stability of these arrangements depends heavily on the strength and integrity of the parent's governing board and its ability to maintain its mission focus and (at least) majority ownership in its businesses over time.

Other examples provided by Cordes *et al.* (2009) reflect the opposite case of nonprofit parent organizations that either run or develop and spin-off businesses internally. The Green Institute runs several programs that promote sustainable economic development, including a green building, a resource center that provides materials and design tools for the use of green technologies, a reuse center and a deconstruction services program. It is financed by a combination of donations and fee revenue. Alternatively, Benetech is a combination of two interconnected nonprofit organizations and a wholly owned profit-making subsidiary which serves as an incubator for new socially useful, technology-based products such as ATMs and vending machines for the visually impaired or literacy tools for autistic children. Benetech solicits donors/investors to support business plans to move projects to commercial viability and ultimately sells them off to for-profit firms that can bring them to market. Benetech is highly dependent on product sales. These two examples provide an interesting contrast in terms of stabilizing and destabilizing forces. They both sit on the stable bottom of the social purpose valley and they both have strong ties to the marketplace. However, the Green Institute copes internally with the pressures of commercially successful ventures, needing to balance continually the temptations to expand profitable ventures and curtail loss-making ones, while Benetech escapes some of this by spinning off its successes and redirecting its energies to new socially useful products. In both cases, however, the overall nonprofit governance structure helps to maintain the mission focus and social purpose orientation over time.

Several more complex social enterprise examples offered by Cordes *et al.* (2009) – New Community Corporation, Manchester-Bidwell Corporation and Housing Works – have the structure of conglomerates consisting of a parent company and a series of nonprofit and for-profit subsidiaries or affiliates with interlocking boards. While these "systems" are governed by a nonprofit umbrella that must maintain the overall social purpose orientation, the potential for going off course seems considerable. Cordes *et al.* (2009, 78) offer a description that suggests both the risks and benefits:

"there are reasons, not necessarily related to mission, for an entity to organize itself into a conglomerate. It is a very fluid organizational structure, allowing resources to flow between affiliates. Creating separate affiliated entities gives an organization leeway to engage in activities that may be only peripherally related to its stated mission or to experiment with new program areas". Two stability-related issues arise here. First, could the overall enterprise tip into the commercial sphere, leaving behind its social goals if, for example, the scheme was used simply to obfuscate the compensation of its leaders? The lack of transparency associated with such complex systems requires great trust to be placed in their leadership to resist the temptations of the commercial marketplace. Second, how strong is the glue that holds a conglomerate system together? If strong tensions exist between its profit-making and nonprofit parts, the system could potentially fly apart, with its components landing in their corresponding social and commercial valleys or dissolving for lack of financial viability or effective governance. To date, experience with these mixed conglomerate social enterprises is insufficient to render judgment on long term stability. Conglomerates in the for-profit sector, of course, have their own checkered history of instability, breaking apart when the component companies fit together poorly or can prosper more effectively on their own (think AOL-Time Warner). While for-profit conglomerates tend to be much larger, nonprofit conglomerates are in some ways more complex, especially in their mixture of nonprofit and for-profit forms.

A final group of social enterprises described by Cordes *et al.* (2009) consist essentially of quid pro quo partnerships between profit-making corporations and mission-focused nonprofits that depend for much of their support on revenues from the corporation in exchange for marketing and other public relations benefits. First Book and several commercial publishers, and City Year and Timberland, illustrate this genre of social enterprise. Cause-related marketing arrangements have become quite common over the past two decades. As previously suggested, the partners to such enterprises are each generically stable in their respective commercial and social purpose valleys. The partnership itself, however, can be tenuous in its balance of social benefits and commercial success or its sustainability as a satisfactory relationship for each partner. At stake from the nonprofit side is reputation and trust, given the risks of associating with a disreputable company or promoting products or services inconsistent with social missions. Both the finance and governance dimensions can be problematic in these arrangements. Governance may depend on the relative bargaining powers of the two partners, a possibly daunting situation for small nonprofits partnering with large corporations. And too heavy financial dependence on one or a few corporate partners can put the nonprofit partner in a vulnerable position, unable to avoid commercial exploitation and/or effectively address its social goals.

Finally, it is well to point out that even these various subsidiary and partnership arrangements do not exhaust the possibilities. For example, Chertok *et al.* (2008) describe partnerships between nonprofit and for-profit organizations that are linked not by ownership per se but rather by common elements of governance such as overlapping board memberships. They give the example of the for-profit World of Good which invests 10 percent of its profits in its partner nonprofit organization World of Good Development Organization. These organizations have overlapping boards and shared managerial staff. The for-profit also has external investors. The stability of this arrangement clearly depends on maintaining the common governance and management links with strong individuals devoted to mission on both sides of the partnership. One can easily envision circumstances that can test this stability, leading either to disintegration, a split that causes each segment to roll down into its respective valley, or an amalgamation in which one partner dominates and essentially pulls the whole partnership down into its own valley.

Solutions

As argued here, every form of social enterprise is subject to tensions that can lead to long term instability of mission, organizational viability or organizational form. I have also argued that attention to the financial incentives and governance arrangements of any particular form of social enterprise is critical to finding those designs that will maintain their desired mixes of social purpose and commercial success over time. While variations are manifold, the number of essentially distinct organizational arrangements for social enterprise is finite, and since some of those arrangements will tend toward instability, the aim of social enterprise designers should be to find those combinations of finance, governance and legal status that will last. The literature on this subject is very thin. Mozier and Tracey (2010) take a good stab by identifying three generic strategies for managing the tensions of a social enterprise contained within a single (nonprofit) organizational entity: (a) separate the mission and commercial components internally and manage them separately; (b) integrate the social and commercial missions; and (c) build alliances with for-profit businesses. These three approaches are not a bad way of summarizing the various organizational forms and arrangements that we have discussed here. The examples of social enterprises arrangements that we have considered above illustrate each of these approaches, and clearly each strategy has its strengths and weaknesses. Strategy (a) implemented within a particular type of nonprofit, for-profit or mixed form is likely to tip one way or another. Strategy (b) is ideal if compatible and symbiotic social and commercial activities can be identified, though it still needs to be implemented within an overall organizational framework with a particular goal orientation – either essentially commercial or essentially social. Strategy (c) depends on the balances that can be struck in managing the alliances between nonprofit and commercial partners. Thus, for each of these strategies the finer particulars of governance and finance need to be considered in order to develop more robust approaches to social enterprise.

In fact, a more direct approach to stability strategies for social enterprise would focus more explicitly on governance and finance. Governance is essentially about stakeholders who exert varying degrees of organizational control and who may have varying interests and goals. Thus, governing arrangements including the composition of a governing board and the rules by which the board operates will greatly influence whether the social enterprise can maintain its balance as commercial and social purpose stakeholders pull in different directions. Similarly, the mix of financial sources of support can make the difference between autonomy and focus on a desired mission balance on the one hand and co-optation by commercial or governmental interests on the other. Finance and governance strategies are matters of intent that presumably can be designed to buffer a social enterprise from conflicting forces in its host and external environments.

For generically stable forms occupying our metaphorical valleys, the strategies need to focus on preventing relatively modest perturbations of mission drift from undermining essentially stable conditions, bearing in mind that in the long run even historically stable forms are subject to considerable adjustment when sufficiently turbulent or fundamental developments take place in the environment, such as globalization, technological innovation and structural changes in the business sector and the role of government. For (hybrid) social enterprises tenuously balanced on the hilltops, the requirements for effective strategy are more demanding and less certain of success, requiring continued attention to the maintenance of counterbalancing forces of governance and finance.

Conclusion

The range of possibilities for the organizational arrangements of social enterprise has sometimes been described as a continuous spectrum ranging from commercial business to entities strictly focused on social goals (Dees and Anderson, 2006; Alter, 2007; Nash, 2010; Teasdale, 2010). The implication of that metaphor is that all combinations are possible and stable and it is simply a matter of choosing the appropriate goals and support structures. Fair-minded and passionate social entrepreneurs and administrators will do the rest.

The hypothesis offered here is somewhat different and it reflects the notion that social enterprises are often caught between two or three different institutional logics (Moore, 2000; Cooney, 2006; Eikenberry, 2009) – between commerce and corporate success on the one hand and social purpose and democratic participation on the other, and possibly captured by governmental interests different from their self-defined social intent (Herranz *et al.*, 2010) In this context, the stability of some of the new hybrid experiments in social enterprise is questionable and careful examination must be given to the long run forces that may tip intendedly "balanced" ventures toward the conventional poles at the extremes of the spectrum. As in chemistry, the periodic table contains lots of elements but some of them are radioactive and have short half-lives. Successful social enterprise requires finding those elements or compounds that are stable over time and the conditions under which they can maintain their stability in the sometimes tenuous balance of social purpose and commercial success. If a spectrum is indeed a valid way to describe the possibilities for social enterprise then it is probably a discrete spectrum, not a continuum, with stable points (our well traveled rhetorical valleys) found at the extremes and perhaps some interesting bright spectral lines (relatively gentle hill tops or plateaus) at points in-between. Research on this question has hardly begun and represents a robust challenge for future explorers of the topography of social enterprise.

Note

* Thanks to Bradley Hill for his able assistance in searching the literature, to my son Barry for his help with the diagram and to Janelle Kerlin, Ben Gidron, Zeke Hasenfeld and Joe Galaskiewicz for their comments and suggestions on earlier drafts.

References

Aiken, Mike. 2010. "Social Enterprises: Challenges from the Field". In Billis op. cit.: 153–174.

Alter, Kim. 2007. *Social Enterprise Typology.* Washington, DC: Virtue Ventures LLC, www.4lenses.org/book/export/html/58

Anderson, Beth Battle and J. Gregory Dees. 2006. "Rhetoric, Reality, and Research: Building a Solid Foundation for the Practice of Social Entrepreneurship". In Alex Nicolls (ed.), *Social Entrepreneurship.* Oxford: Oxford University Press: 144–168.

Bagnoli, Luca and Cecilia Megali. 2009. "Measuring Performance in Social Enterprises". *Nonprofit and Voluntary Sector Quarterly* (December), http://nvs.sagepub.com/content/early/2009/0899764009351111

Billis, David (ed.). 2010. *Hybrid Organizations and the Third Sector.* Basingstoke, UK: Palgrave Macmillan.

Billitteri, Thomas J. 2007. *Mixing Mission and Business: Does Social Enterprise Need a New Legal Approach?* Washington, DC: The Aspen Institute.

Borzaga, Carlo and Jacques Defourny (eds.). 2001. *The Emergence of Social Enterprise.* London: Routledge.

Bosma, Niels and Jonathan Levie. 2009. *Global Entrepreneurship Monitor: 2009 Global Report.* Global Entrepreneurship Research Association, www.gemconsortium.org/

Brody, Evelyn. 2009. "Business Activities of Nonprofit Organizations: Legal Boundary Problems". In Cordes and Steuerle op. cit.: 83–127.

Chertok, Michael, Jeff Hammoui and Eliot Jamison. 2008. "The Funding Gap". *Stanford Social Innovation Review* Spring: 44–51.

Cooney, Kate. 2006. "The Institutional and Technical Structuring of Nonprofit Ventures: Case Study of a U.S. Hybrid Organization Caught Between Two Fields". *Voluntas* 17(2): 143–161.

Cooney, Kate. 2010. "An Exploratory Study of Social Purpose Business Models in the United States". *Nonprofit and Voluntary Sector Quarterly* (January), http://nvs.sagepub.com/content/early/2010/01/22/0899764009351591

Cordes, Joseph J. and C. Eugene Steuerle (eds). 2009. *Nonprofits and Business*. Washington, DC: The Urban Institute Press.

Cordes, Joseph J., Zina Poletz and C. Eugene Steuerle. 2009. "Examples of Nonprofit-For-Profit Hybrid Business Models". In Cordes and Steuerle op. cit.: 69–82.

Cornforth, Chris and Roger Spear. 2010. "The Governance of Hybrid Organizations". In Billis op. cit.: 70–90.

Dees, J. Gregory and Beth Battle Anderson. 2006. "Framing a Theory of Social Entrepreneurship: Building on Two Schools of Practice and Thought". In Rachel Mosher-Williams (ed.), *Research on Social Entrepreneurship*, ARNOVA Occasional Paper Series 1(3): 39–66.

Eikenberry, Angela M. 2009. "Refusing the Market: A Democratic Discourse for Voluntary and Nonproft Organizations". *Nonprofit and Voluntary Sector Quarterly* 38(4): 582–596.

Foster, William and Jeffrey Bradach. 2005. "Should Nonprofits Seek Profits?" *Harvard Business Review* 83: 92–100.

Garrow, Eve. 2010. "A Comparative Case Study of Work Integration Social Enterprises". Paper presented at the Seventh Annual West Coast Nonprofit Data Conference, Portland, OR, April 24.

Gidron, Benjamin. 2010. "Policy Challenges in Light of the Emerging Phenomenon of Social Businesses". *Nonprofit Policy Forum* 1(1), www.degruyter.com/npf.

Hansmann, Henry. 1996. *The Ownership of Enterprise*. Cambridge, MA: Harvard University Press.

Helm, Scott T. 2010. "Social Enterprise and Nonprofit Ventures". In David O. Renz and Associates, *The Jossey-Bass Handbook of Nonprofit Leadership and Management*, 3rd edn. San Francisco: Jossey-Bass: 524–552.

Herranz, Joaquin Jr., Logan R. Council and Brenna McKay. 2010. "Tri-Value Organization as a Form of Social Enterprise: The Case of Seattle's Fare Start". *Nonprofit and Voluntary Sector Quarterly*, forthcoming, http://nvs.sagepub.com/content/early/2010/06/01/0899764010369178

Hodgkinson, Virginia A. and Murray S. Weitzman. 1993. *The Nonprofit Almanac: Dimensions of the Independent Sector*. Washington, DC: Independent Sector.

Jones, Marshall B. 2007. "The Multiple Sources of Mission Drift". *Nonprofit and Voluntary Sector Quarterly* 36(2): 299–307.

Kerlin, Janelle A. 2006. "Social Enterprise in the United States and Europe: Understanding and Learning from the Differences". *Voluntas* 17(3): 247–263.

Kerlin, Janelle A. (ed.). 2009. *Social Enterprise: A Global Comparison*. Medford, MA: Tufts University Press.

Kerlin, Janelle A. 2010a. "A Comparative Analysis of the Global Emergence of Social Enterprise". *Voluntas* 21: 162–179.

Kerlin, Janelle A. 2010b. "Nonprofit Commercial Revenue: A Replacement for Declining Government Grants and Private Contributions". *American Review of Public Administration*.

Kleinberger, Daniel S. 2010. "The Fatal Design Defects of L3Cs". *The Nonprofit Quarterly* 17(2): 38–43.

Krashinsky, M. 2003. "Stakeholder Theories of the Nonprofit Sector: One Cut at the Economic Literature." In H. Anheier and A. Ben-Ner (eds), *The Study of Nonprofit Enterprise*. New York: Kluwer Academic/Plenum Publishers, 2003, pp. 125–136.

Mannan, Manzurul. 2009. "BRAC: Anatomy of a 'Poverty Enterprise'". *Nonprofit Management and Leadership* 20(2): 219–233.

Moore, Mark H. 2000. "Managing for Value: Organizational Strategy in For-Profit, Nonprofit, and Governmental Organizations". *Nonprofit and Voluntary Sector Quarterly* 29: 183–208.

Mozier, Jonathan and Paul Tracey. 2010. "Strategy Making in Social Enterprise: The Role of Resource Allocation and Its Effects on Organizational Sustainability". 2010. *Systems Research and Behavioral Science* 27: 252–266.

Nash, Matthew T. 2010. "Social Entrepreneurship and Social Enterprise". In David O. Renz and Associates, *The Jossey-Bass Handbook of Nonprofit Leadership and Management*, 3rd edn. San Francisco: Jossey-Bass: 262–298.

Oster, Sharon M. 2010. "Product Diversification and Social Enterprise". In Bruce A. Seaman and Dennis R. Young (eds), *Handbook of Research on Nonprofit Economics and Management*. Cheltenham, UK: Edward Elgar.

Oster, Sharon M., Cynthia W. Massarsky and Samantha L. Beinhacker. 2004. *Generating and Sustaining Nonprofit Earned Income*. San Francisco: Jossey-Bass.

Page, Anthony and Robert A. Katz. 2011. "Freezing Out Ben & Jerry: Corporate Law and the Sale of a Social Enterprise Icon". *Vermont Law Review* 35: 211–249.

Reiser, Dana Brakman. 2011. "Blended Enterprise and the Dual Mission Dilemma". *Vermont Law Review* 35(105): 105–116.

Rudney, Gabriel. 1987. "The Scope and Dimensions of Nonprofit Activity". In Walter W. Powell (ed.), *The Nonprofit Sector: A Research Handbook*. New Haven, CT: Yale University Press: 55–64.

Salamon, Lester M., Helmut K. Anheier, Stefan Toepler and S. Wojciech Sokolowski and Associates (eds). 1999. *Global Civil Society: Dimensions of the Nonprofit Sector*. Baltimore, MD: Johns Hopkins Center for Civil Society Studies.

Shockley, Gordon E., Peter M. Frank and Roger R. Stough (eds). 2008. *Non-Market Entrepreneurship*. Cheltenham, UK: Edward Elgar.

Smith, Steven Rathgeb and Michael Lipsky. 1993. *Nonprofits for Hire*. Cambridge, MA: Harvard University Press.

Squazzoni, Flaminio. 2009. "Social Entrepreneurship and Economic Development in Silicon Valley: A Case Study on The Joint Venture: Silicon Valley Network". *Nonprofit and Voluntary Sector Quarterly* 38(5): 869–883.

Steinberg, Richard. 2006. "Economic Theories of Nonprofit Organizations". In Walter W. Powell and Richard Steinberg (eds), *The Nonprofit Sector: A Research Handbook*, 2nd edn. New Haven: Yale University Press: 65–82.

Strom, Stephanie. 2010. "A Marriage of Differing Missions". *New York Times: Business Day*, October 20: B1, B8.

Teasdale, Simon. 2010. "How Can Social Enterprise Address Disadvantage? Evidence from an Inner City Community". *Journal of Nonprofit & Public Sector Marketing* 22: 89–107.

Tuckman, Howard P. 2009. "The Strategic and Economic Value of Hybrid Nonprofit Structures". In Cordes and Steuerle op. cit.: 129–153.

Van Slyke, David M. and Harvey K. Newman. 2006. "Venture Philanthropy and Social Entrepreneurship in Community Redevelopment". *Nonprofit Management and Leadership* 16(3): 345–368.

Weisbrod, Burton A. 1998. *To Profit or Not to Profit?* New York: Cambridge University Press.

Weisbrod, Burton A. 2004. "The Pitfalls of Profits". *Stanford Social Innovation Review* 2(3): 40–47.

Yitshaki, Ronit, Miri Lerner and Moshe Sharir. 2008. "What are Social Ventures? Towards a Theoretical Framework and Empirical Examination of Successful Social Ventures". In Shockley, Frank and Stough op. cit.: 217–241.

Young, Dennis R. (ed.). 2007. *Financing Nonprofits*. Lanham, MD: AltaMira Press.

Young, Dennis R. 2008. "A Unified Theory of Social Enterprise". In Shockley, Frank and Stough op. cit.: 175–205.

Young, Dennis R. 2009. "Alternative Perspectives on Social Enterprise". In Cordes and Steuerle op. cit.: 21–46.

Young, Dennis R. 2011. "The Prospective Role of Economic Stakeholders in the Governance of Nonprofit Organizations". *Voluntas*, online; print version forthcoming.

Young, Dennis R. and Judith Manfredo Legorreta. 1986. "Why Organizations Turn Nonprofit: Lessons from Case Studies". In Susan Rose-Ackerman (ed.), *The Economics of Nonprofit Institutions*. New York: Oxford University Press: 196–204.

Young, Dennis R. and Richard Steinberg. 1995. *Economics for Nonprofit Managers*. New York: The Foundation Center.

2
Social Enterprises and Social Categories

Joseph Galaskiewicz and Sondra N. Barringer*

The discussion of what makes nonprofits and for-profits different from one another is still relevant. Research has touched upon the role of the non-distribution constraint (Hansmann, 1980), values or preferences of leaders (Weisbrod, 1998a), funding streams (Frumkin and Galaskiewicz, 2004) and legal status (Stark, 2010). There is usually the assumption that the identities of the organizations under study are unambiguous and their forms distinct.

The fact is that while organizations may be incorporated as nonprofits or for-profits, many are hybrids. They have elements drawn from different sectors, combined in novel and provocative ways. Indeed almost all nonprofits rely on sales unrelated to their mission activities and provide private as well as public benefits. Also firms often have some public or community service component. Yet some organizations appear to go to extremes and, while embracing one form, they operate according to a logic characteristic of another form. The social enterprise is such a case. Given that the emergence of organizational forms is a topic that has been central to organizational theory from its inception, it is important to spend some time thinking about what makes this form distinct and some of the problems it creates.

In this chapter we put forward two arguments. First, social enterprises are controversial because they are difficult for audiences to categorize and thus difficult for them to hold accountable. The claims of social enterprises do not always match up with what they do. Claims about who they are evoke behavioral norms that social enterprises are evaluated against and which then become the basis for external audiences to validate their claims of authenticity. Because it is a hybrid by definition, the social enterprise is "betwixt and between" different categories. Second, given its marginality, we argue that being a social enterprise is a high risk strategy. On the one hand, straddling two categories (for-profit and nonprofit) allows them to exploit opportunities in these different domains which more "legitimate" businesses and charities cannot tap into. On the other hand, this may confuse audiences and engender distrust. Nonprofits may be "too business-like" or for-profits "too ideological" and thus suspect and better to avoid. So the downside is that stakeholders may find them too confusing, question their legitimacy or simply ignore them, while the potential benefits are the "fruits" which purer forms are forbidden to taste.

Organizational identities

When stakeholders (or audiences) have to interact with organizations there is always the problem of information asymmetries and the potential for opportunism. Over the years different theorists have offered different solutions. Williamson (1975) says the solution is hierarchical control; Ouchi (1979) says culture; Granovetter (1985) says networks; Podolny (1993) says status; Zukerman (1999) and Hsu and Hannan (2005) say identity. While research continues on markets and hierarchies, status and networks, there has been an explosion of research on the topic of organizational identity and categorization in the last ten years.

Early work focused on how managers, employees and volunteers "saw themselves" (e.g. Albert and Whetten, 1985). Organizational identities were part of the organizational culture and were important because mission, routines, structures, technology and marketing strategies are the product of sense-making. Peters and Waterman (1982) were among the first to talk about the strategic importance of culture and identity for business firms. The classic paper by Albert and Whetten (1985) described the identity dilemmas faced by institutions of higher education. Are they primarily revenue generating machines (commercial enterprises) or purveyors of truth and producers of public knowledge (moral enterprises)? In truth, these institutions are hybrids which seek to balance these two contradictory "identities." often resulting in indetermination. The contribution of the Albert and Whetten (1985) paper was to show that this indetermination was the product of fundamental identity conflicts within the organization.

Negro *et al.* (2010) traced the origins of the recent research on organizational identity to work done in the open systems tradition.[1] They cited the work by Meyer and Rowan (1977) and DiMaggio and Powell (1983) on the role of cultural systems in shaping organizational behaviors and giving rise to organizational forms and saw current research evolving out of the cultural and cognitive revolution spearheaded by neo-institutional theory (see DiMaggio and Powell, 1991). The various identities which organizations could assume were not constructed by the organizations themselves or even dictated by their core technology. Rather these existed within the cultural domain and organizations adopted these existing templates. Although DiMaggio and Powell (1983, 1991) did not talk about categories directly, DiMaggio (1987) studied classification systems, how they were formed and their importance in the art world. Friedland and Alford (1991) introduced institutional logics into the organizations literature, Stryker (2000) described how competing logics can co-exist in the same organization, and Clemens (1993) showed how organizational strategists could alter others" perceptions and legitimate their own agendas by borrowing cultural templates from other organizations. Other important contributions were Padgett and Ansell's (1993) study of how contemporaries perceived Cosimo de'Medici in Renaissance Florence and Snow *et al.*'s (1986) research on the role of framing in collective action.

Another important development was the work of Hannan and Freeman (1977) on population ecology, which focused on niches, selection and organizational forms (Negro *et al.*, 2010). Forms were an important part of their theory, because forms were analogous to species in plant and animal ecology. To study population dynamics, the population under study had to have a unitary character: "the most salient kind of unitary character for our concerns is *common dependence on the material and social environment*" (Hannan and Freeman, 1989, 45). But they then asserted that to identify these "common dependencies" one should look at structures of organizations and social boundaries. This was the rationale for using stated goals, authority structure, core technology and marketing strategy to identify organizational forms (ibid., 51). But Carroll and Swaminathan's (2000) paper on the role of audiences in explaining births and deaths in breweries and microbreweries was the important breakthrough. It was the judgments of the beer aficionados about the authenticity of these forms that enabled them to prosper.

Negro *et al.* (2010) pointed out that in the 1980s there was also considerable work on the social structure of markets which combined both material and cultural elements (e.g. White, 1981; Porac and Thomas, 1990). We believe the work on reputation and status is especially salient. Who is influential in organizational fields (Laumann and Knoke, 1987); who is philanthropic (Galaskiewicz, 1985); who is capable of producing quality products (Fombrun and Shanley, 1990)? Subsequent empirical work showed that an organization's effectiveness was contingent on others' opinions and evaluations, e.g. one's status, especially under conditions of uncertainty (Podolny, 1993). Fombrun (1996) made the important distinction between the obvious benefits of reputation for marketing, the role of reputation for inter-organizational collaboration and the importance of reputation for organizational legitimacy. The latter point was a fundamental argument of neo-institutional theory, and many studies looked at referents of legitimacy (e.g. being listed as a charity or in a community directory) and the effects on organizational survival (Singh *et al.*, 1991). The argument was that these referents ensured the sociopolitical legitimacy of organizations in the eyes of stakeholders.

At the same time, the real world was changing and presented serious challenges to anyone trying to identify pure types of organizational forms.

For starters, multidivisional firms often had hundreds of products that they were manufacturing, various technologies in development and operation, different markets they were serving, and it was unclear whether the characteristic authority structure was that of the entire firm or only that within a particular division. As companies built strategic alliances with other firms, it became more and more difficult to know where the legal boundaries of one firm began and the other ended. Firms blended into one another, and distinct red, yellow and blue forms blended into shades of orange, violet and green.

Categories as field-level constructs

Negro *et al.*, (2010, 7) argued that "Zuckerman's (1999, 2000) work was the first to explicitly draw attention to category systems as taken-for-granted constructs that influence market behavior and market outcomes." Zuckerman (1999) linked the ideas of category, form and niche together. Consistent with ecological thinking, forms are defined by niches (structural dependencies), but attached to each form is a set of norms, expectations and standards, and stakeholders use these to classify and make judgments about organizations. An important part of the theory is that the audience or stakeholder needs performance standards which are linked to the categories which organizations make claims to in order to evaluate organizations properly. In his empirical work on firms and stock analysts, Zuckerman showed that firms which didn't exhibit traits that matched any category (because of diversification) were simply ignored because audiences (industry analysts) did not know how to evaluate them against peers. As a consequence, their stock price suffered.

Hsu *et al.* (2009) took us through how the process works (see Figure 2.1). First, the source of identity is not the organization itself but what stakeholders or audiences attribute to the organization. The idea that a restaurant is "really good" may be held by owners and employees, but it is more important that customers have the same idea. Second, audiences do not construct identities but rather they use established category labels to assign identities to organizations. Customers may say "it's a really good Japanese restaurant" using the category "Japanese restaurant" as the benchmark against which they evaluate *this* Japanese restaurant. Third, traits or schemas which are associated with categories are the way audiences assign firms to different categories. If organizations distribute themselves across an elaborate table of cross-classified dimensions, e.g. products (sushi, sake), types of customers (Asians, yuppies), price (expensive), types of workers (Japanese), so that they have enough traits associated with a given category (Japanese restaurant), then audiences assign memberships (or affiliations) to categories. The identity assigned to an organization doesn't necessarily mean that it has all the traits ascribed to an identity (there may be a Caucasian waitress). Just so

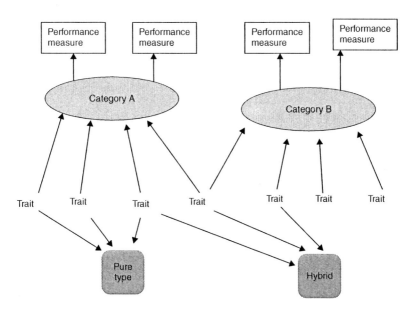

Figure 2.1 Categories, traits, performance measures and organizational forms

long as it doesn't have traits which violate expectations (hot dogs on the menu or reggae music), *audiences assume that it has the other traits.*

Some organizations will easily be categorized – we might call them pure types, while others will have traits that are associated with different forms – we might call these hybrids (pan-Asian cuisine). Categorization is important because a category enables the audience to then draw on rules, standards and measures that can be applied against the organization's performance to evaluate it and hold it accountable. Typically, audiences are uncomfortable with hybrids or boundary spanners, because it challenges the purity of the categories and makes it difficult to hold them accountable. In a pan-Asian restaurant, should the food be evaluated against Japanese, Chinese, Korean or Thai cuisine? As a result, the expectation is that audiences may label them suspect or eat somewhere else.

Finally, the firm is not completely passive in the process. Producers actively try to fit themselves into categories, to make claims, so as to be evaluated "correctly" (Hsu *et al.*, 2009). The goal is to acquire or display enough traits so that your audience perceives you in the right way. Just as organizations will seek to brand themselves, they will also try to impress audiences with external referents of prestige (Perrow, 1961), advertising (Fombrun and Shanley, 1990), affiliations with entities which customers feel positive toward (Cornwell and Coote, 2005) and dissociate from sordid practices and people (e.g. Accenture droppings its sponsorship of Tiger Woods). Thus the process of sorting firms into categories is happening on both sides of the market and should be viewed as a negotiated outcome.

In summary, categorization is good for audiences (it provides them with a coherent way to understand an uncertain world) and good for producers (they do not have to bear the economic burden of carrying all the traits of an identity). Each category has a "story" attached to it which includes its history, traditions and institutional logic(s). Associations, the mass media and industry players both update these stories and embellish them, similar to the way Wikipedia works. Thus these stories both change and remain intact over time. However, audiences need to categorize accurately and with confidence, while firms need to be sure that stakeholders categorize them "correctly." While rooted in cognitive theories, the categorization relies heavily on social processes, institutional memories and market signals.

The peculiar nature of social enterprises

Young (2009, 23) says that a "social enterprise is activity intended to address social goals through the operation of private organizations in the market-place." Light (2008) says that it is an organization that advances social benefit in a "revolutionary way." though the strategy is to maximize profits through traditional business practices, e.g. selling goods and services. We will not review the many nuances of meaning attached to social enterprises inasmuch as Young (Chapter 1) presents an excellent overview of the theory and research on this topic. However, a good working definition of a social enterprise is a private organization working toward a social welfare goal while participating fully in the marketplace.

The social enterprise is special, because it incorporates contradictory institutional logics into its mission and operations. Garrow and Hasenfeld (Chapter 5), McInerney (Chapter 7) and Child (Chapter 8) make the same point. For example, Garrow and Hasenfeld describe in detail how four work integration social enterprises (WISEs) employed and trained less advantaged workers to produce and/or provide goods and services in a competitive market context and struggled with the conflict between commodification and service logics. Other examples of this type of organization include Goodwill Industries and the Greyston Bakery (Young and Salamon 2002; Young, Chapter 1 in this book). Another example is a social enterprise that markets and sells goods and services to disadvantaged populations which will provide long term benefits to them, e.g. low interest loans, disinfectants, simple farm technology, sewing machines, and short term profits to the enterprise. The Grameen Bank is the best known example, and nonprofit and for-profit enterprises embracing Prahalad's (2005) "bottom of the pyramid" strategy also exemplify this approach. Young and Salamon (2002, 433) sum up these latter developments well: "these various experiences with commercial enterprise on the part of nonprofit organizations are beginning to put nonprofit commercial activity into a new light. No longer conceived simply as a revenue generation strategy, these ventures treat market engagement as the most effective way to pursue a nonprofit organizations' mission, to provide marketable skills to the structurally unemployed, or to change behavior in an environmentally sensitive way." These strategies are pursued both by for-profits and by nonprofits alike.

There are many questions surrounding social enterprises. How much is this simply a "left over" from the era when economics and business thought it had all the answers, i.e. nonprofits just need to become more businesslike? Can social enterprises be big, old, bureaucratic organizations as well as small, new organizations run by visionary social entrepreneurs (Light, 2008)? Is goal displacement (or mission drift) a problem (Minkoff and Powell, 2006; Tuckman and Chang, 2006)? Is it possible that disadvantaged workers or the poor will be exploited? At what point does a social enterprise transform into an enterprise or a charity? Who is responsible for ensuring that social enterprises "do the right thing," i.e. are held accountable (Frumkin, 2002)? In the case of for-profits, is it ethical or even legal to expend funds that do not further investors' interests directly (Kahn, 1997)? Can firms really do good and do well (Orlitzky *et al.*, 2003; Galaskiewicz and Colman, 2006)? There are more questions than answers surrounding social enterprises.

Categorization and social enterprises

In this chapter we argue that when evaluating any type of organization, audiences will categorize it based on two sets of traits: organizational inputs and who benefits. On the input side, we are interested in the modality of exchange, e.g. a gift versus an exchange (we label the latter "sales"). On the output side, we are interested in who benefits, e.g. the public, principals or agents. The argument is that audiences figure out the category of the organization by looking at the niche (defined by a multi-dimensional cross-classification of organizational dependencies) in which it is situated (see Hsu *et al.*, 2009).

Figure 2.2 shows what this classification might look like.[2] The horizontal axis describes the input structure ranging from gifts (donations) to exchanges (sales). The vertical axis describes who benefits with the public at large and clients/customers juxtaposed against agents (employees) and principals (owners, investors, donors, etc.). Forms range from traditional charities which produce a high volume of public benefit and are supported by donations and volunteers (United Way, for example) to traditional firms which produce ordinary profits for owners and investors, a livelihood for employees and are funded by sales (Wal-Mart, for example). Each of these organizations is unequivocal, easy for audiences to categorize and has a clear identity. The input and beneficiary traits associated with each are

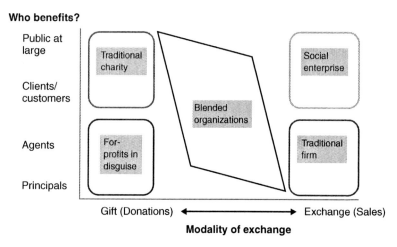

Figure 2.2   The niche defines the criteria for accountability and authenticity
Source: adopted from Blau and Scott (1962).

indisputable and relatively easy to identify. Those in the north-west can claim to be charities and those in the south-east can claim to be firms. Few would challenge these claims.

Hybrid forms include organizations which provide a mix of public and private benefits and are funded by a mix of sales or fees and donations or grants. The pure hybrids, in the center of the graph, might be labeled blended forms, because they encompass a mix of traits. It is common to use profit earned through the sale of goods and services to cross-subsidize unprofitable mission related activity (James, 1983; Weisbrod, 1998a). This strategy is employed both by nonprofits (e.g. using profits from a museum store to keep admission fees low) and for-profits (e.g. corporate philanthropy). However, the former rely on other revenue streams, e.g. contributions and grants, and the latter are still primarily profit oriented. That is, they are blending or blurring the boundaries between the traditional organizational forms.

Because blended organizations are so mixed up, audiences come to expect almost anything from them (but nothing consistent). They are unambiguously ambiguous. Higher education is perhaps the best example. On the one hand, we know that approximately 69.2 percent of the revenue of private nonprofit doctoral and research universities was "earned"[3] on average in 2009 and that 10.5 percent[4] was in the form of gifts, contributions and grants.[5] On the other hand, it is common knowledge that university presidents are paid very handsomely and endowments are flush (Fuller, 2010). For example, the average endowment in 2009 for private nonprofit doctoral and research universities was approximately $1.4 billion according to the National Endowment Study

(NACUBO, 2010). We also know that donors' children often get preferential treatment when applying to college, the so-called legacy admissions (Farrell, 2007). However, on average, 74.9 percent of full-time first-time undergraduate students in four-year private nonprofit colleges and universities received institutional grant aid in the 2008–09 academic year with the average amount being $9,879[6] which is a form of social welfare. Thus the schools bring in funding from a range of sources and provide benefits to principals (donors), agents (university presidents and faculty) and the public (disadvantaged students). Audiences become accustomed to such contradictions, but it is difficult to know exactly what are the universities' agendas.

In the upper right quartile of Figure 2.2, we find our first extreme hybrid, social enterprises. They provide substantial social welfare benefits, do not (or only minimally) distribute residual earnings to owners or investors, but are supported almost exclusively by sales or fees. Based on input traits, they would be categorized as firms, but based on beneficiaries they would be categorized as charities. We have already mentioned nonprofit WISEs and the Grameen Bank. There are also the early incarnations of The Body Shop, Ben & Jerry's, the Kiva Bank and Newman's Own (Frumkin, 2002; Vogel, 2005).

In the lower left quartile, we find our second extreme hybrid, for-profits in disguise (Weisbrod, 1988). They receive donations which are often tax-deductible as charitable contributions, but these are used to produce private, not public, benefits. Based on inputs, they would be categorized as charities, but based on beneficiaries they would be categorized as businesses. That is, while principals make donations or give gifts to the organization, they and/ or administrators and staff derive significant benefits, thus raising the question whether the third parties benefited at all. Examples in the charitable sector are donations to sports booster clubs (in exchange for preferential seating), to arts and museum fund-raisers (in exchange for invitations to receptions and access to artists/performers) and universities (in exchange for naming rights and "legacy admissions"). This also applies to charitables which pay their administrators and staff exorbitant salaries or provide excessive perquisites.[7]

Among these two extreme hybrids, both claims about who benefits and organizational actions are important, because they signal to stakeholders what criteria should be used to evaluate them. If the charity receives donations and claims to be a public benefit organization but provides significant benefits to donors and administrators or staff, it will pass muster on one criterion, being the recipient of tax deductible contributions, but an attorney general may question whether it deserves its public charity status and the privileges that go with it. On the other hand, investors will be content if the social enterprise claims to be a business and sells goods and services in the marketplace, but they will wonder about the motivation of managers who want to "save the world." Again, doubts are raised about the credibility of the organization.

The problem of accountability

Traditional businesses and charities are easy to categorize (based on their revenue streams and the distribution of benefits) and relatively easy to evaluate with metrics that are accessible to audiences. For example, for charities one can calculate the size and number of gifts and grants, executive compensation and fund-raising costs. For businesses one can calculate sales, market share, dividends and stock price. Claims that organizations make about their identities as charities or firms are tested against agreed upon performance measures.

Organizations that operate outside these two, secure niches face problems of credibility and legitimacy. As hybrids they have need to respond to two (or more) different institutional logics working, quite often, at cross purposes to please their audiences. Numerous authors have pointed this out (e.g. Weisbrod, 1998b; Young and Salamon, 2002; Eikenberry and Kluver, 2004; Tuckman and Chang, 2006; Battilana and Dorado, 2010). Illustrations in this book are to be found in: Chapter 7 in McInerney's study of the nonprofit technology assistance provider, NPower NY; Chapter 8 in Child's study of a fair trade for-profit, Coastal Coffees; and Chapter 5 in Garrow and Hasenfeld's study of 11 WISEs and in-depth presentation of four cases. Table 2.1 describes two different institutional logics.

First, in charities a concern about social welfare drives one to address first societal not investor needs. Expenditures expand as the mission expands. Profit-making activities increase to provide subsidies for ever more needy, but unprofitable, mission related activities (James, 1983). In businesses profits drive expenditures. Investments in research and development, marketing and technology are made so as to meet and stimulate demand. If the traditional firm does anything to advance social welfare, it is rationalized in terms of the bottom line, e.g. cause-related marketing (Galaskiewicz and Coleman, 2006).

Second, charities procure revenues by cajoling donors to give to their cause. They must convince them of the value of their mission, their honesty

Table 2.1 Contradictory institutional logics

The charity logic	The business logic
Maximize profits to meet societal needs	Maximize profits to meet owner/investor needs
Providers procure revenues by cajoling donors to help further their mission	Providers procure revenues by competing on the basis of price and quality
Success based on organizational goal attainment, e.g., furthering the public good	Success based on the ability to maximize the spread between revenues and costs, i.e., profit

and trustworthiness, and their ability to "deliver the goods' (Galaskiewicz *et al.*, 2006). Since donors will not benefit directly, it is difficult for them to know if the organization is trustworthy, and nonprofit entrepreneurs will use both informal (referents of prestige and endorsements) and formal (tax status) signals to assure them. In contrast, "the hallmark of commercial transactions is that providers procure revenues by competing on the basis of price and quality, selling goods and services that are excludable and rival" (ibid). Customers have a fairly good idea of what they want and the quality of what's being sold, thus information asymmetry – and the mistrust which accompanies it – is not as serious a problem.

Finally, the criteria for success are different. As a provider of social welfare outputs, the charity must demonstrate that it has achieved its goals and that somehow social welfare has improved. That is, the criteria are the number of students who graduate from college within six years, the reduction in syphilis, cancer or obesity within a population, or the incidence of crime. If these are not available, analysts look at growth in expenditures or donations (Galaskiewicz and Bielefeld, 1998). For-profits have different criteria in mind. Richard *et al.* (2009) describe the criteria most used in business management journals. They include financial performance (profits, return on assets, return on investment, etc.), product market performance (sales, market share, etc.) and shareholder return (total shareholder return, economic value added, etc.). While they mention other criteria, e.g. innovation, efficiency, corporate social responsibility, they are not the principal measures used. Striving to achieve one set of criteria may mean failing on the other.

Since hybrid organizations embody both logics, they are held accountable to performance measures associated with both institutional logics. This sends mixed signals and makes them appear inauthentic. In higher education, there are many examples of stakeholders filing suit or authorities taking action to clarify what these organizations are truly about. For example, nonprofit colleges and universities are facing increased scrutiny regarding their tax exempt status in light of the rising endowment values of some of these institutions and their rising tuition prices (Fain and Wolverton, 2006; Wolverton, 2007; Blumenstyk, 2010a). For-profit colleges and universities provide another useful illustration. A number of these schools are publicly traded for-profit firms; however, they receive heavy government subsidies in the form of federal financial aid and, for this, are expected to provide a public benefit: quality education for the disadvantaged. In effect they are blended organizations which are subject to the constraints of traditional firms (are they profitable?) but also traditional charities (are they providing a quality education to the disadvantaged?). Because of their ambiguous position and their lack of a clear identity they have been subject to additional scrutiny from Congress and have been accused of misusing government funds that were intended to provide a social benefit: education (Blumenstyk, 2010b;

Field, 2010a, 2010b). Some of these organizations such as Kaplan University and the University of Phoenix among others are facing, or in the case of the University of Phoenix faced, federal lawsuits charging that they have defrauded the federal government of billions of dollars (Blumenstyk, 2005, 2008, 2009). Another nonprofit example is the case of hospitals. The nonprofit hospital exists to benefit the public but they rely heavily on sales and fees. Recently a number of these hospitals have had their tax exemption status called into question, and in some cases revoked, because they are seen as not providing enough of a public or social benefit, specifically they are not providing enough charity care (Schwinn, 2004, 2006a, 2006b, 2006c; Williams, 2009).

A for-profit illustration is found in recent shareholder sanctions against Costco, a for-profit retailer. Costco suffered a 4 percent drop in its share price despite reporting better than expected earnings in 2004. This drop was a result of Wall Street and shareholder dissatisfaction at the way Costco treats its employees (Homes and Zellner, 2004; Vogel, 2005). Costco pays substantially higher wages and covers a larger portion of employee health-care and retirement plans than its major competitor Wal-Mart (Homes and Zellner, 2004; Vogel, 2005). In essence Costco faced challenges because analysts and stockholders saw its employee policies as inconsistent with the business logic, and the nonprofit hospitals faced challenges by government regulators because they were not conforming to the charitable logic of meeting societal needs.

Audiences' responses have been negative to for-profits in disguise, i.e. nonprofits that receive donations and gifts and then use the funds to benefit private individuals. If the organization claims to be a charity, there is the assumption that donations will benefit the general public or clients. When the funds or benefits are instead distributed to principals or agents, there is a contradiction. This can happen because executives appropriate the funds for salaries and/or perquisites, e.g. in the case of Aramony at the United Way (Arenson, 1995) and the American Parkinson Disease Association (Richardson, 1996), or executives receive excessive compensation, e.g. Harvard's Fund Managers (Walsh, 2004; Strout, 2007; Hechinger, 2008). In both situations there are doubts about the credibility of the organization being a charity, and, in the extreme, agents are subject to criminal prosecution such as in the Aramony case.

The appearance of being a for-profit in disguise is an issue for most charities. The question is, how much of one's donations should go to benefit the public at large or clients and how much should benefit those providing the service? In the case of natural disasters, what percentage of donations is siphoned off for relief organizations and how much actually benefits the disaster victims? In the wake of 9/11 the Red Cross faced significant scrutiny for its "banking" donations (Brody, 2006), and there were also accusations of misusing flood relief funds in the Red River Valley Flood of 1997 and Hurricane Katrina in 2005 (Belluck, 1998; Strom, 2002, 2005, 2008). There is also the case of veterans' groups and other charity organizations which pretend to raise money for the disadvantaged but in fact take almost all of the donations as "operating expenses" and use only a small amount for charitable activities (Fernandez, 2009; Rivera, 2010; Rothfeld, 2011). But the same can be said about donations to universities (students versus faculty), hospitals (patients versus staff) and athletic programs (athletes versus coaches). Assuming that donors would prefer to aid disaster victims, veterans, students, patients and athletes and not nonprofit executives, fund raisers, faculties, staff or coaches, they can legitimately question the benefits accruing to service providers.

The situation of social enterprises is more complicated. If a nonprofit cross-subsidizes unprofitable, social welfare activities with revenues from profitable commercial transactions, audiences may be wary of mission drift, i.e. giving priority to commercial rather than mission activities. In the 2006 edition of *The Nonprofit Sector: A Research Handbook* (Powell and Steinberg, 2006), Tuckman and Chang (2006) and Minkoff and Powell (2006) described the potential for goal displacement when nonprofit organizations embraced commercial activities, but interestingly they did not present many case studies illustrating this. In a review in the same volume, Galaskiewicz and Colman (2006) cited research by Bowie (1994) on the ethical issues universities faced as they entered into commercial partnerships with industry and Hall's (1990) study of conflict between board members and staff over becoming more businesslike. Yet in neither case did organizations abandon their charitable mission. Thus while most scholars would agree that with commercialization there is the potential for mission drift, research documenting this is surprisingly thin (Froelich, 1999). Efforts to show that "earned income" can result in the better provision of mission-related activities may be more common and an effective way to meet audiences' conflicting expectations (McInerney, Chapter 7).

The situation of social enterprises which make business strategies integral to their mission related activities have faced more criticism. As we noted earlier, the two prototypes are nonprofits which employ and train hard-to-employ disadvantaged workers to produce and/or sell goods and services to boutique markets and for-profits which seek out business opportunities among previously ignored disadvantaged populations. Mannan (2009) described the various challenges which Building Resources Across Community has faced during its nearly 40-year history but particularly since it has achieved prominence as a key player in microfinance. Mannan (2009) described how: the organization has failed to produce evidence that it has moved people out of poverty; the constant need for capital drives it into all sorts of unrelated activities; Islamic society has challenged it for making loans and charging interest. Its bank has attracted scrutiny since the organization is a voluntary association, and the Bangladesh government has issued rulings against its operations. It is an enormously complex organization, and this has exposed it to many attacks on many fronts.

Rangan *et al.* (2011) also described the pitfalls of those working "at the base of the pyramid." Microfinance in India has come under attack because microlending had not resulted in people escaping poverty. They cite Equitas as a company which has responded by earmarking 5 percent of its profits for clients' health care, skill development and education and capping its profits. However, this makes it all the more difficult to make a profit serving this clientele. The authors also described how Proctor & Gamble and Microsoft had to pass off their initiatives of selling water purification packets and scaled down versions of Windows to their corporate social responsibility groups after they failed to make a profit in these impoverished markets. Certainly, there have been many successes in poorer countries, but Rangan *et al.* (2011) also point out that companies have to know when the local people are capable of being customers and coproducers as opposed to clients who need to be helped.

Aneel Karnani (2011) describes how a host of governments and politicians have begun attacking microfinance in places such as Bangladesh, Cambodia, India, Pakistan and Sri Lanka. He also pointed out that microfinance has not proven to be a panacea for alleviating poverty and called for more regulation of the industry. The interest rates being charged are too high and there is a lack of transparency, hidden charges and plenty of abusive loan recovery. But, most importantly, companies are making too much money! He concludes (ibid., 52), "commercial organizations given opportunities for increasing profits usually act in their self-interest ... appeals for self-restraint on the grounds of ethics and values have not been effective in the business world, and there is no reason to believe commercial microcredit organizations will be any different." Indeed, if there was not the claim that these organizations had a mission to alleviate poverty, it would be simply "business as usual." but that ethnics or morality is somehow part of the business plan makes them vulnerable to criticism.

Hypotheses

After presenting our arguments and reviewing selected cases to illustrate our points, it is important now to formulate hypotheses that researchers could test. We assume that an organization's survival and persistence is dependent upon the perceptions of stakeholders in its environment, since they are the ones upon whom the organization is dependent for resources. We also assume that stakeholder support is a function of stakeholder knowledge of and confidence in the organization. This returns us to our initial argument that categorization within organizational fields is relevant for stakeholder decision-making under conditions of uncertainty.

The ecologists hypothesize that under conditions of environmental uncertainty, pure types (firms and traditional charities) should out-compete blended forms (Hsu *et al.*, 2009). The argument is that audiences (investors, donors, customers, regulators, etc.) are better able to understand pure types because they have traits which provide lots of information on the organization. Also claims made by the organization are verifiable. If audiences are able to identify category membership easily, they can easily hold the organization accountable and accountability ensures survival (Hannan and Freeman, 1989). If they are unable to categorize them easily, donors and investors are less likely to support them, regulators are less likely to attest to their legitimacy, and public opinion is more likely to overlook them. As Zukerman (1999) showed, being ignored should hinder their performance.

Furthermore, hybrids that are blended are more likely to outcompete hybrid forms whose traits evoke contradictory logics. The argument is that audiences are harsher on organizations which signal conflicting expectations than organizations where expectations are unclear or ambiguous. Those organizations that are blended are never altogether deviant even though they straddle niches. One has commercial ventures, but one is also receiving donations; one is providing collective goods, but investors and donors are also benefiting. Blended forms are difficult to categorize but they are also difficult to demonize. In contrast, for-profits in disguise and social enterprises are clearly in niches where the logics surrounding their inputs and their beneficiaries contradict one another. Rather than indifference, stakeholder response will be aggressive. Unless the deviant forms "convert" to more legitimate forms or become blended organizations, their survival chances should be lessened.

If, however hybrids are able to signal their "true" identities employing various organizational masques, they will be able to compete as effectively as organizations which are "purer." Indeed, there have evolved a number of organizational strategies to ensure that both nonprofits and for-profits which venture into this territory avoid criticism and controversy. Blended charities have several ways to signal their immunization from the corrupting influence of "profits." For instance, there is considerable attention paid to the leaders', the board members' and the staff's commitment to organizational values. Charities often decouple for-profit subsidiaries and corporate partnerships from the charity organization, building a firewall between the two (Tuckman, 2009). In Chapter 5 Garrow and Hasenfeld describe how the WISEs they studied decoupled social service and business units from each other. Blended charities identify unrelated business income, donors are represented on the board of directors, and charities submit to external monitoring by charitable watchdog groups. Among firms that become involved in social welfare (blended firms), there are comparable efforts to ensure that the firm is not perceived as overly charitable. Executive compensation is linked to company performance through: the issuance of stock options;

corporate foundations and partnerships with nonprofits that are separate legal entities apart from the firm itself; limits on charitable tax deductions; investors sitting on the board of directors; and firms succumbing to external monitoring by shareholder watchdog groups. Unfortunately, there is scant research on the impact of these strategies on shareholders' perceptions and judgments.

Finally, the tactics which an organization pursues are going to be successful or not, depending on the arena or context in which they are pursued. Categories are themselves embedded in larger political and cultural contexts. Distinguishing between organizational types (hospitals, universities, social service agencies) and forms (for-profit and nonprofit) is useful. What may be acceptable commercial activity among one type of organization (recreational centers charging fees) may seem extremely deviant in another (pew fees in churches). Similarly in retail it is common to sponsor neighborhood schools, local nonprofits and the United Way (e.g. Target's pledge to support community causes), but this type of outreach would be odd for hardware companies which typically give support to universities (Galaskiewicz and Coleman, 2006). In addition to being judged as charities or firms, organizations will be judged as universities, churches, day care centers, social service agencies, development agencies, retailers and manufacturers.

The socio-cultural context also needs to be taken into account. This is particularly a problem for NGOs which are trying to reach out to the needy in non-Western countries. Indeed, in some countries commercial activities are less objectionable than in others, while in other cultural contexts, e.g. the Far East, any civic activity that is divorced from government coordination is viewed as risky or even suspect (Ma, 2006; Pekkanen, 2006). More comparative analyses, like Kerlin's (Chapter 4) and Defourny and Nyssens's (Chapter 3), are needed.[8]

Conclusion

The fact that social enterprises exist suggests that the boundaries separating the sectors are becoming blurred. This is not a criticism or a call to return to early times – social enterprises are just a "different" kind of firm and a different kind of charitable organization. Maybe companies need to be a bit more committed to social welfare. Maybe charities need to be more enterprising and self-reliant. Our position is that being a socially responsible firm is desirable even if it means that profits are reduced. It is not a matter of ethics but a matter of social justice where companies pay for externalities they create. If they do not, others will. We also believe that charities need to learn how to sustain themselves, so that they can respond to societal needs during periods when private and/or government funders are unable to subsidize their activities or find them unattractive. Given that nonprofit services are often needed in more difficult times, this seems obvious. However, as a consequence, we should not be surprised if companies find themselves being evaluated like charities and charities find themselves being evaluated like businesses. As the category memberships become blurred, this should be commonplace.

But living up to contradictory performance criteria can be problematic. Accountability is an important issue for any organization (Hannan and Freeman, 1989). Hard and fast categorical distinctions between the sectors allow stakeholders to set clearly the criteria for performance. The traits associated with each sector conjure up a set of expectations. As the categorical distinctions get "fuzzy" it may humanize companies and make nonprofits more efficient. But the cost is audiences' lessened ability to evaluate these organizations and hold them accountable, which calls into question their authenticity and jeopardizes audience support.

What does the future hold? First, classification systems are only one solution to the problem of decision-making under conditions of uncertainty. Networks are equally (if not more) effective if audiences have the time and money to verify authenticity personally. For example, venture philanthropists are famous for their personal involvement in social enterprises (Moody, 2008). Alternatively, a strong hierarchy or a strong culture can also ensure audiences that the organization is "true" to its mission – whether it be social welfare or profit-making. The Catholic Church is an example of this (although not an entirely successful one). Thus to clarify matters audiences may rely on other ways to verify the authenticity of organizations and to make judgments on their legitimacy claims besides traits and categories.

Second, Young (Chapter 1, p. 30) says that social enterprises are always tempted to "follow the money" especially if the governing board has an inclination to maximize profits. But even if the board is public-regarding, Frumkin (2010) suggests that since it is easier to measure the performance and evaluate the authenticity of some forms ("for-profits") than others ("nonprofits"), it is likely that social enterprises will gravitate toward the category where performance is easier to measure. Business performance is easily and quickly quantifiable. Social performance often cannot be evaluated until far into the future and then it is difficult to know the exact contribution of any one organization. Thus if social enterprises find themselves in limbo, they are likely to embrace the for-profit form regardless of the preferences of the governing board. This is an interesting and important prediction but one which does not bode well for the nonprofit sector. It also suggests that more work on nonprofit performance measures is needed.

Third, new categories/forms will emerge and become institutionalized, e.g. L3Cs (the low profit limited liability company), B Corps (a certification that management is committed to social and environmental values and practices), benefit corporations (a business corporation that is formed to pursue some social purpose), SPBs (social purpose businesses) and CICs (community interest companies).[9] That is, entrepreneurs will dream up new categories with their own distinct set of traits, standards and benchmarks to fit the new organizational realities. For example, there are now institutional criteria which audiences can use if they suspect a nonprofit is a proprietary nonprofit, e.g. is there self-dealing or conflicts of interest? Is executive compensation excessive? Is the organization exceeding ceilings on the percentage of donated funds spent on fund-raising? Eventually, the same sort of standards and benchmarks may be put into place for social enterprises. However, we do not expect that these will come about without rancor, and intellectuals, ideologues, foundations, social movement activists, professional schools and governments will all play a role in the process of change and institutionalization (Smith, 2010).

Finally, the sustainability of the social enterprise form depends on the next generation of entrepreneurs and the choices they make. Unfortunately, much that has been written glamorizes social entrepreneurs (e.g. Bornstein, 2007), and there is little social science research on how social enterprises actually operate (for an exception, see Light, 2008). Rubin (1999) showed that often the choice of form is driven by resource needs and resource availability. The mission is not important when choosing the form. Fruchterman (2011) argues that in addition to market and capital concerns an entrepreneur's personal motivations and desired level of control should also be key concerns for those choosing between for-profit, nonprofit and hybrid organizational forms. Tschirhart *et al.* (2008) showed that the experience of the entrepreneur was important. Results from their study of MPA and MBA graduates indicate that an individual's perceived competence within a sector significantly influences their likelihood of working in that sector and that prior experience in a sector was a significant predictor for those working in the nonprofit sector (ibid.). With more research on the benefits and drawbacks of social enterprises, people thinking about starting a social enterprise will be much better equipped to select strategies to overcome the problems which pioneering social entrepreneurs have had to endure.[10]

Notes

*   We would like to thank Benjamin Gidron, Zeke Hasenfeld, Dennis Young, Ezra Zukerman, and Greta Hsu for their comments on earlier drafts of this chapter and the participants at the Exploring Social Enterprises Conference, UCLA School of Public Affairs, October 29–30, 2010, Los Angeles, CA for their useful comments and suggestions. We also acknowledge Burton Weisbrod who greatly influenced our thinking on nonprofit and for-profit forms and Zeke Hasenfeld and Eve Garrow whose early presentations of their research on work- integration social enterprises inspired many of the ideas expressed in this chapter.
 1. The research presented in the next three paragraphs draws heavily from Negro *et al.* (2010) to whom we are indebted.

2. We are indebted to Weisbrod (1988, ch. 4) for direction.
3. Earned income includes tuition and fees, sales and services of educational activities, investment income, hospital revenues, other revenues, and revenues from independent observations. Additional information about the revenues included in each of the categories can be found at http//nces.gov/ipeds /glossary/index.
4. Author's calculations using data from NCES (2010).
5. This includes income from private gifts, grants and contracts and contributions from affiliated groups. Private gifts, grants and contracts includes "revenues from private (non-governmental) entities including revenue from research or training projects and similar activities and all contributions (including contributed services) except those from affiliated entities, which are included in contributions from affiliated entities" (NCES, 2010).
6. Author's calculations using data from NCES (2010).
7. These though are not to be confused with membership nonprofits. In membership nonprofits dues, which are not tax-deductible as charitable contributions, are paid to professional associations, sports and recreation clubs, fraternal associations, and homeowners' associations among others to benefit members. Like Weisbrod (1988), we would categorize them as nonprofit proprietary organizations and place them with firms. They receive fees and they provide member benefits.
8. We would like to thank Dennis Young and Benjamin Gidron for pointing out the importance of other factors which constituents take into account when making judgments about the performance of organizations that operate in different contexts.
9. See Cooney (Chapter 9) for a discussion of their differences and the collective action that led to their establishment.
10. We would like to thank Benjamin Gidron for pointing this out to us.

References

Albert, Stuart and David Whetten. 1985. "Organizational Identity." *Research in Organizational Behavior* 7: 263–95.

Arenson, Karen W. 1995. "Ex-United Way Leader Gets 7 Years for Embezzlement." *The New York Times*, June 23.

Battilana, Julie and Silvia Dorado. 2010. "Building Sustainable Hybrid Organizations: The Case of Commercial Microfinance Organizations." *Academy of Management Journal*. 53(6): 1419–440.

Belluck, Pam. 1998. "Red Cross Accused of Misusing Flood Relief." *The New York Times*, December 16.

Blau, Peter and W. Richard Scott. 1962. *Formal Organizations: A Comparative Approach.* San Francisco, CA: Chandler Publishing Company.

Blumenstyk, Goldie. 2005. "Justice Department Supports $1 Billion False-Claims Suit Against U. of Phoenix." *The Chronicle of Higher Education* 51(21): A32.

Blumenstyk, Goldie. 2008. "Three Former Employees Accuse Kaplan U. of Bilking Government Out of Billions." *The Chronicle of Higher Education* 54(28): A12.

Blumenstyk, Goldie. 2009. "Whistle-Blowers Will Get $19 Million in U. of Phoenix Settlement." *The Chronicle of Higher Education*, December 14.

Blumenstyk, Goldie. 2010a. "Financial Affairs: Why the Endowment-Spending Debate Matters Now more than Ever." *The Chronicle of Higher Education*, March 7.

Blumenstyk, Goldie. 2010b. "Online and For-Profit Colleges Fave Beefed-Up Aid Audits From Education Dept." *The Chronicle of Higher Education*, December 10.

Bornstein, David. 2007. *How to Change the World: Social Entrepreneurs and the Power of New Ideas*. New York: Oxford University Press.

Bowie, Norman. 1994. *University-Business Partnerships: An Assessment*. Lanham, MD: Rowman and Littlefield.

Brody, Evelyn. 2006. "The Legal Framework for Nonprofit Organizations." In Powell, Walter W. and Richard Steinberg (eds), *The Nonprofit Sector: A Research Handbook*, 2nd edn. New Haven, CT: Yale University Press: 243–266.

Carroll, Glenn R. and Anand Swaminathan. 2000. "Why the Microbrewery Movement? Organizational Dynamics of Resource Partitioning in the U.S. Brewing Industry." *American Journal of Sociology*. 106: 715–62.

Clemens, Elisabeth S. 1993. "Organizational Repertoires and Institutional Change: Women's Groups and the Transformation of U.S. Politics, 1890–1920." *American Journal of Sociology*. 98: 755–98.

Cornwell, T. Bettina and Leondard V. Coote. 2005. "Corporate Sponsorship of a Cause: The Role of Identification in Purchase Intent." *Journal of Business Research*. 58: 268–76.

DiMaggio, Paul J. 1987. "Classification of Art." *American Sociological Review*. 52: 440–55.

DiMaggio, Paul J. and Walter W. Powell. 1983. "The Iron Cage Revisited: Institutional Isomorphism and Collective Rational in Organizational Fields." *American Sociological Review*. 48: 147–60.

DiMaggio, Paul J. and Walter W. Powell. 1991. "Introduction." In Powell, Walter W. and Paul J. DiMaggio. *The New Institutionalism in Organizational Analysis*. Chicago: University of Chicago Press: 1–38.

Eikenberry, Angela M. and Jodie Drapal Kluver. 2004. "The Marketization of the Nonprofit Sector: Civil Society at Risk?" *Public Administration Review*. 64(2): 132–40.

Fain, Paul and Brad Wolverton. 2006. "Senate Will Review Tax Status of Colleges." *The Chronicle of Higher Education* 53(14): 31.

Farrell, Elizabeth F. 2007. "When Legacies Are a College's Life Blood." *The Chronicle of Higher Education*, January 19.

Fernandez, Manny. 2009. "Spare Change for Homeless? Cuomo Sees a Sham and Sues." *The New York Times*, November 25.

Field, Kelly. 2010a. "Senators Vow to Crack Down on 'Bad Actors' in the For-Profit Sector." *The Chronicle of Higher Education*, June 24.

Field, Kelly. 2010b. "Key Senator Raises Concerns about Veterans Benefits Flowing to For-Profit Colleges." *The Chronicle of Higher Education*, December 9.

Fombrun, Charles. 1996. *Reputation: Realizing Value from the Corporate Image*. Boston: Harvard Business School Press.

Fombrun, Charles and Mark Shanley. 1990. "What's in a Name? Reputation Building and Corporate Strategy." *The Academy of Management Journal*. 33: 233–58.

Friedland, Roger and Robert R. Alford. 1991. "Bringing Society Back In: Symbols, Practices, and Institutional Contradictions." In Powell, Walter W. and Paul J. DiMaggio. (Eds) *The New Institutionalism in Organizational Analysis*. Chicago: University of Chicago Press: 232–66.

Froelich, K. A. 1999. "Diversification of Revenue Strategies: Evolving Resource Dependence in Nonprofit Organizations." *Nonprofit and Voluntary Sector Quarterly*. 28(3): 246–68.

Fruchterman, Jim. 2011. "For Love or Lucre." *Stanford Social Innovation Review.* 9(2): 42–47.

Frumkin, Peter. 2002. *On Being Nonprofit: A Conceptual and Policy Primer.* Cambridge, MA: Harvard University Press.

Frumkin, Peter. 2010. Personal communication.

Frumkin, Peter and Joseph Galaskiewicz. 2004. "Institutional Isomorphism and Public Sector Organizations." *Journal of Public Administration Research and Theory.* 14: 283–307.

Fuller, Andrea. 2010. "Compensation of 30 Private-College Presidents Topped $1-Million in 2008." *The Chronicle of Higher Education,* November 14.

Galaskiewicz, Joseph. 1985. *Social Organization of an Urban Grants Economy: A Study of Business Philanthropy and Nonprofit Organizations.* Orlando, FL: Academic Press.

Galaskiewicz, Joseph and Wolfgang Bielefeld. 1998. *Nonprofit Organizations in an Age of Uncertainty: A Study of Organizational Change.* Hawthorne, NY: Aldine de Gruyter.

Galaskiewicz, Joseph, Myron Dowell and Wolfgang Bielefeld. 2006. "Networks and Organizational Growth: A Study of Community Based Nonprofits." *Administrative Science Quarterly.* 51: 337–380.

Galaskiewicz, Joseph and Michelle Sinclair Coleman. 2006. "Collaborations between Corporations and Nonprofit Organizations." In Powell, Walter W. and Richard Steinberg. (Eds). *The Nonprofit Sector: A Research Handbook.* 2nd edition. New Haven, CT: Yale University Press: 180–204.

Granovetter, Mark. 1985. "On the Social Embeddedness of Economic Exchange." *American Journal of Sociology.* 91: 481–510.

Hall, Peter D. 1990. "Conflicting Managerial Cultures in Nonprofit Organizations." *Nonprofit Management and Leadership.* 1: 153–65.

Hannan, Michael T. and John H. Freeman. 1977. "The Population Ecology of Organizations." *American Journal of Sociology.* 82: 929–64.

Hannan, Michael T. and John H. Freeman. 1989. *Organizational Ecology.* Cambridge, MA: Harvard University Press.

Hansmann, Henry. 1980. "The Role of Nonprofit Enterprise." *Yale Law Journal.* 89: 835–901.

Hechinger, John. 2008. "Harvard Fund Managers Clear $26.8 Million – Endowment Results, Up 8.6% Through June 30, Don't Reflect Steep Falloff in Performance Since Then." *Wall Street Journal* (Eastern edition), December 20: B.1.

Holmes, Stanley and Wendy Zellner. 2004 "The Costco Way: Higher wages mean higher profits. But try telling Wall Street." *Business Week,* April 12.

Hsu, Greta and Michael T. Hannan. 2005. "Identities, Genres, and Organizational Forms." *Organization Science.* 16: 474–90.

Hsu, Greta and Michael T. Hannan, and O. Özgecan Koçak. 2009. "Multiple Category Memberships in Markets: An Integrative Theory and Two Empirical Tests." *American Sociological Review.* 74: 150–69.

James, Estelle. 1983. "How Nonprofits Grow: A Model." *Journal of Policy Analysis and Management.* 2: 350–65.

Kahn, Faith. 1997. "Pandora's Box: Managerial Discretion and the Problem of Corporate Philanthropy." *UCLA Law Review.* 44(3): 579–676.

Karnani, Aneel. 2011. "Microfinance Needs Regulation." *Stanford Social Innovation Review.* 9: 48–53.

Laumann, Edward O. and David Knoke. 1987. *The Organizational State: Social Choice in National Policy Domains.* Madison, WI: University of Wisconsin Press.

Light, Paul. 2008. *The Search for Social Entrepreneurship.* Washington, DC: Brookings Institution Press.

Ma, Quisha. 2006. *Non-Governmental Organizations in Contemporary China: Paving the Way to Civil Society?* New York: Routledge.

Mannan, Manzurul. 2009. "BRAC: Anatomy of a 'Poverty Enterprise'." *Nonprofit Management and Leadership.* 20(2): 219–33.

Meyer, John and Brian Rowan. 1977. "Institutionalized Organizations: Formal Structure as Myth and Ceremony." *American Journal of Sociology.* 83: 333–63.

Minkoff, Debra C. and Walter W. Powell. 2006. "Nonprofit Mission: Constancy, Responsiveness, or Deflection?" In Powell, Walter W. and Richard Steinberg. (Eds) *The Nonprofit Sector: A Research Handbook.* 2nd edition. New Haven, CT: Yale University Press: 591–611.

Moody, Michael. 2008. "Building a Culture: The Construction and Evolution of Venture Philanthropy as a New Organizational Field." *Nonprofit and Voluntary Sector Quarterly.* 37: 324–52.

NACUBO (National Association of College and University Business Officers). 2010. *2009 NACUBO-Commonfund Study of Endowment Results.* Updated April 8, www. nacubo.org/Research/NACUBO_Endowment_Study/Public_NCSE_Tables_.html

NCES (National Center for Education Statistics). 2010. "Integrated Postsecondary Education Data System: Glossary." http//nces.gov/ipeds/glossary/index

Negro, Giacomo, O. Özgecan Koçak and Greta Hsu. 2010. "Research on Categories in the Sociology of Organizations." *Research in the Sociology of Organizations* 31: 3–35.

Orlitzky, Marc, Frank L. Schmidt, and Sara L. Reyes. 2003. "Corporate Social and Financial Performance: A Meta-analysis." *Organizational Studies.* 24: 403–441.

Ouchi, William G. 1979. "Markets, Bureaucracies, and Clans." *Administrative Science Quarterly.* 25: 129–41.

Padgett, John and Christopher K. Ansell. 1993. "Robust Action and the Rise of the Medici, 1400–1434." *American Journal of Sociology.* 98: 1259–319.

Pekkanen, Robert. 2006. *Japan's Dual Civil Society: Members Without Advocates.* Stanford, CA: Stanford University Press.

Perrow, Charles. 1961. "Organizational Prestige: Some Functions and Dysfunctions." *American Journal of Sociology.* 66: 335–41.

Peters, Thomas J. and Robert H. Waterman, Jr. 1982. *In Search of Excellence.* New York: Harper and Row.

Podolny, Joel. 1993. "A Status-based Model of Market Competition." *American Journal of Sociology.* 98: 829–72.

Porac, Joseph F. and H. Thomas. 1990. "Taxonomic Mental Models in Competitor Definition." *Academy of Management Review.* 15: 224–40.

Powell, Walter W. and Richard Steinberg. 2006. *The Nonprofit Sector: A Research Handbook.* 2nd edn. New Haven, CT: Yale University Press.

Prahalad, C. K. 2005. *The Fortune at the Bottom of the Pyramid: Eradicating Poverty Through Profits.* Upper Saddle River, NJ: Prentice-Hall.

Rangan, V. Kasturi, Michael Chu, and Djordjija Petkoski. 2011. "Segmenting the Base of the Pyramid." *Harvard Business Review.* June: 113–17.

Richard, Pierre J., Timothy M. Devinney, George S. Yip and Gerry Johnson. 2009. "Measuring Organizational Performance: Towards Methodological Best Practice." *Journal of Management.* 35: 718–804.

Richardson, Lynda. 1996. "Former Charity Head Ordered to Prison." *The New York Times,* July 31.

Rivera, Ray. 2010. "Fraud, Theft and other Charges for Operators of a Queens Bingo Hall." *The New York Times*, August 18.

Rothfeld, Michael. 2011. "City News: Charity Accused of Fraud." *Wall Street Journal.* June 29: A21.

Rubin, Julia S. 1999. "Community Development Venture Capital: A Study of Cross-Sector Organizations." Paper presented at the 1999 Independent Sector Spring Research Form, March 25–26, Alexandria, VA.

Schwinn, Elizabeth. 2004. "Hospital Loses State Tax Exemption." *The Chronicle of Philanthropy*, March 4.

Schwinn, Elizabeth. 2006a. "Nonprofit Hospitals Face Scrutiny in Senate." *The Chronicle of Philanthropy*.18(2): 65.

Schwinn, Elizabeth. 2006b. "IRS Takes a Tougher Stance." *The Chronicle of Philanthropy.* 19(1): 25.

Schwinn, Elizabeth. 2006c. "Illinois Hospital Appeals Property-Tax Decision." *The Chronicle of Philanthropy.* 19(3): 31.

Singh, Jitendra W., David J. Tucker, and Agnes G. Meinhard. 1991. "Institutional Change and Ecological Dynamics." In Powell, Walter W. and Paul J. DiMaggio. (Eds) *The New Institutionalism in Organizational Analysis.* Chicago: University of Chicago Press: 390–422.

Smith, Stephen R. 2010. Personal communication.

Snow, David A., E. Burke Rochford Jr, Steven K. Worden, and Robert D. Benford. 1986. Frame Alignment Processes, Micromobilization, and Movement Participation." *American Sociological Review.* 51: 464–81.

Stark, Andrew. 2010. "The Distinction between Public, Nonprofit, and For-Profit: Revisiting the 'Core Legal' Approach." *Journal of Public Administration Research and Theory.* 21: 3–27.

Strom, Stephanie. 2002. "Red Cross Works to Renew Confidence Among Donors." *The New York Times*, June 6.

Strom, Stephanie. 2005. "Senators Press Red Cross for a Full Accounting." *The New York Times.* December 30.

Strom, Stephanie. 2008. "Here's My Check; Spend it All at Once." *The New York Times,* January 20.

Strout, Erin. 2007. "What Harvard Paid its Money Managers." *The Chronicle of Higher Education.* 53(18): A26.

Stryker, Robin. 2000. "Legitimacy Processes as Institutional Politics: Implications for Theory and Research in the Sociology of Organizations." *Research in the Sociology of Organizations.* 17: 179–223.

Tschirhart, Mary, Kira Kristal Reed, Sarah J. Freeman, and Alison Louie Anker. 2008. "Is the Grass Greener? Sector Shifting and Choice of Sector by MPA and MBA Graduates." *Nonprofit and Voluntary Sector Quarterly.* 37(4): 668–88.

Tuckman, Howard P. 2009. "The Strategic and Economic Value of Hybrid Nonprofit Structures." In Cordes, Joseph J. and C. Eugene Steuerle (eds). 2009. *Nonprofits and Business.* Washington, DC: Urban Institute Press: 129–53.

Tuckman, Howard P. and Cyril F. Chang. 2006. "Commercial Activity, Technological Change, and Nonprofit Mission." In Powell, Walter W. and Richard Steinberg. (Eds) *The Nonprofit Sector: A Research Handbook.* 2nd edition. New Haven, CT: Yale University Press: 629–44.

Vogel, David. 2005. *The Market for Virtue: The Potential and Limits of Corporate Social Responsibility.* Washington, DC: Brookings Institution Press.

Walsh, Sharon. 2004. "Harvard's Fund Managers Face Pay Caps." *The Chronicle of Higher Education.* 50(30): A27.

Weisbrod, Burton A. 1988. *The Nonprofit Economy.* Cambridge, MA: Harvard University Press.

Weisbrod, Burton A. 1998a. "Institutional Form and Organizational Behavior." In Powell, Walter W. and Elisabeth S. Clemens. (Eds) *Private Action and the Public Good.* New Haven, CT: Yale University Press: 69–84.

Weisbrod, Burton A. 1998b. "The Nonprofit Mission and Its Financing: Growing Links between Nonprofits and the Rest of the Economy." In Weisbrod, Burton. (Ed.) *To Profit or Not to Profit: The Commercial Transformation of the Nonprofit Sector.* New York: Cambridge University Press: 1–22.

White, Harrison. 1981. "Where Do Markets Come From?" *American Journal of Sociology.* 87: 517–47.

Williams, Grant. 2009. "Senators Consider Changes to Hospitals' Tax Status." *The Chronicle of Philanthropy.* 21(16): 33.

Williamson, Oliver. 1975. *Markets and Hierarchies: Analysis and Antitrust Implications.* New York: Free Press.

Wolverton, Brad. 2007. "Senate Committee Examines Endowments." *The Chronicle of Higher Education.* 53(40): 25.

Young, Dennis R. 2009. "Alternative Perspectives on Social Enterprise." In Cordes, Joseph J and Eugene Steuerle. (Eds). *Nonprofits and Business.* Washington, D.C.: The Urban Institute Press: 21–46.

Young, Dennis R. and Lester M. Salamon. 2002. "Commercialization, Social Ventures, and For-Profit Competition." In Salamon, Lester (Ed). *The State of Nonprofit America.* Washington, DC: Brookings Institution Press: 423–46.

Zuckerman, Ezra W. 1999. "The Categorical Imperative: Securities Analysts and the Illegitimacy Discount." *American Journal of Sociology.* 104: 1398–438.

Zuckerman, Ezra W. 2000. "Focusing the Corporate Product: Securities Analysts and De-diversification." *Administrative Science Quarterly.* 45: 591–619.

3

Conceptions of Social Enterprise in Europe: A Comparative Perspective with the United States

Jacques Defourny and Marthe Nyssens

The concepts of "social enterprise", "social entrepreneurship" and "social entrepreneur" were almost unknown or at least unused some 20 or even ten years ago. In the last decade, however, they have become much more discussed on both sides of the Atlantic, especially in EU countries and the United States. They are also attracting increasing interest in other regions, such as east Asia (Defourny and Kim, 2011) and Latin America.

In Europe, the concept of social enterprise made its first appearance in the very early 1990s, at the very heart of the third sector. According to European tradition (Evers and Laville, 2004), the third sector brings together cooperatives, associations, mutual societies and increasingly foundations, or in other words, all not-for-profit private organizations – such a third sector being labeled the "social economy" in some European countries. More precisely, the impetus was first an Italian one and was closely linked with the cooperative movement: in 1991, the Italian Parliament passed a law creating a specific legal form for "social cooperatives" and the latter went on to experience an extraordinary growth. The concept of social enterprise, which includes social cooperatives as one model among others, doesn't compete at all with the concept of social economy. It rather helps to identify entrepreneurial dynamics at the very heart of the third sector within the various European socio-economic contexts.

In the United States, the concepts of social entrepreneurship and social enterprise also met with a very positive response in the early 1990s. In 1993, for instance, the Harvard Business School launched the "Social Enterprise Initiative", one of the milestones of the period.

Since this early period, the debate has expanded in various types of institutions. Major universities have developed research and training programs. International research networks have been set up, like the EMES European Research Network,[1] which has gathered, since 1996, research centers from most countries of the EU-15, and the Social Enterprise Knowledge Network, which was formed in 2001 by leading Latin American business schools and the Harvard Business School. Various foundations have set up training and support programs for social enterprises or social entrepreneurs. Last but not least, various European countries have passed new laws to promote social enterprises (Roelants, 2009).

However, what is striking is the fact that the debates on both sides of the Atlantic took place in parallel trajectories, with very few connections between them, until the years 2004–2005. From a scientific point of view, the first bridges were built by Nicholls (2006), Mair *et al.* (2006) as well as Steyaert and Hjorth (2006). Kerlin (2006, 2009) also made interesting attempts to compare the concept of social enterprise in different parts of the world.

In this context, the first objective of this chapter is to deepen this trans-atlantic dialogue on social enterprise as embodied in their respective European and US contexts, as well as to underline distinct developments they now tend to experience. However, what seem really at stake beyond conceptual debates are the place and the role of social enterprise within the overall economy and its interaction with the market, the civil society and public policies. So, our second objective is to show that re-embedding social enterprises and social entrepreneurship in their own specific contexts for a better mutual understanding is one of the best ways to raise issues and suggest further lines of research which do not appear clearly when sticking to specific national or regional contexts.

The chapter is structured as follows. In the first part, we describe the different schools of thought in which those concepts took root and their respective contexts. In the second part, we carefully analyze the EMES conception rooted in the historical European third sector tradition. This analysis paves the way for the third part, in which we analyze the conceptual convergences and divergences among the different schools as well as their implications for the debate.

The emergence of social enterprise in various contexts

Let us first examine how conceptualizations of social enterprise and social entrepreneurship were shaped in the United States. Then we will be best placed to highlight the specificities of European approaches to the same notions.

Two major US schools of thought[2]

When looking at the US landscape, what is striking is the diversity of concepts which have been used since the early 1980s to describe entrepreneurial behaviors with social aims that developed in the country, mainly although not exclusively within the nonprofit sector: "nonprofit venture", "nonprofit entrepreneurship", "social-purpose endeavor", "social innovation", "social-purpose business", "community wealth enterprise", "public entrepreneurship", "social enterprise", etc. Although the community of nonprofit studies did use several of such terms, the conceptual debate has been mainly shaped by scholars belonging to business schools. To classify the different conceptions, Dees and Anderson (2006) have proposed distinguishing two major schools of thought. The first school of thought on social enterprise refers to the use of commercial activities by nonprofit organizations in support of their mission. Organizations like Ashoka fed a second major school, named the "social innovation" school of thought.

The "earned income" school of thought

The first school of thought set the grounds for conceptions of social enterprise mainly defined by earned-income strategies. The bulk of its publications was mainly based on the desire of nonprofits to become more commercial (Young and Salamon, 2002) and could be described as "prescriptive": many of them came from consultancy firms and they focused on strategies for starting a business that would earn income in support of the social mission of a nonprofit organization and that could help diversify its funding base (Skloot, 1987). In the late 1990s, the Social Enterprise Alliance, a central player in the field, defined social enterprise as "any earned-income business or strategy undertaken by a non-profit to generate revenue in support of its charitable mission".

In such a perspective, it is straightforward to name that first school the "earned income" school of thought. Within the latter, however, we suggest a distinction between an earlier version, focusing on nonprofits, which we call the "commercial nonprofit approach", and a broader version, embracing all forms of business initiatives, which may be named the "mission-driven business approach". This latter approach refers to the field of social purpose venture as encompassing all organizations that trade for a social purpose, including for-profit companies (Austin *et al.*, 2006).

It should also be noted that some authors, such as Emerson and Twersky (1996), early on provided an analysis shifting from a sole market orientation to a broader vision of business methods as a path toward achieving increased effectiveness (and not just a better funding) of social sector organizations. Even further, various activities undertaken by for-profit firms to assert their corporate social responsibility began to be considered, by some authors, as part of the whole range of initiatives forming the wide spectrum of social entrepreneurship (Boschee, 1995; Austin, 2000). Of course, this raises some fundamental conceptual issues, such as: can any social value-generating activity be considered as an expression of social entrepreneurship, even if this activity remains marginal in the firm's overall strategy?

To a large extent, the concept of social business as promoted by Muhammad Yunus (2010) can also be related to the "mission-driven business approach" although it also involves stronger conditions: "a social business is a non-loss, non-dividend company designed to address a social objective". This concept was mainly developed to describe a business model that focuses on the provision of goods or services to (very) poor customers, a new market segment (often called the "bottom of the pyramid") in the developing countries. The most often quoted case is the Grameen–Danone joint company which provides, at very low prices, highly nutritious yoghurt to vulnerable populations in Bangladesh. Such a social business is supposed to cover all its costs through market resources. It is owned by (often large) investors who, at least in Yunus's version, don't receive any dividend, profits being fully reinvested to support the social mission.

The "social innovation" school of thought

The second school puts the emphasis on the profile and behavior of social entrepreneurs in a Schumpeterian perspective as the one developed by the pioneering work of Young (1986). Along such lines, entrepreneurs in the nonprofit sector are "change makers" as they carry out "new combinations" in at least one of the following ways: new services, new quality of services, new methods of production, new production factors, new forms of organizations or new markets. Social entrepreneurship may therefore be a question of outcomes rather than just a question of incomes. Moreover, the systemic nature of innovation brought about and its impact at a broad societal level are often underlined.

Dees (1998, 4) has proposed the best known definition of a social entrepreneur in that school of thought. He sees the latter as "playing the role of change agents in the social sector by adopting a mission to create and sustain social value, recognizing and relentlessly pursuing new opportunities to serve that mission, engaging in a process of continuous innovation, adaptation and learning, acting boldly without being limited by resources currently in hand, and finally exhibiting a heightened sense of accountability to the constituencies served and for the outcomes created". Today, such outstanding individuals are often portrayed as heroes of the modern times (Bornstein, 2004).

Although many initiatives of social entrepreneurs result in the setting up of nonprofit organizations, many recent works of the social innovation school of thought tend to underline blurred frontiers and the existence of opportunities for entrepreneurial social innovation within the private for-profit sector and the public sphere as well.

Social entrepreneurship at the crossroads of the two schools. Divergences between the "social innovation" school and the "earned income" school should not be overstated, though. Viewing social entrepreneurship as a mission-driven business is increasingly common among business schools and foundations which foster more broadly business methods, not just earned-income strategies, as a path toward social innovation. Various works stress a "double (or triple) bottom line" vision which can be adopted by all types of enterprise as well as the creation of a "blended value" in an effort to really balance and better integrate economic and social purposes and strategies (Emerson, 2006).

The roots of social enterprise in Europe

In Europe, the concept of "social enterprise" as such seems to have first appeared in Italy, where it was promoted through a journal launched in 1990 and entitled *Impresa sociale*. In the late 1980s, new cooperative-like initiatives had emerged in this country to respond to unmet needs, especially in the field of work integration as well as in the field of personal services. As the existing legislation did not allow associations to develop economic activities, the Italian Parliament passed a law in 1991 creating a new legal form of "social cooperative" which proved to be very well adapted to those pioneering social enterprises.

The remarkable development of the latter also inspired various other countries during the following two decades, across Europe and outside the latter (for instance in South Korea). Indeed, several other European countries introduced new legal forms reflecting the entrepreneurial approach adopted by this increasing number of "not-for-profit" organizations, even though the term of "social enterprise" was not always used as such in the legislation (Defourny and Nyssens, 2008). In France, Portugal, Spain and Greece, these new legal forms were of the cooperative type. Some other countries such as Belgium, the UK and Italy (with a second law passed in 2006) chose more open models of social enterprise not just inspired by the cooperative tradition. Of course, there exists a great diversity beyond this basic dichotomy. For instance, the French and Italian legal forms could be qualified as "multi-stakeholder forms" as they bring different stakeholders (employees, users, volunteers, etc.) to work together on a given social purpose project. The Belgian "company with a social purpose" and the Italian law on social enterprise define a label which crosses the boundaries of all legal forms and can be adopted by various types of organization (not only cooperatives and nonprofit organizations, but also investor-owned organizations, for instance), provided they define an explicit social aim and that they are not dedicated to the enrichment of their members.

In the UK, Parliament approved a law creating the "community interest company" in 2004 but, two years earlier, the British government also put forward a definition of social enterprise as "a business with primarily social objectives whose surpluses are principally reinvested for that purpose in the business or in the community, rather than being driven by the need to maximize profit for shareholders and owners" (DTI, 2002).

In many European countries, beside the creation of new legal forms or frameworks, the 1990s have seen the development of specific public programs targeting the field of work integration. It is clear that social enterprises may be active in a wide spectrum of activities, as the "social purpose" they pursue may refer to many different fields. However, since the mid-1990s, one major type of social enterprise has been dominant across Europe, namely "work integration social enterprises" (WISEs). The main objective of these is to help low qualified unemployed people who are at risk of permanent exclusion from the labour market and to integrate them into work and society through a productive activity (Nyssens, 2006). This has even led, in several cases, to the concept of social enterprise being systematically associated with such employment creation initiatives.

Although field initiatives blossomed up across Europe, with Italian social cooperatives as an inspiring model in the early 1990s, the concept of social enterprise as such did not really spread during those years. In the academic sphere, major analytical efforts were undertaken from the second part of the 1990s, both at the conceptual and empirical levels, especially by the EMES European Research Network, gathering mainly social science scholars. Indeed, as soon as 1996, i.e. before most of the European public policies were launched, a major research program funded by the European Commission was undertaken by a group of scholars coming from all EU member states. That group progressively has developed an approach, which we will expand in the next section, to identify organizations likely to be called "social enterprises" in each of the 15 countries forming the EU at that time.

It should also be noted that recent years have witnessed a growing mutual influence of each side of the Atlantic upon the other, probably with a stronger influence of the US upon Europe than the other way round. More precisely, various authors from European business schools, such as Mair and Marti (2006), Mair *et al.* (2006) as well as Nicholls (2006) among others, contributed to the debate, relying on the concept of social entrepreneurship as it took roots in the US context, although they of course brought in their own backgrounds as Europeans. Nicholls (2006), for example, suggests a continuum to describe social entrepreneurship from voluntary activism to corporate social innovation which is defined by venture capital targeted to a social mission. Between these opposite models, different nonprofit organizations may be found on the continuum, from those fully funded by grants to those entirely self-financed. In his analysis, only the latter deserve the label of "social enterprise", in line with the earned income school of thought.

The EMES approach of social enterprise

In Europe, the EMES European Research Network has developed the first theoretical and empirical milestones of social enterprise analysis. The EMES approach derives from extensive dialog among several disciplines (economics, sociology, political science and management) as well as among the various national traditions and sensitivities present in the European

Union. Moreover, guided by a project that was both theoretical and empirical, it preferred from the outset the identification and clarification of indicators over a concise and elegant definition.

Three sets of indicators for three distinct dimensions

Such indicators were never intended to represent the set of conditions that an organization should meet to qualify as a social enterprise. Rather than constituting prescriptive criteria, they describe an "ideal-type" in Weber's terms, i.e. an abstract construction that enables researchers to position themselves within the "galaxy" of social enterprises. In other words, they constitute a tool, somewhat analogous to a compass, which helps analysts locate the position of the observed entities relative to one another and eventually identify subsets of social enterprises they want to study more deeply. Those indicators allow identifying brand new social enterprises, but they can also lead to designating as social enterprises older organizations being reshaped by new internal dynamics.

The indicators have so far been presented in two subsets: a list of four economic indicators and a list of five social indicators (Defourny, 2001, 16–18). In a comparative perspective, however, it seems more appropriate to distinguish three subsets rather than two, which allows highlighting particular forms of governance specific to the EMES ideal type of social enterprise. In doing so, we will also recognize more easily many of the usual characteristics of social economy organizations which are refined here in order to highlight new entrepreneurial dynamics within the third sector (Borzaga and Defourny, 2001).

In such a slightly reshaped EMES approach, three criteria reflect *the economic and entrepreneurial dimensions* of social enterprises:

- **A continuous activity producing goods and/or selling services.** Social enterprises, unlike some traditional nonprofit organizations, do not normally have advocacy activities or the redistribution of financial flows (as, for example, many foundations) as their major activity, but they are directly involved in the production of goods or the provision of services to people on a continuous basis. The productive activity thus represents the reason, or one of the main reasons, for the existence of social enterprises.
- **A significant level of economic risk.** Those who establish a social enterprise assume totally or partly the risk inherent in the initiative. Unlike most public institutions, their financial viability depends on the efforts of their members and workers to secure adequate resources.
- **A minimum amount of paid work.** As in the case of most traditional nonprofit organizations, social enterprises may also combine monetary and nonmonetary resources, voluntary and paid workers. However, the activity carried out in social enterprises requires a minimum level of paid workers.

Three indicators encapsulate the *social dimensions* of such enterprises:

- **An explicit aim to benefit the community.** One of the principal aims of social enterprises is to serve the community or a specific group of people. In the same perspective, a feature of social enterprises is their desire to promote a sense of social responsibility at the local level.
- **An initiative launched by a group of citizens or civil society organizations.** Social enterprises are the result of collective dynamics involving people belonging to a community or to a group that shares a well-defined need or aim; this collective dimension must be maintained over time in one way or another, even though the importance of leadership (by an individual or a small group of leaders) must not be neglected.
- **A limited profit distribution.** The primacy of the social aim is reflected in a constraint on the distribution of profits. However, social enterprises not only include organizations that are characterized by a total nondistribution constraint, but also organizations which – like cooperatives in many countries – may distribute profits, but only to a limited extent, thus allowing an avoidance of profit-maximizing behavior.

Finally, three indicators reflect the *participatory governance* of such enterprises:

- **A high degree of autonomy.** Social enterprises are created by a group of people on the basis of an autonomous project and they are governed by these people. They may depend on public subsidies but they are not managed, be it directly or indirectly, by public authorities or other organizations (federations, private firms, etc.). They have both the right to take up their own position ("voice") and to terminate their activity ("exit").
- **A decision-making power not based on capital ownership.** This criterion generally refers to the principle of "one member, one vote" or at least to a decision-making process in which voting power is not distributed according to capital shares on the governing body which has the ultimate decision-making rights.
- **A participatory nature, which involves various parties affected by the activity.** Representation and participation of users or customers, influence of various stakeholders on decision-making and a participative management often constitute important characteristics of social enterprises. In many cases, one of the aims of social enterprises is to further democracy at the local level through economic activity.

As already underlined, these indicators can be used to identify totally new social enterprises, but they can also lead to designating as social enterprises older organizations which have been reshaped by new internal dynamics. The EMES approach proved to be empirically fertile. This has been the conceptual basis for several EMES researches across different industries, such as personal services or local development (Borzaga and Defourny, 2001) or work integration (Davister *et al.*, 2004; Nyssens, 2006), sometimes enlarged to Central and Eastern Europe (Borzaga *et al.*, 2008). When J.-F. Draperi (2003) studied 151 organizations subsidized over a 20-year period by France's Fondation du Crédit Coopératif, he found in varying degrees most of the features outlined above.

Paving the way to a theory of social enterprise

In the last phase of its first major research, the EMES Network took the initial steps toward the progressive development of a specific theory of social enterprise. In such a perspective, Bacchiega and Borzaga (2001) used tools from the new institutional economic theory to highlight the innovative character of social enterprises: the characteristics defining the social enterprise were interpreted as forming an original system of incentives that takes into account the potentially conflicting objectives pursued by the various categories of stakeholders. Evers (2001) developed a more socio-political analysis to demonstrate that such a "multi-stakeholder, multiple-goal" structure was more easily understood if making use of the concept of "social capital". For Evers, creating social capital can also constitute an explicit objective of organizations such as social enterprises. Laville and Nyssens (2001) came up with elements for an integrated theory of an "ideal type" combining the economic, social and political dimensions of social enterprise. Like Evers, they emphasized the role of social capital, which is mobilized and reproduced in specific forms by social enterprises. In addition, they stressed the particularly hybrid and composite nature of the resources of social enterprises (made of market, nonmarket and nonmonetary resources such as volunteering), viewing this as a major asset of these organizations for resisting the trend toward "institutional isomorphism" that threatens all social economy organizations. Those theoretical lines were transformed into hypotheses to be tested for WISEs through a large survey conducted in 12 EU countries (Nyssens, 2006).

Theoretically, the social enterprise concept could also point the way toward a more integrated approach to the entire social economy. As a matter of fact, when apprehending the social economy, two sources of tension appear as recurrent and difficult to overcome. One source of tension originates in the gap between enterprises offering their entire output for sale on the market (as do most cooperatives) and associations whose activities do not have a strong economic character (such as advocacy) and whose resources are totally nonmarket (grants, subsidies, etc.), or even nonmonetary (volunteering). A second tension exists between so-called mutual interest organizations (cooperatives, mutual societies and a large part of associations) which, at least in principle, aim to serve their members, and general interest organizations, serving the broader community or specific target groups outside their membership (such as organizations fighting poverty and exclusion, or those involved in development cooperation, environmental protection and so on). However, we must not exaggerate this second tension, which reflects more of a different historical heritage between two models of action than a clear-cut difference between contemporary practices. For example, when they expand themselves, numerous mutual societies and user cooperatives offer their goods and services to customers which are not members, with similar benefits than those of the members.

These two sources of tension are partly illustrated in Figure 3.1. The first source of tension is represented by the coexistence of two distinct spheres: one sphere represents the cooperative tradition (which generated specific literature and schools of thought), while the other sphere represents the tradition of associative initiatives and movements (which has also inspired numerous sociologists and political scientists, especially in the North American literature on nonprofit organizations). The second source of tension is more difficult to depict: it may be seen, although partly, within each of the two spheres, where general interest organizations are rather located quite close to the diagram's center, whereas the mutual interest organizations tend to be located either on the left or on the right of the diagram (although some advocacy NPOs may of course be of general interest).

The unifying role of the social enterprise concept resides primarily in the fact that it generates mutual attraction between the two spheres. It accomplishes this by drawing certain organizations within each sphere toward the central zone and by including them into a single group of organizations because they actually are very close to each other. Whether they choose a

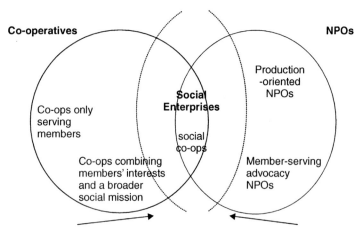

Figure 3.1 Social enterprises at the crossroads of the cooperative and nonprofit sectors

Source: adapted from Defourny (2001, 22).

cooperative legal form or an associative legal form depends primarily on the legal mechanisms provided by national legislations.

On the left hand (cooperative) side, social enterprises may be seen as more oriented to the whole community and putting more emphasis on the dimension of general interest than many traditional cooperatives. This is of course the case for enterprises registered as social cooperatives in Italy. On the right hand (nonprofit) side, social enterprises place a higher value on economic risk-taking related to an ongoing productive activity than many traditional associations, including advocacy or grant-making organizations.

Lastly, by going beyond the two spheres, the dotted lines suggest yet another point to be considered: although most social enterprises take the form of cooperatives or associations across Europe, they can also develop, as already mentioned, within the framework of other legal forms.

European conceptions in a comparative perspective

The different conceptions of social enterprise coexist to varying extents in most parts of the world including Europe. So we would certainly not claim the EMES approach is fully representative of the conceptual landscape in Europe. We do think however that it provides quite useful lenses to identify major convergences and divergences between Europe and the United States, not only as to social enterprise conceptions but also as regards the place and role of public policies.

The governance structure

As we have seen, social enterprises are, across Europe, mainly embedded in the third sector tradition which is itself marked by a long-lasting quest for more democracy in the economy. As a result, the governance structure of social enterprise has attracted much more attention in Europe than in the United States, as shown by the EMES approach as well as by various public policies, across Europe, promoting social enterprises. As the governance structure can be seen as the set of organizational devices that ensure the pursuit of the organization's mission, it can be analyzed along several dimensions.

Autonomy of governance bodies

First, in a typical European approach, social enterprises are characterized by a high degree of autonomy. According to the EMES definition, they are generally created by a group of people and are governed by them in the framework of an autonomous project. This condition of autonomy clearly diverges from the conception of the "Social Enterprise Knowledge Network" (launched by Harvard in Latin America), according to which a short-term project with a social value undertaken by a for-profit enterprise or a public body can be considered as a social enterprise (Austin *et al.*, 2004, xxv).

A participative dynamic

Second, the ideal-typical social enterprise defined by EMES is based on a collective dynamics and the involvement of different stakeholders in the governance of the organization. The various categories of stakeholders may include beneficiaries, employees, volunteers, public authorities and donors, among others. They can be involved in the membership or in the board of the social enterprise, thereby creating a "multi-stakeholder ownership" (Bacchiega and Borzaga, 2003). Such a multi-stakeholder ownership is even recognized or required by national legislations in various countries (Italy, Portugal, Greece and France).[3] Stakeholders can also participate through channels that are less formal than membership, such as representation and participation of users and workers in different committees in the everyday life of the enterprise. In many cases indeed, one of the aims of social enterprises is to foster democracy at the local level through economic activity. To that extent, this approach to social enterprise remains clearly in line with the third sector literature, especially when the latter focuses on community development. Such a way to stress a collective dynamics clearly contrasts with the emphasis put on the individual profile of the social entrepreneur and his or her central role, especially by the social innovation school. Let us note however that these two points of view are not necessarily incompatible: the importance of a strong leadership by one or several founders may also be found in truly collective dynamics.[4]

Limitations to the rights of shareholders

Third, one of the EMES criteria states that the decision-making power is not based on capital ownership, again reflecting the quest for more economic democracy that characterizes the field of social enterprise in Europe along with the cooperative tradition. This generally means that the organization applies the principle of "one member, one vote", or at least that the voting rights in the governing body that has the ultimate decision-making power is not distributed according to capital shares. Once more, such rules are reflected in most legal frameworks designed for social enterprises, the majority of them requiring the rule of "one member, one vote".[5]

Constraints on profit distribution

Fourth, the rights of shareholders are also firmly limited regarding the appropriation of profits. Indeed, according to EMES criteria, the field of social enterprises includes organizations that are characterized by a total non-distribution constraint and organizations which may only distribute profits to a limited extent, thus avoiding a profit-maximizing behavior. European legal frameworks also reduce the power of the shareholders of social enterprises by prohibiting[6] or limiting[7] the distribution of profits. A convergence must be noted here with the US "commercial nonprofit approach" (within the "earned income" school of thought) which explicitly locates social enterprise in the field of nonprofit organizations, i.e. entities whose surplus is entirely retained by the organization for the fulfillment of its social mission. This is also in line with the way Yunus defines a social business as shareholders must accept not to receive any dividend. On the contrary, for the "mission-driven business approach" as well as for the "social innovation school of thought", social enterprises may adopt any kind of legal framework and may therefore distribute surplus to shareholders. It is possible here to argue that such a profit distribution in some cases might put into question the primacy of social objectives: in very broad conceptions of social enterprise, the latter may include an increasing number of firms which claim to look at a double or triple bottom line (Savitz, 2006) but actual practices may reveal the economic line clearly dominates the other (social and environmental) dimensions.

To sum up these four dimensions, as Young and Salamon (2002, 433) state, "in Europe, the notion of social enterprise focuses more heavily on the way an organisation is governed and what its purpose is rather than on whether it strictly adheres to the non-distribution constraint of a formal non-profit organisation". As a matter of fact, although the EMES approach of social enterprise also includes this feature by its "limited profit distribution" criterion, it goes further than that by incorporating other aspects which are central to characterizing the governance structure of social enterprise and to guaranteeing its social mission, whereas the other schools do not underline so much organizational features as key tools to maintain the primacy of the social mission.[8]

The concept of economic risk

Social enterprises are generally viewed as organizations characterized by a significant level of economic risk. According to EMES criteria, this means that the financial viability of social enterprises depends on the efforts of their members to secure adequate resources for supporting the enterprise's social mission. These resources can have a hybrid character: they may come from trading activities, from public subsidies or from voluntary resources.[9] Although public opinion tends to associate the concept of economic risk to a market orientation, rigorous definitions, including for instance definitions in EU legislation, see an enterprise as an organization or an undertaking bearing some risk but not necessarily seeking sole market resources.

This conception appears to be shared to a large extent by the "social innovation" school of thought. Indeed, according to Dees (1998), the centrality of the social mission implies a very specific mix of human and financial resources, and social entrepreneurs explore all types of resources, from donations to commercial revenues. Bearing economic risks does not necessarily mean that economic sustainability must be achieved only through a trading activity; it rather refers to the fact that those who establish the enterprise assume the risk of the initiative.

By contrast, for the "commercial nonprofit approach" and "mission-driven business approach" (forming together the "earned income" school of thought), to be a social enterprise means relying mainly on market resources. For the authors belonging to this school, the economic risk tends to be correlated with the amount or the share of income generated through trade. This vision is shared by some public policies, which tend to require a market orientation from social enterprises. In the United Kingdom, for example, social enterprises are seen first and foremost as businesses (see p. 75). The Finish Act on social enterprise and the social economy program in Ireland also describe these organizations as market-oriented enterprises. Many Italian social cooperatives are financed through contracts which are passed with the public authorities in a more or less competitive market.[10]

The divergence between the "social innovation" school and the "earned income" school as to the economic risk should not be overstated, though. Viewing social entrepreneurship as a mission-driven business is increasingly common among business schools and foundations which foster more broadly business methods, not just earned-income strategies, for achieving social impacts. In this last perspective, we are coming back to the efforts made by Dees and Anderson (2006) and Emerson (2006) among others to stress converging trends between both major US schools, at least in parts of the academic debate.

The production of goods and services and their relation to the social mission

In a rather classical way, most approaches use the term "enterprise" to refer to the production of goods and/or services. Accordingly, social enterprises, unlike some nonprofit organizations, are normally neither engaged in advocacy, at least not as a major goal, nor in the redistribution of financial flows (as, for example, grant-giving foundations) as their major activity; instead, they are directly involved in the production of goods or the provision of services on a continuous basis.[11]

However, differences appear between the various schools of thought when considering the nature of this production activity. When speaking of social enterprise in Europe, it appears that the production of goods and/or services does itself constitute the way in which the social mission is pursued. In other words, the nature of the economic activity is closely connected to the social mission: for instance, the production process involves low-qualified people if the goal is to create jobs for that target group; if the social enterprise's mission is to develop social services, the economic activity is actually the delivery of such social services, and so on. This type of approach is also found in the social innovation school, which considers that social enterprises implement innovative strategies to tackle social needs through the provision of goods or services. Although the innovating behavior may only refer to the production process or to the way goods or services are delivered, it always remains linked to the latter, the provision of such goods or services therefore representing the reason, or one of the main reasons, for the existence of the social enterprise.

By contrast, for the "commercial nonprofit approach", the trading activity is often simply considered as a source of income, and the nature of the traded goods or services does not really matter as such. So, in this perspective, social enterprises can develop business activities which are only related to the social mission through the financial resources they help to secure. More precisely, it is common for a US nonprofit to establish a separate business entity under its control, to generate revenue from sales. Only this latter entity can then be labeled as a social enterprise.

Channels for the diffusion of social innovation
The key role of public policies

In the European context, the process of institutionalization of social enterprises has often been closely linked to the evolution of public policies. Following authors like DiMaggio and Powell (1983), objectives and practices of organizations are partly shaped by the external environment, including the regulations under which they operate. Such a perspective however neglects an essential dynamic of social enterprises: the relationships the latter have with public policies are not one-sided: social enterprises are not just residual actors filling the gaps of the market or the state. In fact, social enterprises significantly influence their institutional environment, and they contribute to shaping institutions including public policies.

For example, social enterprises were pioneers in promoting the integration of excluded persons through a productive activity. A historical perspective shows that they have contributed to the development of new public schemes and legal frameworks, which in turn became channels for social innovation. The conditions imposed on social enterprises by the different European legal frameworks can be seen as signals often first created by social enterprises themselves and furthermore as guarantees that allow governments to provide financial support to social enterprises. Without such guarantees (often involving a strict non-distribution constraint), the risk would be greater that public subsidies just induce more profits to be distributed among owners or managers. In turn, such public support often allows social enterprises to avoid purely market-oriented strategies, which, in many cases, would lead them away from those who cannot afford market prices yet nevertheless constitute the group that they target in accordance with their social mission

The support of foundations

In other contexts, such as the United States, the scaling up of social innovation has also been a concern from the outset, especially for the "social innovation" school of thought, historically led by Ashoka. However, social innovation in the US is typically expected to expand through the growth of the enterprise itself[12] and/or with the support of foundations. Such ways to grow include social venture capital bringing a leverage effect to the initiative through increased financial means and professional skills as well as celebration and demonstration strategies, through some success stories, of social entrepreneurs (Bornstein, 2004). Public policies could also play a role but the recent initiative of President Obama to create a Social Innovation Fund to boost the best achievements of the nonprofit sector rather appears, in the US, as an exception across the last decades.

Conclusion

Even if all practices encompassing social entrepreneurship and social enterprises are not new, these concepts are on the rise. As we have seen, this field is characterized by a wide diversity from a point of view of organizational models, industries and geographical areas. The diversity and openness of the concept are probably some of the reasons for its success. The debate now concerns both the public and the private agenda. Indeed, both the public sector and the private sector, each in its own way, are discovering or rediscovering new opportunities to promote, simultaneously, entrepreneurial spirit and the pursuit of the public good.

The perspective we have adopted in this chapter suggests that the various conceptions of social enterprise and social entrepreneurship are deeply rooted in the social, economic, political and cultural contexts in which such dynamics take place. This implies that supporting the development of social enterprise cannot be done just through exporting US or European approaches.[13] Unless they are embedded in local contexts, social enterprises will just be replications of formulas that will last only as long as they are fashionable. However, international comparisons can prove to be a fertile source of mutual questioning and can help to identify major challenges that social enterprise has to face.

Each context produces specific debates. In the US context, the strong reliance on private actors might result from a kind of implicitly shared confidence in market forces to solve an increasing part of social issues in modern societies. Even if various scholars stress the need to mobilize various types of resources, it is not impossible that the current wave of social entrepreneurship may act as a priority-setting process and a selection process of social challenges deserving to be addressed because of their potential in terms of earned income. This type of questioning is also increasingly relevant in the

European context, particularly in countries where the logic of privatization and marketization of social services are more developed. In the European context, strict regulations and direct intervention of public authorities in the field of social enterprises might reduce the latter to instruments for achieving specific goals which are given priority on the political agenda, with a risk of bridling the dynamics of social innovation.

Notes

1. The letters EMES stand for Emergence des Enterprises Sociales en Europe, i.e. the title in French of the vast research project carried out from 1996 through 2000 by the network. The acronym EMES was subsequently retained when the network decided to become a formal international association. See www.emes. net.
2. See Defourny and Nyssens (2010).
3. In Italian social cooperatives, workers are members of the cooperative and disadvantaged workers should be members of the B-type cooperative that employs them, if this is compatible with their situation. The statutes may also require the presence of volunteers in the membership. In Portuguese "social solidarity cooperatives", users and workers must be effective members. In French "collective interest cooperative societies", at least three types of stakeholders must be represented: workers, users and at least a third category, defined according to the project carried out by the cooperative. As to Greek social cooperatives, they are based on a partnership between individuals of the "target group", psychiatric hospital workers and institutions from the community, and such different stakeholders have to be represented in the board of the organization.
4. Nicholls (2006) explains that Banks (1972), interestingly, first coined the term "social entrepreneur" while referring to management approaches inspired by values such as those promoted by Robert Owen, a major utopian widely considered as a father of the cooperative movement.
5. This is the case for the Italian "social cooperative", the Portuguese "social solidarity cooperative", the Spanish "social initiative cooperative" and the French "collective interest cooperative society". In the Belgian "social purpose company", no single person can have more than one-tenth of the total number of votes linked to the shares being represented. It also provides for procedures allowing each employee to participate in the enterprise's governance through the ownership of capital shares.
6. In Portuguese "social solidarity cooperatives" and Spanish "social initiative cooperatives", any distribution of profit is forbidden.
7. Distribution of profit is limited by strong rules in Italian social cooperatives and Belgian social purpose companies. The British "community interest company" includes an asset lock which restricts the distribution of profits and assets to its members; the dividend payable on the shares is subject to a cap set by the regulator.
8. Such a European specificity seems to be increasingly acknowledged at the level of the whole European Union: in November 2011, the European Commission organized a Conference to prepare a Social Business Initiative, and the Communication it issued was to serve as a basis explicitly stating that "a social enterprise is an operator in the social economy whose main objective is to have

a social impact rather than make a profit for their owners or shareholders. It operates by providing goods and services for the market in an entrepreneurial and innovative fashion and uses its profits primarily to achieve social objectives. It is managed in an open and responsible manner and, in particular, involves employees, consumers and stakeholders affected by its commercial activities". A bit further on, it is also stated that the Commission uses the term "social enterprise" (and "social business" with the same meaning) to cover types of businesses for which the social or societal objective is the reason for the commercial activity, where profits are mainly reinvested with a view to achieving this social objective and where the method of organization or ownership reflects their mission, using democratic or participatory principles or focusing on social justice (European Commission, 2011).

9. For an empirical analysis of the resource mixes in European WISEs, see Gardin (2006).

10. Such a market orientation is also clear in the above-mentioned Communication of the European Commission, which is by the way explicitly related to the Single Market Act. However, the Commission acknowledges the fact that such a market orientation should be considered broadly as public procurement and that it is an important source of income for many social enterprises. In addition EU legislations on state aids need to be reconsidered in various cases of provision of social or local services by social enterprises.

11. We are aware that it can be argued that advocacy nonprofits may also be described, to a certain extent, as service providers.

12. A key example, often referred to, is provided by the Grameen Bank, which underwent a remarkable growth before it inspired other microfinance initiatives across the world.

13. For instance, when collaborating with the UNDP to analyze the potential for promoting social enterprise in Central and Eastern European countries and in the Community of Independent States, the EMES Network decided to simplify radically its approach based on Western European experiences (Borzaga *et al.*, 2008).

References

Austin, J.E., 2000, *The Collaboration Challenge: How Nonprofits and Businesses Succeed through Strategic Alliances*, San Francisco: Jossey-Bass.

Austin, J.E. and the SEKN Team, 2004, *Social Partnering in Latin America*, Cambridge, MA: Harvard University.

Austin, J.E, Leonard, B., Reficc, E. and Wei-Skillern, J., 2006, "Social Entrepreneurship: It's for Corporations too", in A. Nicholls, ed., *Social Entrepreneurship, New Models of Sustainable Social Change*, Oxford University Press, 169–180.

Bacchiega, A. and Borzaga, C., 2001, "Social Enterprises as Incentive Structures: An Economic Analysis", in C. Borzaga and J. Defourny, eds, *The Emergence of Social Enterprise*, London and New York: Routledge, 273–294.

Bachiegga, A. and Borzaga, C., 2003, "The Economics of the Third Sector," in H.K. Anheier and A. Ben-Ner, eds, *The Study of the Nonprofit Enterprise, Theories and Approaches*, New York: Kluwer Academic/Plenum Publishers.

Bornstein, D., 2004, *How to Change the World: Social Entrepreneurs and the Power of New Ideas*, New York: Oxford University Press.

Borzaga, C. and Defourny, J., eds, 2001, *The Emergence of Social Enterprise*, London and New York: Routledge.

Borzaga, C., Galera, G. and Nogales, R., eds, 2008, *Social Enterprise: A New Model for Poverty Reduction and Employment Generation*, Bratislava: United Nations Development Programme.

Boschee, J., 1995, "Social Entrepreneurship", *Across the Board*, March 20–25.

Davister, C., Defourny, J. and Grégoire, O., 2004, "Les entreprises sociales d'insertion dans l'Union européenne: un aperçu général", *RECMA*, 293, 24–50.

Dees, J.G., 1998, *The Meaning of Social Entrepreneurship*, Stanford University, mimeo.

Dees, J.G. and Anderson, B.B., 2006, "Framing a Theory of Social Entrepreneurship: Building on Two Schools of Practice and Thought", *Research on Social Entrepreneurship*, ARNOVA Occasional Paper Series, 1(3), 39–66.

Defourny, J., 2001, "From Third Sector to Social Enterprise", in C. Borzaga and J. Defourny, eds, *The Emergence of Social Enterprise*, London and New York: Routledge, 1–28.

Defourny, J. and Kim, S.-Y., 2011, "Emerging Models of Social Enterprise in Eastern Asia: A Cross-Country Analysis", *Social Enterprise Journal*, 7(1), 86–111.

Defourny, J. and Nyssens, M., 2008, "Social Enterprise in Europe: Recent Trends and Developments", *Social Enterprise Journal*, 4(3), 202–228.

Defourny, J. and Nyssens, M., 2010, "Conceptions of Social Enterprise and Social Entrepreneurship in Europe and the United States: Convergences and Divergences", *Journal of Social Entrepreneurship*, 1(1), 32–53.

DiMaggio, P.J. and Powell, W., 1983, "The Iron Cage Revisited: Institutional Isomorphism and Collective Rationality in Organisational Fields", *American Sociological Review*, 48, 147–160.

Draperi, J.-F., 2003, "L'entreprise sociale en France, entre économie sociale et action sociale", *RECMA*, 288, 48–66.

DTI (Department of Trade and Industry), 2002, "Social Enterprise: A Strategy for Success", London: Department of Trade and Industry, www.dti.gov.uk/socialenterprise/strategy.htm

Emerson, J., 2006, "Moving Ahead Together: Implications of a Blended Value Framework for the Future of Social Entrepreneurship", in A. Nicholls, ed., *Social Entrepreneurship, New Models of Sustainable Social Change*, New York: Oxford University Press, 391–406.

Emerson, J. and Twersky, F., 1996, *New Social Entrepreneurs: The Success, Challenge and Lessons of Non-profit Enterprise Creation*, San Francisco: Roberts Foundation.

European Commission, 2011, "Social Business Initiative", Communication from the Commission to the European Parliament, the Council, the European Economic and Social Committee and the Committee of the Regions, Brussels.

Evers, A., 2001, "The Significance of Social Capital in the Multiple Goal and Resource Structure of Social Enterprise", in C. Borzaga and J. Defourny, eds, *The Emergence of Social Enterprise*, London and New York: Routledge, 296–311.

Evers, A. and Laville, J.-L., eds, 2004. *The Third Sector in Europe*, Cheltenham: Edward Elgar.

Gardin, L., 2006, "A Variety of Resource Mixes inside Social Enterprises", in M. Nyssens, ed., *Social Enterprise: At the Crossroads of Market, Public Policies and Civil Society*, London and New York: Routledge, 111–136.

Kerlin, J., 2006, "Social Enterprise in the United States and Europe: Understanding and Learning from the Differences," *Voluntas*, 17(3): 247–263.

Kerlin, J., 2009, *Social Enterprise: A Global Perspective*, Lebanon: University Press of New England.

Laville, J.-L. and Nyssens, M., 2001, "The Social Enterprise: Towards a Theoretical Socio-Economic Approach", in C. Borzaga and J. Defourny, eds, *The Emergence of Social Enterprise*, London and New York: Routledge, 312–332.

Mair, J. and Marti, I., 2006, "Social Entrepreneurship Research: a Source of Explanation, Prediction and Delight", *Journal of World Business*, 41, 36–41.

Mair, J., Robinson, J. and Hockerts, K., eds., 2006, *Social Entrepreneurship*, New York: Palgrave Macmillan.

Nicholls, A., ed., 2006, *Social Entrepreneurship: New Models of Sustainable Social Change*, New York: Oxford University Press.

Nyssens, M., ed., 2006, *Social Enterprise: At the Crossroads of Market, Public Policies and Civil Society*, London and New York: Routledge.

Roelants, B., 2009, *Cooperatives and Social Enterprises: Governance and Normative Frameworks*, Brussels : CECOP Publications.

Savitz, A., 2006, *The Triple Bottom Line: How Today's Best-Run Companies are Achieving Economic, Social, and Environmental Success – And How You Can Too*, San Francisco: Jossey-Bass/Wiley.

Skloot, E., 1987, "Enterprise and Commerce in Non-profit Organizations" in W.W. Powell ed., *The Non-profit Sector: A Research Handbook*, New Haven, CT: Yale University Press, 380–393.

Steyaert, C. and Hjorth, D., eds., 2006, *Entrepreneurship as Social Change*, Cheltenham: Edward Elgar.

Young, D., 1986, "Entrepreneurship and the Behavior of Non-profit Organizations: Elements of a Theory", in S. Rose-Ackerman, ed., *The Economics of Non-profit Institutions*, New York: Oxford University Press, 161–184.

Young, D. and Salamon, L.M., 2002, "Commercialization, Social Ventures, and For-Profit Competition", in L.M. Salamon, ed., *The State of Nonprofit America*, Washington, DC : Brookings Institution, 423–446.

Yunus, M., 2010, *Building Social Business: Capitalism That Can Serve Humanity's Most Pressing Needs*, New York: Public Affairs.

4
Defining Social Enterprise across Different Contexts: A Conceptual Framework Based on Institutional Factors

Janelle A. Kerlin

Over the past several decades the concept of social enterprise has grown dramatically in many regions of the world. Defined as the use of nongovernmental, market-based approaches to address social issues, social enterprise often provides a "business" source of revenue for many types of socially oriented organizations and activities.[1] However, within these broad parameters, world regions have come to identify different definitions and concepts with the social enterprise movement in their areas (Kerlin, 2006). This variation has also resulted in considerable debate among researchers and practitioners on how to define the concept (Mair *et al.*, 2006; Light, 2008). To address these difficulties, this research draws on the theory of historical institutionalism to advance understanding of how context influences the development of social enterprise as well as to propose a preliminary conceptual framework for social enterprise that spans regional differences in the term.

Recent research has shown that variations in social enterprise around the world are in part due to their connection with the specific socio-economic conditions of their context (Kerlin, 2009). Such research aligns with Salamon *et al.* (2000) and Salamon and Sokolowski's (2010) social origins approach that proposes that existing institutions influence the development of nonprofit sectors in different countries. It also aligns with research connecting national trends in entrepreneurship with government and society (Baumol, 1990; Bosma and Levie, 2010). While broad connections between levels of civil society, government, market and international aid have been associated with variance in social enterprise (Nyssens, 2006; Nicholls, 2006; Kerlin, 2009), little is known about how these institutions directly shape, as well as constrain, social enterprise structures. Indeed, this chapter begins to address research questions raised by Austin (2006) involving the need for the comparison of social enterprise across dimensions of place and form.

Most literature on social enterprise in relation to place focuses on single country or regional analyses and/or case studies rather than a global comparison (Borzaga and Defourny, 2001; Young, 2003; Dacanay, 2004; Les and Jeliazkova, 2005; Mulgan, 2006; Nyssens, 2006; Squazzoni, 2009; Cooney, 2011; Bagnoli and Megali, 2011; Liu and Ko, forthcoming). Indirectly, Salamon *et al.* (2004) provide comparative data on social enterprise in nonprofit organizations. They find that for 34 countries an average of 53 percent of nonprofit income comes "from fees and charges for the services that these organizations provide and the related commercial income they receive from investments, dues, and other commercial sources" (ibid., 30). In particular, they note that the dominance of commercial revenue was most prevalent among transition and developing countries where civil society sectors are small. For these countries, fees represented, on average, 61 percent of civil society organization income compared to 45 percent for developed countries (ibid.), suggesting that the context for social enterprise can influence its occurrence. Salamon *et al.*'s research also indicates that many similar types of social enterprise can be found across countries, most commonly nonprofits supported by commercial revenue. The focus of the present research, however, is on differences in the forms of social enterprise across countries whether it be variation in nonprofit and for-profit structures, the focus of their outcomes or differences in resource mixes.

This study draws on theoretical findings and national-level survey research on societal institutions as well as descriptive accounts of country contexts for social enterprise to construct a preliminary framework for large institutional processes shaping social enterprise. This conceptual framework points to a preliminary typology of social enterprise models in different countries that relate to and provide explanatory power for the types of social enterprises found there. The study then preliminarily checks the framework against empirically based case studies of five countries' current institutional patterns and how they relate to the types of social enterprises in each country. In practical terms, rather than a restrictive definition of social enterprise, the study leads to an initial conceptual framework by which a broad range of social enterprise activity can be understood.

Methodology

This study makes use of comparative historical analysis, a mode of investigation borrowed from sociology and political science (Mahoney and Rueschemeyer, 2003). Within this approach, the study draws on the theory of historical institutionalism which is based on the premise that existing institutional processes and patterns constrain the options available to actors in the innovation of institutions across time (Thelen, 1999). Researchers drawing on this theory focus on the qualitative analysis of case studies of nations and regions to compare the interaction of large-scale, societal institutions over time to understand institutional outcomes better.

In line with this approach, the initial construction of a conceptual framework relies on qualitative and quantitative macrolevel information on country institutions. The qualitative aspect draws on Kerlin (2009) and other authors for information on social enterprise and its context in different regions and countries. For quantitative data, the study makes use of survey data and empirically based models from the Global Entrepreneurship Monitor (GEM),[2] the Global Competitiveness Report (models include three stages of economic development) (Sala-i-Martin *et al.*, 2010) and the Johns Hopkins Comparative Nonprofit Sector Project (including its proposed five civil society sector models).

Due to space constraints, supporting case studies consist of an empirical overview of measures of current macrolevel institutions and how they appear to be shaping specific social enterprise models in five countries: the United States, Italy, Sweden, Argentina and Zimbabwe. Information for the empirical overviews was taken from the above referenced studies as well as from the World Development Indicators (World Bank, 2008), the Worldwide Governance Indicators (World Bank, 2010) and the GLOBE Research Project on culture in 61 countries (House *et al.*, 2004).

From macro-institutional processes to a conceptual framework for social enterprise, theoretically

This study proposes that macro-institutions and processes can account for a large part of the variation in social enterprise across different countries. Recent evolving theory suggests that institutions, both formal and informal, can create causal paths whereby the development of newer institutions is shaped by both the constraints and the supports offered by prior and present institutions. By "institutions" I mean both formal and informal rules that are consciously or unconsciously known by individuals, as defined by Rueschemeyer (2009, 210): "institutions are clusters of norms with strong but variable mechanisms of support and enforcement that regulate and sustain an important area of social life".

Our approach to institutions emphasizes the importance of underlying power relationships, both in terms of how power is involved in the creation of institutions and how institutions then create and structure power in different ways. This approach aligns with the theoretical frame of historical institutionalism, which asserts that "effective institutions influence – at the individual as well as the collective level – beliefs, normative commitments, and preferences. Their major effect at the macrolevel is to create and maintain power disparities and to broadly structure shared and antagonistic interests" (ibid., 207). Power in this study is therefore understood to support the continuing existence of institutions, but also to condition disparities that may ultimately work to shift power to previously subordinate groups, the latter providing the explanation for changes that occur in institutions over time. In short, in line with the historical institutionalism theory frame, this discussion focuses on how power relationships among institutions explain institutional reproduction and change, following Mahoney's description as outlined in Table 4.1.

Evolving theory in this area suggests that current institutions largely responsible for shaping different models of social enterprise initially arose from a rich mix of culture; local (including social classes), regional and global hierarchies; and political–economic histories. These elements structured the development of the present day state, which then helped shape the current economic situation and civil society, which in turn both influence social enterprise development. Thus, I argue that the state ultimately plays a key role in understanding a country's social enterprise model. In the following discussion I draw on theory that shows how antecedent events and processes shaped the type of state in power. I then discuss research on how the state in turn influences economic development and civil society. Figure 4.1 illustrates these macrolevel institutions and their proposed causal paths.

The question of how states come to be democratic or authoritarian in nature is addressed by many social scientists in the comparative historical analysis tradition (Mahoney, 2003). Moore (1966), in his ground breaking book *Social Origins of Dictatorship and Democracy*, spurred on research in this area, though his original hypotheses were later found to be limited (Skocpol, 1973; Mahoney, 2003). Arguably the most important work to date is Rueschemeyer *et al.*'s (1992) *Capitalist Development and Democracy*, which found that capitalist development is associated with democracy due to its alteration of the balance of power between the working class and the landed elite. Other groundbreaking research in this vein includes Skocpol's (1979) *States and Social Revolutions*, which finds three necessary and sufficient conditions for social revolutions: "international pressure from a more advanced state or states; economic or political elites who had the power to resist state-led reforms and create a political crisis; and organizations

Table 4.1   Power explanation of institutional reproduction

Mechanism of reproduction	Institution is reproduced because it is supported by an elite group of actors.
Potential characteristics of institution	Institution may empower an elite group that was previously subordinate.
Mechanism of change	Weakening of elites and strengthening of subordinate groups.

Source: Excerpted from Mahoney (2000, 517, table 1).

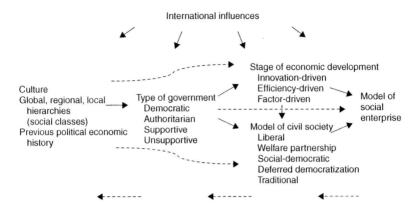

Figure 4.1 Macro-institutional processes and causal paths for models of social enterprise.

(either village or party) that were capable of mobilizing peasants for popular uprisings against local authorities" (Goldstone, 2003, 64).

Theorists have also long supported the idea that institutions at meso and microlevels, which in this case include social enterprise, business and civil society organizations, are highly structured by state institutions and policies. As Rueschemeyer (2009, 258) states:

> Taken together, the effects of purposeful state policies (even if they may often have unintended or not fully intended outcomes) and the indirect, Tocquevillean consequences of the very presence of state structures and policies leave no doubt that states and state-society relations constitute a powerful and influential environment for social and economic dynamics at the meso- and micro-levels of social life.

Indeed, authors writing within the specific fields of business and civil society often point to the importance of state institutions and policies in shaping their respective sectors over time.

In terms of business, Baumol (1990) questions the prevailing under-standing about the numbers of entrepreneurs and their effect on economic growth by showing that productive entrepreneurship (as opposed to unpro-ductive black market or rent seeking) is likely determined by the rules of society. His hypothesis is that "it is the set of rules [and not the supply of entrepreneurs *or the nature of their objectives*] that undergoes significant changes from one period to another and helps to dictate the ultimate effect on the economy via the *allocation* of entrepreneurial resources" (ibid., 894; my parentheses). Using a historical approach, he provides evidence from four periods in history that institutions, rules and norms in societies are a determining factor in the kind of entrepreneurship and economic development a society experiences. Most of these institutions and rules are generated by those governing society.

On the civil society side, in a key statement on the influence of democratic versus authoritarian governance on civil society, Salamon and Sokolowski (2009, 26) summarize their comparative historical analysis of the sector as follows:

> In sum, the key dimension that shapes the state–civil society relationship is democratic governance. The presence of such governance protects the civil sector from arbitrary state control and repressions, thus allowing it to function … the absence of democratic governance, however, entails authoritarian measures that governments take to restrain political opposition which impede the functioning and development of the civil society sector.

Overall, the literature lends significant support to the idea that, due to their connection to civil society and the economy, models for social enterprise may be indirectly shaped to a great degree by what government chooses to do and not to do over time. This is illustrated by the links between the state and economic stages and models of civil society, which are then linked to the models of social enterprise in Figure 4.1. Due to its importance, in the following sections we examine the *empirical* research available on the government connection with the economy, entrepreneurship and civil society. We then propose models of social enterprise that combine the characteristics of both the economic stage and the civil society model on the argued premise that the latter have largely been shaped by the state, though also by antecedent events and culture.[3]

From government to type of economy and entrepreneurship, empirically

Recent empirical data on government factors associated with economic development also point to the role of society's institutions in shaping economies. The Global Competitiveness Report (GCR) outlines many of these state factors in its "twelve pillars of competitiveness", including public institutions, infrastructure, health and education, and fiscal policy. Each of the 12 pillars "rests on solid theoretical foundations" in economics (Sala-i-Martin *et al.*, 2009, 4). The GCR also provides a typology of stages of economic development (see Table 4.2). The factor-driven stage is characterized by reliance on the export of mineral goods and poor supportive policies and infrastructure. The efficiency-driven stage is characterized by industrialization where productive efficiency is expanded and product quality improved, both facilitated by improving state policies. The innovation-driven stage is found in countries

Table 4.2 The Global Competitiveness Report's criteria for stages of economic development

	GDP per capita (in US$) OR	
Stage 1: Factor-driven	<2,000	If 100% of a country's total
Transition from stage 1 to 2	2,000–3,000	exports are in mineral goods[1] the country is assumed to be in
Stage 2: Efficiency-driven	3,000–9,000	the factor-driven stage (if over
Transition from stage 2 to 3	9,000–17,000	70%, the GDP-based stage rating is adjusted downwards)
Stage 3: Innovation-driven	>17,000	

Notes: Measured using a five-year average 2003–07. Total exports includes goods and services. Mineral goods include crude oil, gas, other petroleum products, metal ores and other minerals, liquefied gas, coal and precious stones. For additional explanation see Sala-i-Martin *et al.* (2009, 42, footnote 24).
Source: Adapted from Sala-i-Martin *et al.* (2010, 10, table 2).

where a high standard of living and growth is supported by the continued introduction of unique and innovative products in a sophisticated business environment. Though largely categorized on the basis of GDP per capita, each individual country assessment shows how strengths and weaknesses in the country's 12 pillars are often indicative of that country's GDP and further helps to explain the country's current stage of economic development (Sala-i-Martin *et al.*, 2010). Though the GCR categorization is currently viewed as one of the most comprehensive cross-country economic comparisons – hence its inclusion in this study – we acknowledge its limitations, including its linear determinism and failure to recognize the influence that a country's economic development can have on its institutional framework.

Drawing on the GCR's 12 pillars of competitiveness, GEM provides recommendations for each stage of economic development (see the lists below) that give further insight into what are often government-related conditions needed for a country to enhance entrepreneurship and economic growth at its present stage and move into the next. The recommendations are supplemented by GEM's own Entrepreneurial Framework Conditions in the innovation-driven stage, which were developed against a theoretical base to identify conditions relevant for innovation and entrepreneurship specifically (see Levie and Autio, 2008). In the 2009 survey, these conditions, including those that are government-related, were found to be at expected levels for countries in each of the three stages of economic development (Bosma and Levie, 2010).

Basic requirements (key focus for factor-driven economies):

• Institutions (legal and administrative);
• Infrastructure;

- Macroeconomic stability;
- Health and primary education.

Efficiency enhancers (key focus for efficiency-driven economies):

- · Higher education and training;
- Goods market efficiency;
- Labor market efficiency;
- Financial market sophistication;
- Technological readiness;
- Market size.

Innovation and entrepreneurship (key focus for innovation-driven economies):

- Entrepreneurial finance;
- Government policies;
- Government entrepreneurship programs;
- Entrepreneurship education;
- Research and development transfer;
- Commercial, legal infrastructure for entrepreneurship;
- Internal market openness;
- Physical infrastructure for entrepreneurship;
- Cultural, social norms.[4]

The GEM Report for 2009 (Bosma and Levie, 2010) also describes the role of entrepreneurship at the different stages of economic development. Of particular interest to this study, they find that for factor-driven economies the decline of agricultural work and movement of workers to extractive industries results in an oversupply of labor that leads to subsistence entrepreneurship. Indeed, the report finds that this kind of self-employment driven by necessity tends to be more prominent in less developed economies. For efficiency-driven economies, the move toward large-scale industrialization for increased productivity goes along with national economic policies that increasingly favor large businesses. Favorable conditions for emerging economic and financial institutions and openings in industrial supply chains support the development of entrepreneurship in small- and medium-sized manufacturing sectors. In innovation-driven economies, increasing wealth and desires of high-income societies support the expansion of the service sector at the same time as knowledge and research and development institutions support the aspirations of innovative entrepreneurs who are then willing to challenge larger, established economic players.

A side note on culture and entrepreneurship

Given the broad nature of culture, this research preliminarily explores the two aspects discussed in the culture literature deemed most likely to influence social enterprise: the level of in-group collectivism (vs. individualism) and the level of uncertainty avoidance in terms of what a society values.[5] In particular, this research takes the view supported by Tiessen (1997) that collectivism and individualism each support different key functions of entrepreneurialism. While the literature has long supported the idea that individualism supports entrepreneurial behavior broadly construed, Tiessen argues that individualism specifically supports the generation of variety through innovation (see Shane 1992, 1993) while collectivism supports the leveraging of resources internally and through external ties. Both the generation of new ideas and the ability to leverage resources are key to economic success on a societal level, which helps to explain why some largely collectivist countries (the Asian tigers for example) have experienced economic success (Franke *et al.*, 1991). Low levels of uncertainty avoidance have also been associated with innovation (Shane, 1993). Thus the cultural aspects discussed here influence two different functions of entrepreneurship – innovation and networked resources – each of which has a positive effect on economic activity.

From government (and economy) to civil society, empirically

Government actions also appear to be a leading factor shaping civil societies around the world. Based on two decades of empirical research, Salamon and Sokolowski's (2010) models of civil society sectors differentiate five different types (see Table 4.3). The first three, liberal, welfare partnership and social democratic, are all found in developed countries and to a significant degree are shaped by the structure of the welfare state. The last two, deferred democratization and traditional, are influenced to a lesser extent by the welfare state and more so by identifying characteristics of other aspects of government, including its absence in certain spheres. The economy is inherently important in the discussion to the degree that it makes possible the different types of welfare states or does not provide resources for one. In the latter situation, international aid may fill the gap, which has its own influence on civil society and ultimately social enterprise (Appendix 1 provides descriptions of the models as well as country examples).

From economy and civil society to models of social enterprise

In Table 4.4, the typologies for economic development and civil society are combined to create models for social enterprise that incorporate how both

Table 4.3   Salamon and Sokolowski's models of civil society sector structure

Model	Dimension				
	Workforce size	Volunteer share	Government support	Philanthropic support	Expressive share
I. Liberal	Large	Medium–high	Medium–small	Medium–high	Smaller than service
II. Welfare partnership	Large	Low–medium	High	Low	Smaller than service
III. Social democratic	Large	High	Medium	Medium	Larger than service
IV. Deferred democrati-zation	Small	Low	Low		Limited advocacy
V. Tradi-tional	Small	Medium–high	Low		Medium

Notes: Defining characteristics are shaded.
Source: Salamon and Sokolowski (2010).

Table 4.4   Models of social enterprise

Civil society	Economy		
	Factor-driven	Efficiency-driven	Innovation-driven
Liberal	–	–	Autonomous, diverse, ex. United States
Welfare partnership	–	–	Dependent, focused, ex. Italy, Germany
Social-democratic	–	–	Enmeshed, focused, ex. Sweden, Austria
Deferred democratiza-tion	–	Autonomous, mutualism, ex. Argentina, Ukraine	(Transitional) ex. Slovak Republic
Traditional	Sustainable, subsistence, ex. Zimbabwe, Uganda	(Transitional) ex. South Africa (B)	–

Notes: B = Borderline country for model of civil society.

contexts shape the organizational patterns for social enterprise in a given country. Models were identified only for those cross-sections between the two typologies where countries actually fell. The cross-sections where only one or two countries fell were labeled "transitional" (these countries were often identified as being in transition in terms of either their economy or civil society). The specific characteristics of social enterprise were drawn from the descriptions of social enterprise found in Kerlin (2009) for countries in the particular models (additional sources used are cited in the model descriptions). These models are meant to function as ideal types for social enterprise. Thus, in some cases countries may diverge somewhat from outlined characteristics though still be considered largely aligned with the indicated model.

For the **sustainable subsistence** model, social enterprise is characterized by individualized small group efforts of entrepreneurs to provide poverty relief through subsistence employment for themselves and their families. These activities are supported by international aid and often appear in the form of microfinance-supported projects due to the need to provide a sustainable form of assistance and improve small-scale economic development. This model of social enterprise fits with the factor-driven stage of economic development because of the low GDP per capita that necessitates need-based entrepreneurialism and the traditional civil society model that builds on traditional forms of social interaction in the small village group.

The **autonomous mutualism** social enterprise model is characterized by a post-authoritarian emerging civil society that comes together to fill gaps left in the economy and state social welfare. Cooperatives, recuperated companies and other mutual assistance activities that provide needed services and employment are predominant forms of social enterprise. More so than other models, social enterprises may participate in and be viewed as a form of social activism, in part because of a past tradition of civil society working in opposition to an authoritarian state coupled with present efforts to provide a form of social justice for those left behind by the market and state. This model fits with the efficiency-driven stage because entrepreneurial activities often take the form of small- and medium-sized businesses and, in the case of recuperated companies, are involved in larger scale manufacturing activities commonly attributed to this stage. With a higher GDP per capita there is also more possibility for drawing on larger pooled resources for entrepreneurship, either formally or informally. The model also aligns with the deferred democracy model because social enterprises work autonomously from and sometimes in opposition to the state to address perceived deficiencies in state policies.

Both the **dependent focused** and **enmeshed focused** social enterprise models are characterized by the large presence of the welfare state, leaving in the first instance a narrow space for the development of social enterprise activities. Although social enterprise ideas may develop in the civil society sphere to provide a unique service, once proven, they can become captured in state welfare policy and be dependent on state funding for their activities. Thus, social enterprise runs the danger of only being associated with the narrow sphere of services popularized and supported by the state. There may also be occurrences of local municipalities running social enterprises or partnering with civil society organizations to do so.

The difference between the two models involves the number, connection to public policy, and at times the origin of social enterprises. While both models rely on state subsidies for implementation, in the enmeshed focused model there are fewer and less diverse kinds of social enterprises, many of which have close ties with specific public policies that may have spurred their development. Moreover, a small number of social enterprises have originated from the top down due to state privatization of sheltered workshop programs (Spear and Bidet, 2005). The two models fit with the innovation-driven stage because of the availability of a high degree of wealth necessary to support a large welfare state, as well as government policies and other institutions supportive of innovative entrepreneurship. They each fit their respective civil society models because social enterprise has assumed a relationship with the state that aligns with the relationship between social service nonprofits and the state in each case.

The **autonomous diverse** model of social enterprise is characterized by a broader array of types of social enterprise activities in large part because of its autonomy from government due to a smaller welfare state. This autonomy from the state, in terms of the limited subsidies provided, also encourages the use of social enterprise as an income generator for organizations that at times is independent of programming for participants. There is also a highly supportive environment for innovative entrepreneurialism. Thus, this model fits with the innovation-driven stage due to the latter, but also due to the high level of wealth that supports private philanthropy for social enterprise. There may also be greater supply and demand for diverse social enterprise services due to a high-income society's desire for them and ability to pay. The model fits with the liberal model of civil society because of its autonomy from the state.

Country case studies

Finally I examine the empirical features of key institutions representing social enterprise models in five countries to see whether and how institutional factors may be shaping social enterprise in specific countries according to the models. Table 4.5 shows the socio-economic data for the five countries used in tracking large-scale differences across the five institutions relevant to social enterprise. Table 4.6 draws on currently available empirical evidence to show the differences in characteristics of social enterprise for the same five countries.[6]

Zimbabwe

Zimbabwe has a long and varied history of precolonial, colonial and then authoritarian restrictions that interrupted and limited the development of the economy and civil society and helped shape the present state, a largely authoritarian "democracy". However, cultural indicators show that citizens have a strong tradition of supportive collective activity. According to the GLOBE analysis Zimbabweans rate the highest of the five countries in terms of in-group collectivism (House *et al.*, 2004). Here, collectivism is theorized to support social innovation and enterprise through the generation of "variety through group-based, incremental improvements and changes" and the leveraging of "their own resources by harnessing 'clanlike' affiliations" (Tiessen, 1997, 368). Given the current instability in Zimbabwe, a feeling or need for more uncertainty avoidance aligns with the situation in the country (House *et al.*, 2004).

Indeed, World Governance Indicators and the Global Competitiveness Index in Table 4.5 show that Zimbabwe has one of the poorest institutional environments in the world. In 2009 it had a GDP per capita of $375 and is currently categorized as a factor-driven economy (Schwab, 2010, 350). Given its high poverty level, the country receives international aid estimated at $49 per person in 2008 (World Bank, 2008). In terms of civil society, in 2010 the Zimbabwe National Association of Non-Governmental Organisations (NANGO) described government suspicion, mistrust of the sector and recent victimization of civil society through arrests and intimidation as well as restrictions on its freedom of expression in the independent media (NANGO, 2010). As a civil society sector model, Zimbabwe best aligns with countries belonging to the traditional model though it is a borderline case because it varies from them due to repression likely limiting the share of volunteer participation (Salamon and Sokolowski, 2010).

The failure of political and economic institutions and a weak civil society in Zimbabwe have led to a necessity-driven type of social enterprise characterized by microfinance supported by international aid. As such, immediate outcomes for social enterprise are focused on individual self-sustainability and the maintenance of livelihoods. Indeed, Masendeke and Mugova (2009) report that high levels of unemployment and the negative social impact of structural adjustment reforms promoted by international financial institutions have led to the recent movement toward social enterprise solutions. Not surprisingly, given the high collectivism rating, descriptions of social enterprise in Zimbabwe do indeed have a strong emphasis on collective microfinance forms of social enterprise that receive initial direction and support from international aid (ibid.). With little recourse to welfare state or philanthropic support, social enterprise is heavily reliant on commercial revenue. With its high level of poverty, lack of a supportive state and need for sustainable livelihoods, Zimbabwe's situation most closely aligns with the sustainable subsistence social enterprise model.

Argentina

Argentina transitioned from authoritarian to democratic rule in 1983. That event, as well as structural adjustment programs in the late 1990s and

Table 4.5 Socioeconomic data for five countries

	Culture[1]		Welfare State[2]	Governance[3] (percentile rank/ governance score)			Economy[4]		Civil Society[5]	Int'l Aid[6]
	In-Group Collectivism (Practices)	Uncertainty Avoidance (Values)	Public Spending on Health/ Education (% of GDP)	Regulatory Quality (0–100/ −2.5 to +2.5)	Rule of Law (0–100/ −2.5 to +2.5)	Control of Corruption (0–100/ −2.5 to +2.5)	Economic Development Stage	GCI Ranking (1= most competitive)	Sector Model (B=Borderline)	per capita (in US $)
Zimbabwe	5.57	4.73	5.16	1.4/−2.29	.9/−1.91	1.9/−1.49	Factor	136	Traditional (B) (assumed)	49
Argentina	5.51	4.66	9.94	21/−.9	29.7/−.66	38.1/−.49	Efficiency	87	Deferred (B) Democratization	3
Italy	4.94	4.47	10.60	77.6/+.9	62.7/+.39	59/+.05	Innovation	48	Welfare Partnership (B)	–
United States	4.25	4	12.43	89.5/+1.36	91.5/+1.53	85.2/+1.18	Innovation	4	Liberal	–
Sweden	3.66	3.60	13.68	96.7/+1.66	99.5/+1.93	98.6/+2.23	Innovation	2	Social Democratic	–

1. *Source:* The Global Leadership and Organizational Behavior Effectiveness (GLOBE) Research Project is a study of 61 cultures/countries reported in, *Culture, Leadership, and Organizations: The GLOBE Study of 62 Societies* (House et al., 2004). The study examines culture through nine different dimensions each in terms of practices and values. This paper uses the study's findings for two dimensions: In-Group Collectivism in societal practices, which is "the degree to which individuals express pride, loyalty, and cohesiveness in their organizations or families" (p. 12) (on a scale of 1–7 where higher scores indicate greater In-Group Collectivism in practice) and Uncertainty Avoidance in societal values which is "the extent to which members of an organization or society *should* strive to avoid uncertainty by relying on established social norms, rituals, and bureaucratic practices" (p. 11) (on a scale of 1–7 where higher scores indicate greater Uncertainty Avoidance). Findings for both dimensions correlate with findings for similar dimensions in Geert Hofstede's (1980, 2001) pioneering work, *Culture's Consequences*. Thus work based on Hofstede's dimensions and findings is also likely to hold true for GLOBE findings in these areas.

2. *Source:* World Development Indicators. Education spending data are from the United Nations Educational, Scientific, and Cultural Organization (UNESCO) Institute for Statistics. Health spending data are from the World Health Organization, World Health Report and updates and from the OECD for its member countries, supplemented by World Bank poverty assessments and country and sector studies. Education and health spending data are from 2007 except Zimbabwe with data from 2001. Retrieved from http://databank.worldbank.org/ddp/home.do.

Definition: Public expenditure on education consists of current and capital public expenditure on education plus subsidies to private education at the primary, secondary, and tertiary levels. Public health expenditure consists of recurrent and capital spending from government (central and local) budgets, external borrowings and grants (including donations from international agencies and nongovernmental organizations), and social (or compulsory) health insurance funds.

3. *Source*: World Bank (2010) World Wide Governance Indicators: Governance Matters 2010. Report provides six governance indicators for 212 of the world's countries and territories. Four of these indicators are referred to in this paper: Government Effectiveness is the quality of public services, the capacity of the civil service and its independence from political pressures, and the quality of policy formulation. Regulatory Quality is the ability of the government to provide sound policies and regulations that enable and promote private sector development. Rule of Law is the extent to which agents have confidence in and abide by the rules of society, including the quality of contract enforcement and property rights, the police, and the courts, as well as the likelihood of crime and violence. Control of Corruption is the extent to which public power is exercised for private gain, including both petty and grand forms of corruption, as well as "capture" of the state by elites and private interests (retrieved from http://info.worldbank.org/governance/wgi/pdf/WBL_GovInd.pdf).

4. *Source*: 2010–2011 Global Competitiveness Report, in addition to a competitiveness ranking of 139 countries, provides a typology of stages of economic development largely based on GDP per capita (Sala-i-Martin *et al.*, 2010).

5. *Source*: Johns Hopkins Comparative Nonprofit Sector Project. Based on two decades of empirical research in over 40 countries, Salamon and Sokolowski's (2010) models of civil society sectors distinguish five types based on differences in empirical data across five dimensions: workforce size, volunteer share, government support, philanthropic support, and expressive share. Zimbabwe was not included in the Johns Hopkins project however its civil society characteristics largely match other African countries that belong in the Traditional model thus Zimbabwe's alignment with this model is assumed.

6. *Source*: World Bank (2008) World Development Indicators. International aid data is from the Development Assistance Committee (DAC) of the Organization for Economic Co-operation and Development (OECD), and population estimates from the World Bank. Data are from 2008. Notes: International aid per capita includes net official development assistance (loans and grants from DAC member countries, multilateral organizations, and non-DAC donors) divided by the midyear population estimate. Italy and the United States did not receive international aid (data retrieved from the World Bank's World Databank at http://databank.worldbank.org/ddp/home.do?Step=12&id=4&CNO=2).

Table 4.6 Social enterprise characteristics for five countries

	Outcome Emphasis	Common Form	Variation in Types of Activities	Reliance on Commercial Revenue	Government Involvement		Civil Society Presence
					SE Policies/ Subsidies	SE Legal Form	
Zimbabwe[1] Sustainable Subsistence	Individual Self-Sustainability	Microfinance/ Nonprofit	Low	High	No	No	Moderate (works w/intl aid)
Argentina[2] Autonomous Mutualism	Group Self-Sufficiency	Cooperative/ Mutual Benefit	Moderate	High	No	No	Strong
Italy[3] Dependent Focused	Social Benefit	Cooperative	Low	Moderate – Low (reliant on govt subsidies)	High	Yes	Moderate (partnered w/govt)
United States[4] Autonomous Diverse	Organizational Sustainability	Nonprofit/ Business	High	Moderate (mixed w/charity & govt revenue)	No	No	Strong
Sweden[5] Enmeshed Focused	Social Benefit	Cooperative/ Business*	Low	Low (very reliant on govt subsidies)	Very High	No	Low (highly partnered w/govt)

1. *Source*: Masendeke, A. & Mugova, A., 2009
2. *Source*: Roitter & Vivas, 2009.
3. *Source*: Borzaga & Santuari, 2001; Nyssens, 2009.
4. *Source*: Kerlin & Gagnaire, 2009.
5. *Source*: Stryjan, 2001, 2004; Spear & Bidet, 2005; Gawell et al., 2009.
* While government-supported social cooperatives have been the dominant social enterprise form in Sweden, recently some businesses with a social purpose have appeared that are less engaged with government. See Gawell et al., 2009.

the 2001 economic crisis, had a dramatic effect on government policies, the economy and civil society. Culturally, Argentina has a moderate risk avoidance rating and a high collectivism orientation, the latter manifesting itself in many forms of mutual association that have a long tradition. Reflective of recent events, Worldwide Governance Indicators for 2010 (see Table 4.5) show that Argentina has experienced declines in a number of areas since 1996 (World Bank, 2010). The 2010–2011 GCR finds that economic factors in Argentina have only recently improved in some respects (Schwab, 2010). The report, which places the country in the efficiency-driven stage of economic development, puts GDP per capita in at $7,726 in 2009 (ibid., 80).

According to Salamon and Sokolowski (2010), Argentina has a borderline deferred democratization civil society sector model. The recent changes in government and the economy have encouraged a restructuring of the relationship between civil society and the state. With the return of democracy in 1983, many associations were restored, though they were largely tied to the welfare state. Structural adjustment reforms in the 1990s, however, brought privatization and a dismantling of the welfare state, dramatically changing the landscape for civil society (Jacobs and Maldonado, 2005). When coupled with the 2001 economic crisis, the situation encouraged a (re)turn to mutual forms of civil society organizations (Roitter and Vivas, 2009).

With little recourse to the state or the economy during economic downturns, social enterprise in Argentina has developed in part around mutual benefit forms of organization that have a historical legacy in the country, including cooperatives, mutual benefit associations and cooperative recuperated companies.[7] Thus the immediate outcome emphasis of social enterprise is group self-sufficiency. Indeed, higher levels of GDP than Zimbabwe likely make it possible for groups to aggregate resources for mutual benefit and also be in less need of international assistance. Interestingly these larger-scale social enterprise structures, at times including entire factories, align with the aggregation of production reflective of the efficiency-driven economic stage Argentina is currently in. With little support from the welfare state, philanthropy or even international aid, social enterprise is characterized by the large presence of civil society. The institutional context and their connection to social enterprise in Argentina thus best align with the autonomous mutualism social enterprise model.

Italy

With the start of the 21st century, Italy has experienced greater overall political and economic stability than in previous decades, though problems of corruption persist. Similar to other West European countries, Italy has a strong welfare state. Culturally, however, unlike other West European countries that value low uncertainty avoidance and have low collectivism, Italy values moderate uncertainty avoidance and practices moderate in-group collectivism. Worldwide Governance Indicators consistently rank Italy in the sixtieth and seventieth percentile on a number of important indicators (see Table 4.5) (World Bank, 2010). Categorized as an innovation-driven economy, the Global Competitiveness Index ranked Italy forty-eighth out of 139 countries in 2010. In 2009 Italy had an average GDP per capita of $35,435 (Sala-i-Martin, 2010, 27).

The civil society sector in Italy is considered to be a borderline welfare partnership model (Salamon and Sokolowski, 2010). Historically, the foundation for civil society in Italy[8] was city corporations or guilds among other entities. These were self-managed forms of mutual assistance that had legal and financial autonomy. More recently the development of the welfare state meant many service-oriented civil society organizations became public entities. In the 1980s, however, budget restrictions and dissatisfaction with welfare state services spurred the development of new forms of civil society organizations, including social cooperatives (Barbetta *et al.* 2004).

The rise of social enterprise in Italy provides an example of a re-emerged collective civil society tradition in the form of social cooperatives.[9] As Barbetta *et al.* (2004, 251) note, social cooperatives "revitalized the mutuality sentiments of the guild, and at the same time sought to merge market means with charitable purpose". Initially a civil society response to a crisis of unemployment among hard-to-employ populations, the success of social cooperatives brought the attention and support of the welfare state which used them to help further its policy agenda in the area of work integration for the hard-to-employ. Thus immediate outcomes for social enterprise in Italy focus on social benefit and social cooperatives that have a reliance on government subsidies and supportive policies. Indeed, in 1991 Italy became the first country in Western Europe to pass legislation designating a legal form for social enterprise known as "type B" social cooperatives (Borzaga, 1996; Borzaga and Santuari, 2001; Nyssens, 2009). Given the mutual dependence of the welfare state and social cooperatives and the focus on work integration, the Italian case best aligns with the dependent focused model of social enterprise.

The United States

In the United States, the stability and strength of its institutions over long periods of time have supported innovation and high economic growth, though the 2008–2009 economic recession has brought new challenges. Compared to West European countries, the US has a small welfare state but similarly rates low on uncertainty avoidance and low on collectivism, both indicating a culture that drives innovation through the generation of variety. On government performance, the US slipped into the high eightieth percentile in 2010 after a decade in the ninetieth percentile on a number of factors due to the economic recession. Similarly, according to the 2010–2011

GCR, the US ranked fourth of 139 countries, down from second place in 2009–2010 and first place in 2008–2009 (Sala-i-Martin, 2010). In the innovation-driven stage, its domestic economy remains the world's largest with a 2009 GDP per capita of $46,381 (Schwab, 2010, 340).

According to Salamon and Sokolowski (2010), the civil society sector in the US belongs to the liberal model and is characterized by its large size, diverse activities, volunteer support and autonomy from the state. Over the past few decades, it has experienced dramatic growth, making it difficult for traditional forms of nonprofit revenue (philanthropy and government) to keep up with the increased demand. Kerlin and Gagnaire (2009) suggest that this situation may have been a factor in a 20-year increase in commercial revenue supporting nonprofits (see also Kerlin and Pollak, 2011).

Like civil society, social enterprise in the US is characterized by its autonomy from government due to lack of involvement of the welfare state as well as diverse activities. In addition to for-profit forms of social enterprise, it also has a growing foundation in the increasing number of nonprofits that are pursuing commercial activities as a revenue maintenance and growth strategy due to stagnation in government and philanthropic sources. Given this function, unlike most other countries, social enterprise in the US at times provides revenue generation without a programming component, though it can also provide both. Thus, the immediate outcome for social enterprise is often organizational sustainability which then supports social benefit. In the US, innovation and effective governance spurs wealth that supports social enterprise development through private philanthropy and some government funding leading to a moderate but increasing reliance on commercial revenue. Given these institutional outcomes, social enterprise in the US aligns with the autonomous diverse model.

Sweden

Sweden is known for its strong, stable institutions that include a healthy economy and a large welfare state that offers a high degree of social protection. Though the last few decades have witnessed a divestiture of some state responsibilities, this effort is ongoing. Culturally, Sweden scores the lowest among the five countries on both in-group collectivism and uncertainty avoidance in terms of what society values, the latter perhaps assisted by state social protections.

Sweden ranks among the highest in the world on both governance and economic factors. As the governance figures show in Table 4.5, it has among the highest rankings in government effectiveness, regulatory quality, rule of law and control of corruption. In terms of its economy, Sweden moved from fourth to second in the 2010 Global Competitiveness Ranking, replacing the US in the number two position. This ranking can be attributed, among other variables, to highly efficient and transparent public institutions, trust in public officials, innovation and a low level of corruption. The country falls into the innovation-driven economic stage and had a GDP per capita of $43,986 in 2009 (Schwab, 2010, 310).

In terms of civil society, Sweden has a social democratic model characterized by less diversity but a high degree of volunteering (Lundstrom and Wijkstrom, 1995; Salamon and Sokolowski, 2010). The large presence of the welfare state in Sweden means that service delivery in certain areas such as health, education and social welfare is almost entirely provided by the state. According to some theorists this has led to a smaller nonprofit sector that is focused on activities such as culture, adult education and sports. However, for those few social service nonprofits that overlap with the state's social welfare domain there is a high degree of financial and in-kind state support (Wijkstrom, 2000). Indeed, cooperation is so close that "it can be difficult to separate these entities one from the other" (Lundstrom and Wijkstrom, 1995, 22).

The dominance of the welfare state in Sweden has led to fewer social enterprises that operate in fewer spheres of activity. Because many of the work integration social enterprises that dominate social enterprise activity in Sweden fall into the welfare state's sphere of activity (like some nonprofits), they have close ties with specific public policies and government institutions that in some cases spurred their development. These include social work cooperatives and community development businesses. Thus, in Sweden, social enterprise in many ways is a labor market policy tool that the welfare state uses to address problems of unemployment (Stryjan, 2001, 2004; Levander, 2010). Innovation and effective governance have supported a strong economy that in turn supports a strong welfare state. We may also note, however, that recently in Sweden some businesses with a social purpose have appeared that are less engaged with government (Gawell *et al.*, 2009). Overall it appears though that macrolevel institutions in the Swedish context have helped shape larger outcomes for social enterprise that align it with the enmeshed focused model.

Conclusion

The five case studies attempt to illustrate how macrolevel institutions (or at times the lack of them), including culture, the state, the economy and civil society, put pressure on social enterprise organizations to fulfill particular functions and be structured in specific ways. Thus, generally speaking this discussion has attempted to show that the resulting types of social enterprises appear to fit the particular needs as well as the institutional structures of each country. These case studies provide preliminary evidence for the existence of distinct models of social enterprise presented earlier. The models were formulated on the basis of a dynamic framework showing how socioeconomic institutions shape social enterprises in different countries. As supported by the theory of historical institutionalism, it can be expected that these socioeconomic institutions will change over time due to shifts in power relations and that social enterprise models for different countries will change over time as well. Future research is needed to investigate current and additional country case studies from a deeper historical perspective. Indeed, the present study is only a preliminary overview based on the most widely available information. Such research will help validate the grouping of countries into like social enterprise models and also identify any new models. Other countries with significantly different contexts yet to be explored include Asian and Middle Eastern countries. Moreover, additional in-depth research may reveal greater differentiation within the models presented here. For example, differences across countries within the autonomous Mutualism model may call for separate models for Latin American and East European countries. More rigorous formal testing of the models, including the extent to which they minimize within-group differences and maximize between-group differences, will be undertaken once models for social enterprise have been more fully expanded and fine-tuned. Though to a large extent theoretically based, this research has practical implications for the facilitation of cross-regional dialogue, the transfer and replication of social enterprise ideas, and the structures developed for their support.

Appendix: Descriptions of Salamon and Sokolowski's five models of civil society sectors[10]

Liberal

In this model civil society is large due to greater reliance on non-governmental services in the face of a relatively small welfare state (compared to other industrialized countries). Government funding is more limited and there is a sizeable reliance on private support including volunteers. Examples include the United States, the United Kingdom and Australia.

Welfare partnership

Here civil society is large due to government reliance on the sector for implementation of its sizable welfare state policies. Funding is characterized by a large share of government revenue rather than resources coming from private sources including volunteers. Examples include Belgium, Germany and Israel.

Social democratic

Civil society in this model can be large but circumscribed to expressive roles and activities due to a sizable welfare state that both funds and delivers social services. Expressive functions include advocacy, sports, recreation and culture, supported by a high level of volunteering and fees-for-service. Examples include Austria, Norway and Sweden.

Deferred democratization

Here civil society remains small due to repressive or neglectful policies of a state that views certain forms of civil society activity as a threat to itself and/or economic development. With little government support, the sector relies on fees where it provides services for the upper class and international aid where it serves the poor. Volunteerism is limited. Examples include Brazil, Colombia and Poland.

Traditional

In this model civil society is small and is characterized by the persistence of traditional social relationships and forms of helping. With the government providing little support even for welfare services, the sector focuses on anti-poverty services and maintains itself primarily through fees and international aid. Volunteerism can be sizable because there is little opposition from the state. Examples include Kenya, Pakistan and Uganda.

Notes

1. See Nicholls (2006), Mair *et al.* (2006) and Light (2008) for literature reviews on the definition of social enterprise and social entrepreneurship.
2. The GEM consortium of 56 countries conducts annual surveys of individuals on the topic of entrepreneurship. The 2009 survey included a section on social entrepreneurship activity in 49 countries.
3. Regarding the question of endogeneity (expressed as reverse arrows at the bottom of Figure 4.1), while there is likely some influence of latter institutions backwards along the causal path, theorists speculate this to be minimal (Rueschemeyer, 2009, 244; see also Evans *et al.*, 1985, ch. 1).
4. Excerpted from Bosma and Levie (2010, 15, figure 3). For a description of components under basic requirements and efficiency enhancers see Sala-i-Martin *et al.* (2009, 4–7). For innovation and entrepreneurship see Bosma and Levie (2010, 33).
5. See note 1 in Table 4.1 for the source and definitions of these variables.
6. Information on social enterprise was drawn from the writings of social enterprise researchers from each of the countries in question. See cited references.
7. Failed companies that have been reorganized into self-managed cooperatives at times in opposition to local authorities. Roitter and Vivas (2009) find that 170 recuperated companies have emerged in Argentina since the end of the 1990s.
8. Putnam (1993) provides an in-depth study of civil society in Italy and notes strong regional variation between northern and southern parts of the country.
9. Social cooperatives, common in Western Europe, are characterized by multi-stakeholder ownership and democratic management involving workers, managers, volunteers, costumers, donors and public authorities.
10. The following is taken from Salamon and Sokolowski (2010).
11. The following is taken from Salamon and Sokolowski (2010).
12. The following is taken from Salamon and Sokolowski (2010).

References

Austin, J.E. (2006). "Three Avenues for Social Entrepreneurship Research." In J. Mair, J. Robinson and K. Hockerts (eds), *Social Entrepreneurship*. New York: Palgrave Macmillan: 22–33.

Bagnoli, L. and Megali, C. (2011). "Measuring Performance in Social Enterprises." *Nonprofit and Voluntary Sector Quarterly* 40(1): 149–165.

Barbetta, G.P., Cima, S., Nereo, Z., Sokolowski, S.W. and Salamon, L.M. (2004). "Italy." In L. Salamon and S. Sokolowski (eds), *Global Civil Society. Dimensions of the Nonprofit Sector, vol. 2.* Bloomfield, CT: Kumarian Press.

Baumol, W.J. (1990). "Entrepreneurship: Productive, Unproductive and Destructive." *Journal of Political Economy,* 98(5): 893–921.

Borzaga, C. (1996). "Social Cooperatives and Work Integration in Italy." *Annals of Public and Cooperative Economics,* 67(2): 209–234.

Borzaga, C., & Defourny, J. (Eds.). (2001). *The Emergence of Social Enterprise.* New York: Routledge.

Borzaga, C. & Santuari, A. (2001). Italy: From traditional co-operatives to innovative social enterprises. In Borzaga, C., & Defourny, J. (Eds.), *The Emergence of Social Enterprise* (pp. 166–181). New York: Routledge.

Bosma, N. and Levie, J. (2010). *Global Entrepreneurship Monitor 2009 Global Report.* www.gemconsortium.org/about.aspx?page=pub_gem_global_reports

Cooney, K. (2011). "An Exploratory Study of Social Purpose Business Models in the United States." *Nonprofit and Voluntary Sector Quarterly,* 40(1): 185–196.

Dacanay, M. (Ed.). (2004). *Creating Space in the Market: Social Enterprise Stories in Asia.* Makati City, Philippines: Asian Institute of Management and Conference of Asian Foundations and Organizations.

Evans, P. B., Rueschemeyer, D., & Skocpol, T. (1985). *Bringing the State Back in.* Cambridge, UK: Cambridge University Press.

Franke, R.H., Hofstede, G., & Bond, M.H. (1991). "Cultural Roots of Economic Performance: A Research Note." *Strategic Management Journal,* 12:165–173.

Gawell, M., Johannisson, B., & Lundqvist, M. (Eds.) (2009). *Entrepreneurship in the Name of Society.* Stockholm, Sweden: Knowledge Foundation.

Goldstone, J. (2003). "Comparative Historical Analysis and Knowledge Accumulation in the Study of Revolutions." In J. Mahoney & D. Rueschemeyer (Eds.), *Comparative historical analysis in the social sciences* (pp. 41–90). Cambridge, UK: Cambridge University Press.

Hofstede, G. (1980). *Culture's Consequences: International Differences in Work Related Values.* Beverly Hills, CA: Sage.

Hofstede, G. (2001). *Culture's Consequences: Comparing Values, Behaviors, Institutions, and Organizations across Nations.* Thousand Oaks, CA: Sage.

House, R. J., Hanges, P. J., Javidan, M., Dorfman, P. W., & Gupta, V. (2004). *Culture, leadership, and organizations: The GLOBE study of 62 societies.* Thousand Oaks, CA: Sage.

Jacobs, J. E. & Maldonado, M. (2005). "Civil Society in Argentina: Opportunities and Challenges for National and Transnational Organisation." *Journal of Latin American Studies,* 37: 141–172.

Kerlin, J. A. (2006). Social enterprise in the United States and Europe: Understanding and learning from the differences. *Voluntas,* 17(3): 247–263.

Kerlin, J. A. (Ed.). (2009). *Social Enterprise: a Global Comparison.* Lebanon, NH: Tufts University Press.

Kerlin, J. A., & Gagnaire, K. (2009). United States. In Kerlin, J. (Ed.), *Social Enterprise: a Global Comparison.* Lebanon, NH: Tufts University Press.

Kerlin, J. A., & Pollak, T. (2011). "Nonprofit Commercial Revenue: a Replacement for Declining Government Grants and Private Contributions?" *American Review of Public Administration,* 41(6): 686–705.

Les, E. and Jeliazkova, M. (2005). "The Social Economy in Central, East and South East Europe." In *The Social Economy as a Tool of Social Innovation and Local Development.* Background Report. Paris: OECD.

Levander, U. (2010). "Social Enterprise: Implications of Emerging Institutionalized Constructions." *Journal of Social Entrepreneurship*, 1(2): 213–230.

Levie, J., & Autio, E. (2008). a Theoretical Grounding and Test of the gem Model. *Small Business Economics*, 31(3): 235–263.

Light, P. C. (2008). *The Search for Social Entrepreneurship*. Washington, DC: Brookings Institution Press.

Liu, G., & Ko, W. W. (forthcoming). "Organizational learning and marketing capability development: A study of the charity retailing operations of British social enterprise. " *Nonprofit and Voluntary Sector Quarterly*.

Lundstrom, T. and Wijkstrom, F. (1995). "Defining the Nonprofit Sector: Sweden." Working Papers of the Johns Hopkins Comparative Nonprofit Sector Project, no. 16. Baltimore: The Johns Hopkins Institute for Policy Studies.

Mahoney, J. (2000). "Path Dependence in Historical Sociology." *Theory and Society*, 29(4), 507–548.

Mahoney, J. (2003). "Knowledge Accumulation in Comparative Historical Research: The Case of Democracy and Authoritarianism." In J. Mahoney & D. Rueschemeyer (Eds.), *Comparative Historical Analysis in the Social Sciences* (pp. 131–176). Cambridge, UK: Cambridge University Press.

Mahoney, J., & Rueschemeyer, D. (Eds.). (2003). *Comparative Historical Analysis in the Social Sciences*. Cambridge, UK: Cambridge University Press.

Mair, J., Robinson, J., & Hockerts, K. (2006). "Introduction." In J. Mair, J. Robinson, & K. Hockerts (Eds.), *Social Entrepreneurship* (pp. 1–13). New York: Palgrave Macmillan.

Masendeke, A., & Mugova, A. (2009). "Zimbabwe and Zambia." In J. Kerlin (Ed.), *Social Enterprise: a Global Comparison* (pp. 114–138). Lebanon, NH: Tufts University Press.

Moore, B. Jr. (1966). Social Origins of Dictatorship and Democracy: Lord and Peasant in the Making of the Modern World. Boston: Beacon Press.

Mulgan, G. (2006). "Cultivating the Other Invisible Hand of Social Entrepreneurship: Comparative Advantage, Public Policy, and Future Research Priorities." In A. Nicholls (Ed.), *Social Entrepreneurship: New Models of Sustainable Change* (pp. 74–95). Oxford: Oxford University Press.

NANGO ((Zimbabwe) National Association of Non-Governmental Organisations). (2010). *Early Warning System Report Reporting Period October 2009–February 2010*, www.nango.org.zw/index.php?option=com_content&view=article&id=72&Itemid=265

Nicholls, A. (2006). "Introduction." In A. Nicholls (Ed.), *Social Entrepreneurship: New Models of Sustainable Change* (pp. 1–36). Oxford: Oxford University Press.

Nyssens, M. (Ed.). (2006). "Social Enterprise: at the Crossroads of Market, Public Policies and Civil Society." New York: Routledge.

Nyssens. M. (2009). "Western Europe." In Kerlin, J. (Ed.), *Social Enterprise: a Global Comparison*. Lebanon, NH: Tufts University Press.

Putnam, R. (1993). *Making Democracy Work: Civic Traditions in Modern Italy*. Princeton: Princeton University Press.

Roitter, M., & Vivas, A. (2009). "Argentina." In J. Kerlin (Ed.), *Social Enterprise: a Global Comparison* (pp. 139–162). Lebanon, NH: Tufts University Press.

Rueschemeyer, D. (2009). "Usable Theory: Analytic Tools for Social and Political Research. " Princeton: Princeton University Press.

Rueschemeyer, D., Stephens, E. H., & Stephens, J.D. (1992). *Capitalist Development and Democracy*. Chicago: Chicago University Press.

Sala-i-Martin, X., Blanke, J., Hanouz, M., Geiger, T., & Mia, I. (2009). The Global Competitiveness Index 2009–2010: "Contributing to Long-Term Prosperity Amid the Global Economic Crisis." In K. Schwab (Ed.), *The Global Competitiveness Report 2009–2010*. Geneva: World Economic Forum: 3–47, www.weforum.org/pdf/GCR09/GCR20092010fullreport

Sala-i-Martin, X., Blanke, J., Hanouz, M., Geiger, T., & Mia, I. (2010). "The Global Competitiveness Index 2010–2011: Looking beyond the Global Economic Crisis." In K. Schwab (Ed.), *The Global Competitiveness Report 2010–2011*. Geneva: World Economic Forum: 3–55, http://www3.weforum.org/docs/WEF_GlobalCompetitivenessReport_2010–11.pdf.

Salamon, L. and Sokolowski, S. (2009). "Bringing the 'Social' and the 'Political' to Civil Society: Social Origins of Civil Society Sectors in 40 Countries." Paper presented at the 38th Annual Conference of the Association for Research on Nonprofit Organizations and Voluntary Action, November 12–21, Cleveland, OH.

Salamon, L. and Sokolowski, S. (2010). "The Social Origins of Civil Society: Explaining Variations in the Size and Structure of the Global Civil Society Sector." Paper presented at the 9th International Conference of the International Society for Third Sector Research, July 7–10, Istanbul, Turkey.

Salamon, L., Sokolowski, S.W. and Anheier, H.K. (2000). "Social Origins of Civil Society: An Overview." Working Paper of the Johns Hopkins Comparative Nonprofit Sector Project, no. 38. Baltimore: The Johns Hopkins Center for Civil Society Studies.

Salamon, L., Anheier, H., List, R., Toepler, S., Sokolowski, S., & Associates. (2004). *Global Civil Society: Dimensions of the Nonprofit Sector*, vol. 2. Bloomfield, CT: Kumarian Press.

Schwab, K. (ed.) (2010). *The Global Competitiveness Report 2010–2011*. Geneva: World Economic Forum: 3–55), http://www3.weforum.org/docs/WEF_GlobalCompetitivenessReport_2010–11.pdf

Shane, S. (1992). "Why Do Some Countries Invent More Than Others?" *Journal of Business Venturing*, 7: 29–46.

Shane, S. (1993). "Cultural Influences on National Rates of Innovation." *Journal of Business Venturing*, 8: 59–73.

Skocpol, T. (1973). "A Critical Review of Barrington Moore's Social Origins of Dictatorship and Democracy." *Politics and Society*, 4(1): 1–34.

Skocpol, T. (1979) *States and Social Revolutions*. Cambridge, UK: Cambridge University Press.

Spear, R., & Bidet, E. (2005). "Social Enterprise for Work Integration in 12 European Countries: a Descriptive Analysis." *Annals of Public and Cooperative Economics*, 76(2): 195–231.

Squazzoni, F. (2009). "Social Entrepreneurship and Economic Development in Silicon Valley. " *Nonprofit and Voluntary Sector Quarterly*, 38(5): 869–883.

Stryjan, Y. (2001). "Sweden: the Emergence of Work-Integration Social Enterprises." In Borzaga, C., & Defourny, J. (Eds.), *The Emergence of Social Enterprise* (pp. 220–235). New York: Routledge.

Stryjan, Y. (2004). "Work Integration Social Enterprises in Sweden." Working Papers Series, no. 04/02, Liège: EMES European Research Network.

Thelen, K. (1999). "Historical Institutionalism in Comparative Politics." *Annual Review of Political Science*, 2, 369–404.

Tiessen, J. H. (1997). "Individualism, Collectivism, and Entrepreneurship: a Framework for International Comparative Research." *Journal of Business Venturing*, 12: 367–384.

Wijkstrom, F. (2000). "Changing Focus Or Changing Role? the Swedish Nonprofit Sector in the 1990s." *German Policy Studies.* 1(2): 161–188.

World Bank (2008). *World Development Indicators.* World Bank World Databank accessed at http://databank.worldbank.org/ddp/home.do?Step=12&id=4&CNO=2

World Bank (2010). *Governance Matters 2010: Worldwide Governance Indicators, 1996–2008. Country Data Reports,* http://info.worldbank.org/governance/wgi/pdf/WBI_GovInd.pdf

Young, D. (2003). "New Trends in the U.S. Non-profit Sector: Towards Market Integration?" In *The Nonprofit Sector in a Changing Economy* (pp. 61–77). Paris: OECD.

Part II
Empirical Studies

5
Managing Conflicting Institutional Logics: Social Service versus Market

*Eve Garrow and Yeheskel Hasenfeld**

Work integration social enterprises (WISEs) are human service organizations that provide employment opportunities and job training to people with employment barriers. Although the work experiences function primarily as a component of their social services, WISEs also produce and sell products or services on the market. Thus the social enterprise functions as both social service and revenue generator. In pursuing the "double bottom line", the WISE is frequently heralded as a potentially self-sustaining economic model in which the market is cleverly harnessed in service of a social mission (see e.g. Borzaga and Defourny, 2001; Schorr, 2006; Brozek, 2009). In fact, it is often noted that commercial earnings in excess of operating costs can cross-subsidize other social programs, rendering additional social value (Alter, 2006).

Institutional theory departs from this prevailing economic model to provide a more complicated portrait of WISEs. Viewed through an institutional lens, pursuit of the "double bottom line" positions WISEs in two organizational fields – human services and market – governed by competing institutional logics, or sets of organizing principles that provide organizations and individuals with means, motives and identities (Friedland and Alford, 1991, 248). Consequently, WISEs must assume two different, institutionally derived identities. In the human services field the WISE's primary identity is that of a human service organization. Stakeholders in this field, including funders and collaborators, interact with the organization because they support its social mission. Consistent with a logic of social service, the organization justifies its work experiences as therapy for clients. By contrast, within the context of the market the WISE, in its ideal form, is a business; work experiences are production jobs; and clients are instruments of production who help to generate goods or services that are exchanged for money. While some business customers may engage in exchange relations with the WISE as a means of supporting the social mission, other customers may adhere to the market logic, holding the WISE accountable to standards of quality, efficiency and price that prevail in the market – standards that the WISE may struggle to meet given that it "employs" clients with barriers to work.

In the face of competing logics, WISEs run the risk of subordinating the therapeutic purpose of the work experience to its production function. When a market logic prevails, clients become *commodified* and their value as instruments of production supersedes their role as service recipients. Table 5.1 illustrates the contrasting treatment of clients under a logic of social service and a market logic.

In contrast to the "win–win" metaphor implicit in the prevailing economic model of social enterprise, then, the metaphor is now one of political and ideological struggle between irreconcilable sets of cultural meanings and associated practices. The political and cultural implications offered up by the institutional lens are clear: at the intersection of market and nonmarket spheres, WISEs are a potential conduit for the seepage of market meanings across institutional boundaries into arenas previously structured by a social service logic.

Yet subordination to market meanings, while a distinct threat, is not the only possible outcome of institutional conflict. As WISEs derive their core identity in the field of human services and (at least outwardly) justify their

Table 5.1   Client commodification

When clients are commodified	When clients are decommodified
They are selected because they meet the needs of the enterprise.	They are selected because the work opportunities meet their service needs.
They are retained because they are productive workers.	They are retained even if they are less productive, because they require training/experience.
They are fired or dismissed because they are not productive, fail or violate work norms.	They are "graduated" from the work program when they become productive or otherwise no longer require the therapeutic benefits of the work experience.
Their work experiences are determined by the needs of the business.	Their work experience is determined by their therapeutic needs.
Their tasks, work schedule and pay are determined by the requirements of the work site. Therapeutic issues are viewed as a distraction from work.	They may be diverted from the work experience if they have therapeutic issues that require additional social services.
Ancillary social services are viewed as less important, especially if such services do not increase or interfere with productivity.	Ancillary services are viewed as just as important as the work experience.

work experiences in therapeutic terms, we might expect the logic of social service to prevail at least some of the time. In addition, as Kraatz and Block (2008) have argued, institutional conflict opens the possibility for not only subordination of one institutionally derived identity or another, but also for compartmentalization of rival identities, balance between identities, or the emergence of novel hybrid identities.

Despite an awareness of an institutional conflict for WISEs, there has been surprisingly little effort to assess its theoretical and empirical implications. We are particularly interested in the implications of cognitive or constitutive institutional conflict – that is, conflict between institutional logics that are constitutive of individuals and organizations. The specter of constitutive institutional conflict raises the following questions for the study of WISEs: Under what conditions do WISEs subordinate their preferred logic of social service to a market logic? That is, when do they preserve their core identity as a human service organization, and when do they become a de facto business? When do they construct and treat their clients as service recipients, and when do they commodify their clients?

Drawing linkages across institutional logics and political economy theories, we first develop a theoretical model that attempts to answer these questions. Through a comparative case study of WISEs, we then present an empirical evaluation of the causal hypotheses derived from the model. A detailed description of four WISEs serves to illustrate the model. We conclude by offering some theoretical and practical implications of the study. Our aim is, both theoretically and empirically, to advance understanding of the institutional and political influences on WISEs and the consequences for clients.

Theoretical framework

At the core of our framework is the insight, drawn from institutional theory, that organizations are deeply influenced by the structuring logics that govern the fields in which they participate. If the institutional logics that organize fields are broadly conceived as "rules of the game", then WISEs operate in two different games structured by varying and sometimes conflicting rules, meanings and interests (Bourdieu and Wacquant, 1992; Kraatz and Block, 2008; Thornton and Ocasio, 2008). However, the degree to which WISEs are influenced by the field depends on their exposure to field-level logics. Given the constitutive nature of institutional logics, our main hypothesis is: the greater the exposure to a market logic, with its emphasis on profit, productivity and efficiency, the greater the risk of displacement of the mission-motive of work experience and the role of clients as service recipients. Exposure to a market logic will increase the likelihood that the work experiences are construed as production jobs and clients are viewed as production workers. Below, we develop a model that attempts to identify the organizational and environmental factors that mediate exposure to the market logic.

Service Logic

We start by proposing that the organization's service logic will influence the degree to which the organization is exposed to a market logic. At the organizational level, service logics are the sets of symbolic arrangements and material practices that guide the services provided for clients. At the symbolic level the service logic socially constructs clients in terms of the types of problems they are thought to have, what should be done to address these problems, and the desired outcomes of the intervention (Hasenfeld, 1983). These classificatory principles provide a blueprint for the service technology by distinguishing the kinds of services and practices that are deemed appropriate for particular categories of clients (Mohr and Duquenne, 1997)

The service logic is constituted by a set of normative assumptions about the clients and practices that embody these assumptions. In WISEs, an important aspect of the service logic is the organizational construction of the capabilities of the clients as production workers. Clients who are viewed as able-bodied are more likely to be constructed by the organization as production workers, while those thought of as less able-bodied are likely to be construed as inappropriate for market participation and in need of a protected work environment (Figure 5.1).

These cultural assumptions at the symbolic level then inform the selection of the material practices (i.e. the work experience model). When the WISE constructs clients as relatively productive and potentially capable of full market participation, the organization may select work experiences

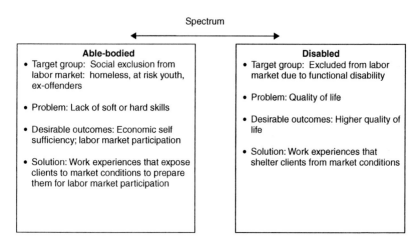

Figure 5.1 Perceived ability of clients

that directly expose clients to customers and their demands (such as strict production deadlines and high quality control), rationalizing them as both appropriate to the client's ability level and as valuable preparation for market participation. Under such conditions the clients are more likely to be commodified.

Relative embeddedness across fields

While the service logic provides the rationale for the business enterprise and the degree to which clients are directly exposed to customer demands, we must also consider the organization's relations with its environment and especially its relative embeddedness across market and human service fields. The model of embeddedness developed in this chapter views institutional pressure as generated in the relationships between field participants who may have divergent interests (Bourdieu and Wacquant, 1992; Wooten and Hoffman, 2008) Therefore, we focus on the field, not in totality, but as experienced by the WISE. That is, recognizing that fields are heterogeneous, we pay attention to the actors in the field with which the WISE interacts.

We also recognize that the bifurcated nature of the organization's environment is likely to be replicated in its internal structure through the creation of different organizational units to manage disparate institutional pressures. Indeed, a key characteristic of the internal structure of WISEs is the existence of a social service unit and a production unit whose relations to each other will echo and replicate the external relations of the organization. Thus we focus on the embeddedness of each unit in its respective field.

Embeddedness in the market

To assess the WISE's embeddedness in the market, we differentiate between business fields in which the actors with which the production unit interacts enforce a market logic and business fields in which the actors attenuate the market logic by recognizing and respecting the social mission of the organization.

When the business enterprise operates in what it experiences as a market dominated field, the buyers or customers expect to receive the goods and services at a competitive price and quality, and delivered as explicated by a specific contract. That is, the relationship is that of seller and buyer. Moreover, the business enterprise faces competition from other commercial providers to whom the customers can turn if they are dissatisfied with the product or service. When the WISE connects to a market dominated field, it is embedded in the market.

When the business enterprise experiences a market moderated business field, the customers enter into the exchange to support the social mission of the organization. They are less concerned with contractual obligations of price and deliverables. They recognize the value of the services or products for the clients served by the organization. Competition is attenuated because the customers are less likely to turn to competitors unless the products or services fail to meet some minimal expected standards. Therefore, the business enterprise is less likely to face competition from other commercial providers. We expect that the market logic will be more attenuated within the business enterprise in such settings. We view WISEs that are connected to a market moderated business field as weakly embedded in the market.

Embeddedness in the social services field

We also differentiate between social service units that are strongly or weakly embedded in the social services field. Such embeddedness is expressed by having contracts and other types of exchange relations (e.g. referrals, collaboration) with service providers that the unit can mobilize on behalf of the clients, or by having stakeholders, such as foundations or government contractors, that impose a social service logic on the organization by, for example, demanding evidence of progress toward specific social goals.

Relative embeddedness

If embeddedness mediates the organization's exposure to field level logics and their expression in the organization, then the degree to which the market or the social services logic becomes dominant depends on the strength of embeddedness of the social enterprise in the market vs. the strength of embeddedness of the social services unit in the service field. That is, when the business enterprise is strongly embedded in the market field while the social services unit is weakly embedded in the human services field, the market logic will become more dominant. Conversely, when the social services unit is strongly embedded in the human services field while the business enterprise is weakly embedded in the market field, the social service logic is likely to dominate. When both units are embedded in their respective fields, a political struggle will ensue as to which logic will become dominant and be settled by political and economic factors as noted below.

The political economy of the organization

The conflict between field level logics is played out internally in the interactions and power struggles between the units representing the fields in which the organization participates. When both units – social services and business enterprise – are highly embedded in their respective fields, their logics compete with each other for dominance. Following a political economy perspective, we propose that the resulting dominance of either logic will depend on the power position of each unit within the organization. Such power is a function of the importance of the unit to the maintenance and survival of the organization, particularly its dependence on the resources mobilized by the unit (Salancik and Pfeffer, 1974; Pfeffer and

Salancik, 1978). In particular, the greater the dependence of the organization on revenues from the business enterprise, the more dominant it will become in the organization. Therefore, when the organization is highly embedded in both the market and the social service fields, exposure to the market logic is greater when the business enterprise has a power advantage over the social services unit within the organization. Conversely, when the organization depends more on the revenues of its social services, the social services unit and its service logic will become dominant.

The moderating role of organizational form

We propose that the processes and outcomes of power struggles over competing logics are conditioned on the organization's form. First, the organization can manage external conflict by compartmentalizing the logics in separate units (Kraatz and Block, 2008). Compartmentalization avoids conflict between units by buffering the less powerful unit from the logic upheld by the more powerful unit, allowing the less powerful unit to express the logic of the field in which that unit is embedded (Weick, 1976). Now, the conflict shifts onto the client, who must assume dual identities in the organization as a production worker and a service recipient. It is the client rather than the organization that now needs to negotiate environmental contradictions. Alternatively, when the logics compete and the units are tightly coupled (i.e. integrated), the two units must compete for dominance. The greater the power advantage of one unit over the other, the more likely that the logic that structures that unit will become hegemonic within the organization and the more likely that the organization will subordinate the conflicting logic. The full model is provided in Figure 5.2.

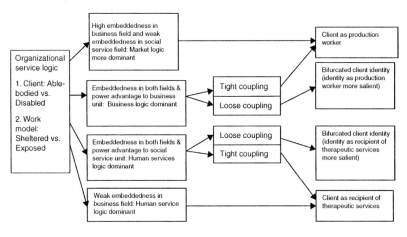

Figure 5.2   Casual model

Methods

To test the causal model presented in the previous section, we employed a comparative case study approach. We selected a purposive sample of 11 WISEs located in two large metropolitan areas to maximize variability along the dimensions of the theoretical model. Organizations were identified through searches on various websites such as Guidestar and informants in the field of social enterprises. Person(s) in charge of the business enterprise and service sides were interviewed using a semi-structured interview protocol. We also collected archival data on all organizations, including brochures, articles about the organizations, financial reports, strategic plans, financial data from IRS tax returns and annual reports. We coded the data along the following factors.

We define *service logic* along two dimensions. First, clients are defined as disabled when eligibility for services is based on a diagnosis of cognitive, mental or physical disability. They are defined as able-bodied when eligibility for services is based on social barriers to labor market participation (e.g. homelessness, poverty or criminal history) but not disability. Work model is operationalized as "sheltered" when clients do not have direct contact with suppliers or customers and as "exposed to market pressures" when clients do directly interact with suppliers or customers.

We operationalize *embeddedness* in the business field as the degree to which the business field actors with which the production unit interacts enforce a market logic. Business field actors channel a market logic when they view the relationship with the WISE primarily as a market exchange and/or threaten to withdraw their business if the social enterprise does not meet contractual commitments. We scored the variable as "low", "medium" or "high" embeddedness. Embeddedness in the social services field is operationalized as the degree to which actors with which the social service unit interacts reinforce or enforce a social service logic, and is also scored "low", "medium" or "high".

Power advantage refers to the relative degree to which the organization depends on the social service and business units for financial resources. For example, if the production unit represents 30 percent of the total budget and the service unit represents 5 percent of the total budget then the production unit has the power advantage. We define "power advantage" as either "social service unit" or "business unit".

Coupling is operationalized as the extent to which the business and social service units integrate their services. The organizational units are tightly coupled when the two units are in regular communication about clients' case plans. For example, they may attend weekly meetings to discuss their shared clients, collaborate on case plans for the clients, and problem solve together when client issues emerge at either the workplace or social service setting. The businesses and social service units are loosely coupled when they interact little if at all during the client's tenure in the work experience. The variable is defined as tightly or loosely coupled.

To measure *client commodification* we identified the organization's practices with the worker clients as displayed in Table 5.1. Organizations exhibited practices that primarily fell in the commodified or decommodified categories and were classified accordingly. The variable is scored as "commodification" and "decommodification".

The two authors and two research assistants coded the variables separately and checked for inter-rater reliability, which was about 80 percent. We then discussed and recoded the discrepant cases.

To test the model we ascertain the presence or absence of each of the causal conditions and outcomes for each case. We then determine whether the various factors combine with one another to yield particular outcomes and which hypothesized factors are irrelevant to the outcome. When a factor does not systematically relate to an outcome as hypothesized it is considered to be irrelevant.

Findings

Our analysis of the 11 cases suggests that, in contrast to expectations, service logic (i.e. construction of clients' abilities and work model) and client commodification are not associated. First, we find that constructing clients as "disabled" does not prevent organizations from putting into place work experiences that directly expose them to the demands of customers. At the same time, sheltered work models are sometimes applied to "able-bodied" clients. Second, commodification often coexists with a service logic that constructs clients as "disabled" and/or with a sheltered work model. Conversely, decommodification can coexist with a service logic that constructs clients as able-bodied and/or with an exposed work model.

Other dimensions of the model, however, receive strong support. First, in support of the idea that field logics are a precondition of commodification, we find that clients are only commodified when the organization is embedded in a market dominated business field. Similarly, when the embeddedness of the organization in the social services field is strong while weak in the business field, the clients are not commodified. Second, the predicted relationship between coupling and embeddedness is supported. In most cases, the presence of conflicting logics is associated with decoupling of the social service and business units, suggesting that organizations often manage potential conflict through compartmentalization of competing pressures. In support of our model, we find that in such cases conflict shifts to the client, who negotiates a dual identity as service recipient (on the social service side) and instrument of production (on the business side). Only one organization resolved conflict through political struggle rather than compartmentalization. As expected, the logic of the more powerful unit subordinated the logic of the less powerful unit. Next we present several cases that illuminate our findings in greater depth.

Cases

Employment Inc.: able-bodied, sheltered work model, market embeddedness, weak embeddedness in social service field, commodification

Employment Inc. exemplifies the WISE as a de facto business. It is a multiservice agency that provides educational, home healthcare and rehabilitative services in addition to work opportunities. We focused on the organization's contract with the state Department of Corrections prisoner reentry program, which engages ex-offenders in three months of work experience once they transition from prison to the community. The work experience functions to enhance the employability of clients, who are expected to transition to jobs in the labor market.

Service logic

Construction of client abilities: While the organization serves clients with a wide spectrum of disability, ex-offenders referred from the prisoner reentry program are constructed by the organization as "able-bodied" and they assume the most difficult and demanding tasks. Although the ex-offenders may experience various personal problems, the organization does not officially categorize them as "disabled" and they do not receive mental health or rehabilitative services in-house.

Work model: Employment Inc. provides three-month transitional work opportunities through the operation of a production facility that is a certified supplier to the auto industry. Although its revenues do not quite cover costs, the production facility represents about a third of the organization's $6 million budget, and offers work experiences in assembly, packaging, light machining, inspection and sorting. From what we observed, much of the work on the production floor is quite dangerous and physically demanding, requiring heavy lifting, driving forklifts, using toxic chemicals and working at a fast pace with heavy machinery. Yet, the work model is "sheltered" because the clients do not come in direct contact with customers and their demands.

Clients also receive case management services from workers who have been hired as part of the contract with the prison reentry program. The case managers monitor clients' performance in the production facility and encourage them to engage in job search throughout their tenure in the program. They also refer clients to their "resource specialist" with the state prisoner reentry program, should additional needs emerge such as housing or mental health issues.

Embeddedness

By virtue of its contracts with automobile manufacturers, Employment Inc. is firmly embedded in the business field. The main customer places enormous pressure on its contractors to bid low, and in response the organization constantly searches for efficiencies. According to Pat, the production manager, the competition for bids is intense. He feels that Employment Inc. has been successful in securing contracts year after year because it is able to bid low and it has a 25-year relationship with the auto industry. However, he indicates that the facility could lose the contracts at any time. He repeatedly remarks that the biggest customer doesn't do them any favors. It treats Employment Inc. just like any other contractor. Pat says, "They ask for things that are impossible" and "They give us no special consideration."

By contrast, the case management program for ex-offenders is only weakly embedded in the social service field. The case managers have backgrounds in criminal justice and interact mostly with the prisoner reentry program and parole, which are both closely connected to the criminal justice system. Thus although the aim of the program is to meet the social needs of ex-offenders and, ideally, keep them in the community, the program is an extension of the criminal justice system which functions as an instrument of punishment and control.

Commodification

Because the case management side is weakly embedded in the social service field, a social service logic is only weakly represented in the organization. Meanwhile, the auto makers impose a strong market logic on the business side. According to our model, in such cases the market logic will prevail in the absence of a competing social service logic, irrespective of power dynamics or coupling of the service and business sides. Indeed, this seems to be the case at Employment Inc., where power struggles, past or present, are not in evidence, the case management services are coupled (i.e. integrated) with the production side, and the case manager reinforces the market logic channeled by the production unit.

On the business side, the organization has put into place several practices designed to maximize the productivity of client workers. For example, Sue, the vice president of production, and Pat ensure quality control with this challenging workforce by encouraging clients to report unproductive behavior of other clients, and by providing "strong supervision". Pat explained that he conducts time studies every day and implements strict quality control procedures. He noted that workers need to be "fast and good". By this he meant that they need to work at a fast pace to meet deadlines, but they also need to meet quality standards. Some people work rapidly but make mistakes, and some want to do a perfect job but work too slow. Neither is acceptable. As Pat explained to us,

> Some people just don't have the fine finger dexterity, and there are other tasks they can do. We have some assembly production lines where they are running a stamping machine, it's an imposed pace. Some people do really well at that but you put them on the feed end of another thing and they are very unproductive. Because they can't drive themselves.

Rather than fitting the work experiences to the service needs of clients, the purpose of such shuffling is to fit the skills of the client-worker to the needs of the production facility – that is, to maximize productivity.

If clients exhibit behavioral issues such as the inability to be supervised, anger in the workplace, absenteeism or otherwise disturbing the work environment, they are "released" early. According to Sue, these clients, lacking other means of financial support, often end up back in prison. She maintained that such clients fail in the work experience because are "not ready" to live on the outside.

While non-productive workers are released, productive workers can apply for the "long term transitional program" and stay on with the production facility past the three-month time limit. Periodically full-time supervisor positions open up and the long term transitional workers may apply for them. Pat figured that about 11 out of the 70 workers on the floor were from the prisoner reentry program. He said that about eight were long term because they "did such a good job".

At Employment Inc. the case managers view their role primarily as collaborating with the business side to maintain productivity of the facility. According to Julie, a case manager, while they visit the facility a minimum of once a week, case managers will schedule extra time to meet individually with clients when Pat alerts them that "there are some issues with attendance, [the clients'] production rate, things like that." When describing the most important aspects of her role, Julie said:

> for the [prisoner reentry program] role...we are giving them a lot of supportive feedback to make sure – if maybe they are performing a specific job incorrectly we are giving them that corrective feedback. If they need to increase their production rate, we are talking about them with that. Any attendance issues, I mean we, myself, the production supervisor or manager, we sit down, himself and I, the team, we will sit down to talk with these people and provide them feedback.

Sharon, another case manager, stressed the importance of being "on the same page" with Pat and presenting a united front to the client:

> Well here's the great thing about Pat and myself, is we sit down and we talk, and I mean it could be constantly via phone, e-mail regarding anything that might come up…we come to some type of common ground before we meet with that particular client. So that way we are both on the same page in that we don't conflict, so between us we will do that one-on-one by phone or e-mail before we meet with that client.

People Inc.: Able-bodied, sheltered work model, market attenuated, social services embeddedness, tight coupling, decommodification

People Inc. constructs its clients as able-boded and adopts a work model that is sheltered. Nonetheless, the clients are hardly commodified. With a mission to provide at-risk young adults with opportunities to integrate into the labor market through job skills training, education and work experience, People Inc. has contracts with various government agencies to plant trees, build community gardens, divert recyclable materials from landfills, restore habitats and remove graffiti. Its total budget is over $20 million.

Service logic

Construction of client abilities: The organization recognizes that many of the young adults lack a high school degree, ran away from home, might have used drugs or have a criminal record. Even so, they are constructed as able-bodied workers. They are all expected to alternate between working for two months and going to school for two months. While the clients can opt out of work, they cannot opt out of going to school which is a prerequisite for successful completion of the program.

Work model: Clients work in crews doing physical manual work on various contracted projects such as clearing brushes, removing trash from public parks, clearing hiking trails and planting trees. After orientation, the young adults get through a trial work week after which they are hired into various projects. The work model is sheltered because the clients do not come in direct contact with government contractors. Yet, the work is challenging. As noted by George, the director of the business enterprise,

> It's basically hard labor work so, what we are looking for is whether they can handle it. We are not looking for speed. What we are looking for is for somebody who can. What we want to accomplish is first and foremost to have them get their high school diploma and finish their education, and

we also try to teach them basic work ethic. We have some job training programs that they can take advantage of so they become more marketable when they leave here.

Embeddedness

Most of the work projects are contracted from various local, state and federal government agencies. The contractors recognize the social mission of People Inc. and take that into account in awarding the contracts to the organization. As a result, the organization is embedded in a market moderated field. Indeed, the organization relies heavily on political connections to get the contracts. George put it this way: "We work heavily with politicians. We work heavily with county and with government officials to fill their needs. Our executive director, the founder of the organization, is very well politically connected." At the same time, the business enterprise is concerned about meeting the contract requirements, not losing money and making sure that the enterprise can be self-sufficient. It tries hard to diversify in order to attract more contracts, and it is concerned about its line of credit in order to ensure that it can raise the capital needed to successfully bid and fund its work projects. Still, its exposure to market logic is quite moderate.

Because the young adults are required to attend school as a perquisite for working, the organization is highly embedded in the educational field. It is also embedded in the related social services field through its extensive support services department. Contracts with Workforce Investment Act and with the justice department require the organization to assign case managers to each client. In addition, the department handles mental health and substance abuse issues. The case managers are in charge of intake and determine whether the person is appropriate for the program. Because the program has strict attendance policies, the case managers are in charge of enforcing them. Young adults who fail to attend school three days in a row without notifying their case managers are likely to be dismissed from the program. Frank, the director of support services notes that "We definitely get kids who have psychological challenges and if we cannot provide supportive services, we will refer them out to the other agencies."

Coupling

There is close coupling between the social services and the business enterprise. There are regular communications between the worksite supervisors and the case managers. There are weekly managerial meetings of the teachers, case managers and work supervisors to go over cases. As George put it:

> As a collective from both work, school and supportive service sides we meet and we go over specific clients' needs. We go over the most pressing or over some of the successes that we have ... We talk about who is going

to transition out because staff have a lot of input as they know their kids well and they have information that others don't.

Commodification

Given that the organization is strongly embedded in the social service field and weakly embedded in the business field we would expect that clients are not commodified at People Inc. The findings confirm this expectation. Because completing high school is the primary objective for the young adults in the program, and they can only work if they attend school, they are buffered from commodification pressures. To be sure, when there are contract pressures to complete certain projects, more clients are likely to be assigned to them. However, the requirement that the clients rotate every two months between work and school ensures that the work requirements do not take precedence.

Rehabilitation Inc.: clients disabled, exposed/sheltered work model, market attenuated, social service embeddedness, decommodification

Rehabilitation Inc. provides housing, educational programs, mental health treatment and work experiences for persons with mental health diagnoses. As discussed below, the organization is another example of a social enterprise that retains the therapeutic focus of its work experiences.

Service logic

Construction of client abilities: Rehabilitation Inc. constructs its clients as mentally disabled. Jan, the program manager for vocational services, acknowledged that at least some of the clients will never work in the labor market, although the organization aims to help clients do so if labor market participation is one of their goals.

   Work model: Rehabilitation Inc. operates a kitchen and convenience store which are integrated into their main service location. The kitchen is backstage work which is sheltered from customers, and the convenience store, where client workers interact directly with customers, is exposed. Clients can also engage in in-house janitorial work. On-site mental health case managers refer interested clients to the work experiences, where they first receive an orientation and a two-week rotation through the various jobs. Then, clients decide whether they want to work and select their preferred job. Some jobs are more complex than others, and if clients become overwhelmed they can opt to switch to a less stressful position.

Embeddedness

Rehabilitation Inc. is embedded in a *market moderated* business field, where customers enter into the market exchange to support the social mission of the organization. This field simply does not expose the business side to strong market pressures. When asked to describe the customer base, Jan, the director of the business enterprise, said,

> Quite a few clients – members here – buy the lunch special. And quite a few businesses down the street come in most every day. We have some people who just walk in off the street. They just walk in and buy. [Customers] can write it off for charitable donations. They are contributing to the community. It makes them feel better, you know, because they are supporting Rehabilitation Inc.

By contrast, the case management unit is heavily embedded in the social service field. Case managers are responsible for monitoring the clients' overall case plan, including the work experience, and they run therapy groups on a daily basis. They interact with a larger team of service providers, both internal and external to the organization, which collaborates to provide a package of services ranging from life skills coaching, supported employment training and placement, psychiatric services, medication support, transportation, computer training, an art studio, and socialization.

Commodification

Because the social services unit is strongly embedded while the business enterprise is weakly embedded, we would expect the social services logic to dominate. At Rehabilitation Inc. this seems to be the case. As mentioned previously, by allowing the clients to sample the various work experiences and then select for themselves, the organization tries to ensure that work experiences meet the specific service needs of clients. Further, the business managers view nonproductive behavior as a learning opportunity and occasion for skill building rather than as a threat to productivity and cause for termination. Clients may be diverted from the work experience if they have therapeutic issues that require additional social services, but they are rarely fired. As noted by the vocational manager:

> The only real difference between our employment and outside employment is [that we use] consequences as guide...So, if the client crashes and burns here...we'll pull him off the schedule...we can get him connected with case services...we [are] going to give them help that they need...[clients] are not going to get fired for their mental health breakdown. They are going to get fired if they steal from me, but they are not going to get fired because they did not show up for three days. But my hope is that these things happen here so that I can teach them skill sets to [do well in the outside world].

Work industries: clients disabled, exposed work model, market embeddedness, social service embeddedness, power advantage to social services, loose coupling, commodification

On the surface, Work Industries is quite similar to Rehabilitation Inc. Both organizations serve clients with serious mental illness, both are heavily embedded in the social service field and both operate businesses in the food service industry. Yet while the business side of Rehabilitation Inc. treats its clients as service recipients, Work Industries treats them as instruments of production.

Service logic

Construction of client abilities: Work Industries, like Rehabilitation Inc., constructs clients as chronically mentally disabled. The organization targets economically vulnerable persons with mental illness, including homeless adults, foster care youth aging out of the system, incarcerated persons leaving jail or prison, or people at risk of homelessness or incarceration. It strives to ensure that clients engage in productive work that may lead to labor market participation, although not all clients may make this transition.

Work model: A deli offers work experiences, such as over the counter, serving breakfast and lunch, washing dishes and running the cash register. Many of the positions are exposed to customers and their demands. The organization also has a catering business where clients interact directly with customers. Finally, it runs a cookie shop, where clients participate in serving, baking and packaging. Clients are referred to the work experience by case managers at Work Industries and from the Department of Rehabilitation. They work in the positions for around six months and then are transferred to a job developer who helps them obtain employment in the community.

Embeddedness

The business field experienced by Work Industries is a mix between market dominated and market moderated. On the one hand, many of the business customers are not particularly market oriented and seem to engage in exchange relations with Work Industries to support its social mission. The catering business, for example, counts among its customers other social service agencies, public agencies and schools that align with the social mission of Work Industries. This said, Work Industries does encounter market pressures. Sometimes, for example, long term relations with customers built on a common appreciation of Work Industries' social purpose are disrupted when the customers retain new management who view the organization through a market lens. When asked if the catering business ever lost long term customers, for example, Jane, the manager, said,

> Absolutely. Because of poor services. Sometimes they give us over-whelming orders. [Name of company] is one of those. They will probably

come back to us. So often, they get new administrators [who don't support Work Industries' mission]. I believe last year they were just not happy with our catering.

The case management side is heavily embedded in the social service field. Case managers are part of a larger team of mental health providers including psychiatrists, financial planners, community integration specialists and registered nurses. They also interact with counselors at the Department of Rehabilitation.

Power advantage

At Work Industries, the power advantage rests with the case management side. Most of the organization's multi-million dollar budget comes from grants and contracts to support their social and mental health services, which case managers help to provide. The business enterprises contribute a relatively small share of the organization's total revenue, and consequently the businesses are less important to its survival. As reported by an executive on the business side,

> We made [less than $200,000] last year. That's gross. That is not net. I will say that $30,000 came from the cookie business, and probably the rest of it is split even between catering and in-house breakfast/lunch.

Coupling

At Work Industries, the social service and business units are decoupled. While many clients are actively involved in both mental health therapy and work, Jane notes that contact between the social services side and business side is kept to a minimum to prevent the social services from interfering with what goes on in the work place:

> We try to separate what is going on in the businesses from everything else that goes on, in terms of the social work activities here and supports that are given...um...because we want to teach them the real world work skills.

Adhering to the decoupled structure, the business managers draw a firm line between work and therapy. They see themselves as "bosses" and treat the clients accordingly. When clients have behavioral issues related to their mental illness, the business managers alert the case management side, but do not get involved with the clients' case plans, nor allow the case plans to interfere with work practices in the business units. According to Jane,

> I am a boss. I am not a social worker. [When behavioral issues arise] I call their case managers without [clients] knowing, because I need to maintain that professional job – because this is a job structure. We can't do

that [engaging clients in discussions about their social needs] because we dilute the use of this place. We dilute [our] power.

Commodification

In the face of competing logics, we expect that the unit with greater power resources within the organization holds the power advantage and therefore has the capacity to impose its logic on the subordinate unit. However, we also expect that the less powerful unit can buffer itself through compartmentalization, allowing expression of the logic that structures the field in which that unit is embedded with minimal interference from the more powerful unit. Work Industries decouples the social service and business sides, thus providing a test for this expectation.

In support of our expectations, the data suggest that on the business side clients are commodified and a market logic prevails. According to Jane, "We need to be able to say that we take our business so seriously [that] we do more, we expect more, and we get more." By "expect more", Jane meant that clients are held to the same standards as any worker:

> When they come to the bosses, the bosses treat them like any other [employees]. We expect them to show up to work on time, have their uniforms clean – hair – all that. And we expect certain behaviors as well. If they violate any of those areas, they can be warned, maybe. It depends on what it is. And the bosses, like any other bosses, have complete discretion to do whatever. They can be sent home for a day, suspended for a day or two, or they can be fired.

Jane recognizes that some of the behavioral issues of her client workers are mental health related. Yet, this does not prevent her from firing them, leading to high turnover:

> You have many daily issues that you are dealing with. Basically, all the employees' related personal problems. I can give you today's example: We sent an employee home because he came here incorrectly dressed, and he doesn't remember to wear a specific uniform. And we lost our dishwasher. He was terminated. So, now I need to get four [workers]. [He was terminated] because of his experience level and his mental illnesses. So we have a lot of turnover, for that reason. And it makes it difficult.

The business side alerts the client's case manager when the client is terminated, to help the client adjust to the termination and to create a new case plan. As they exit the work site, the client switches from worker to service recipient and is now viewed through a therapeutic lens. Therefore clients, who must assume dual identities in the organization as a production worker and a service recipient, shoulder the burden of environmental conflict. Clients may experience considerable distress when they are fired from the business enterprises. As Jane noted,

> When they are terminated...we will go back at some point of the day and call their case worker and say, "this is what happened. We need your help." It is our responsibility to let the case worker know that we need support and this person needs support. If it is pretty urgent, we will call right away, and say "[The client] is going to downstairs. We terminated him. We need to intercept them before they leave the building, because this is very urgent." We get support [from the case manager] like that.

Discussion

WISEs operate in two fields structured by conflicting institutional logics – social service and market. They must therefore assume competing institutionally derived identities as human service organization and business. We propose that exposure to a market logic threatens to undermine the therapeutic purpose of client work opportunities and may lead the organization to treat client workers more as instruments of production and less as service recipients with therapeutic needs. In this chapter we have developed and conducted a preliminary test of a theoretical framework that explains the conditions under which the organization becomes exposed to a market logic. We find strong support for some aspects of the framework and no support for others.

First, in contrast to expectations, we find no evidence that the organization's expressed service logic is related to commodification of clients. We expected that clients who are viewed as able-bodied and/or exposed to customer demands are more likely to be constructed by the organization as production workers, while those thought of as less able-bodied and/or sheltered from customer demands are likely to be construed as inappropriate for market participation and in need of a protected work environment. To the contrary, we find examples of commodification when clients are constructed as disabled and/or sheltered from customer demands and examples of client decommodification when clients are constructed as able-bodied and/or exposed to customer demands.

Second, we find compelling support for the central role of field embeddedness in client commodification. We find that WISEs commodify their clients only when they are at least moderately embedded in a market dominated business field. Absent exposure to a field level market logic, WISEs treat clients as service recipients rather than as production workers. Our analysis thus points to the primacy of the organizational field as the origin of organizational practices and suggests that when field level logics find expression internally they supersede the organization's professed service logic.

Third, the results suggest that WISEs often manage external conflict by compartmentalizing competing logics in separate units. Among the cases we studied, the decoupling of social service and business units allows expression of the less dominant logic and pushes environmental contradiction onto the clients. In the case of Work Industries, for example, clients negotiate between identities as instrument of production (on the business side) and service recipient (on the social service side). In other words, by decoupling the business enterprise from social services, WISEs can respond to market pressures by commodifying the clients without interference from the social service unit.

In an extension of our model, we find evidence of practice ideologies that function as a rationale for exploitative organizational practices. First, we find that organizational members often justify practices that commodify clients by framing such practices as therapeutic. At Work Industries, for example, termination of nonproductive clients is justified as confronting clients with "consequences" that prepare them for the reality of the labor market. Yet termination could just as easily be understood as the withdrawal of services from clients in greatest need of the skills the program is designed to impart. Additionally, terminated clients are sometimes reframed as unsuitable for the work experiences, as we see at Employment Inc., where fired ex-offenders are sometimes constructed as "institutionalized" by the prison system and therefore "not ready" for life outside of prison. We suggest that these practice ideologies arise to close the moral and cognitive disjuncture between what the workers know they should do (the service logic) and what they actually do for their clients (Brodkin, 1997). They make it possible to reconcile exploitative economic arrangements with the organization's professed ideals as reflected in its service logic. Consequently, they make it difficult for the organization to analyze critically and to reflect on its own practices.

The study presents a cautionary tale to policymakers and social entrepreneurs. It demonstrates that a commitment to a social mission is no guarantee that the organizational practices will actually implement it. Rather, how the leaders of the organization position the program in the two conflicting fields – social and business – will have considerable impact as to which logic will prevail. Unless the organizational leaders and its stakeholders ensure that the organization is heavily embedded in the social service field and gives the social service unit a power advantage within the organization, the organization risks a mission drift toward commodification of the clients.

More importantly, while WISEs rarely make a profit from their business enterprises, nonetheless to be competitive in the market field, they must meet production demands while paying their clients at most minimum wages with no additional benefits. Supposedly, the clients benefit from the therapeutic aspects of the work experience when these experiences are integrated with the array of social services the clients obtain. But when these aspects are endangered or disappear as the enterprise becomes captured by the market, the clients become truly exploited workers. They lose the protection they rightfully expect from the social service component. This can happen in two ways. First, this happens when the social service unit is detached and isolated from the work component. Second, it can happen when the social service unit becomes co-opted by the market logic that governs the work component. As a result, clients' intended advocates, the social services workers, may incorporate practice ideologies in their daily routines that mask and justify what is effectively an exploitative work environment. Without such advocates, being quite vulnerable and morally devalued, these clients have little voice. They cannot protest their working conditions, and if they exit the program they return to the ranks of the homeless, ex-offenders or the disabled who have little if any social protection. The challenge for WISEs, then, is how to protect their clients from becoming exploited, and how to ensure that they are treated as clients rather than as production workers.

Note

* We thank Kate Cooney for her suggestions during the early stages of our study.

References

Alter, Sutia Kim. 2006. "Social Enterprise Models and their Mission and Money Relationships." In Alex Nicholls (ed.), *Social Entrepreneurship: New Models of Sustainable Social Change*. Oxford: Oxford University Press: 205–232.

Borzaga, Carlo and Jacques Defourny. 2001. *The Emergence of Social Enterprise*. London: Routledge.

Bourdieu, Pierre and Loïc J. D. Wacquant. 1992. *An Invitation to Reflexive Sociology*. Chicago: University of Chicago Press.

Brodkin, Evelyn Z. 1997. "Inside the Welfare Contract: Discretion and Accountability in State Welfare Administration." *Social Service Review* 71(1): 1–33.

Brozek, Kathy O. 2009. "Exploring the Continuum of Social and Financial Returns: When Does a Nonprofit become a Social Enterprise?" *Community Development Investment Review* 5(2): 7–17.

Friedland, Roger and Robert R. Alford. 1991. "Bringing Society Back in: Symbols, Practices, and Institutional Contradictions." In Walter W. Powell and Paul J. DiMaggio (eds), *The New Institutionalism*. Chicago: University of Chicago Press: 232–263.

Hasenfeld, Yeheskel. 1983. *Human Service Organizations*. Englewood Cliffs, NJ: Prentice-Hall.

Kraatz, Matthew S. and Emily Block. 2008. "Organizational Implications of Institutional Pluralism." In Royston Greenwood, Christine Oliver, Roy Suddaby, and Kerstin Sahlin (eds), *The Sage Handbook of Organizational Institutionalism*. Los Angeles: Sage Publications: 243–275.

Mohr, John W. and Vincent Duquenne. 1997. "The Duality of Culture and Practice: Poverty Relief in New York City, 1888–1917." *Theory and Society* 26(2–3): 305–356.

Pfeffer, Jeffrey and Gerald R. Salancik. 1978. *The External Control of Organizations: A Resource Dependence Perspective.* New York: Harper & Row.

Salancik, Gerald R. and Jeffrey Pfeffer. 1974. "The Bases and Use of Power in Organizational Decision Making: The Case of a University." *Administrative Science Quarterly* 19 (4): 453–473.

Schorr, Jim. 2006. "Point of View – Social Enterprise 2.0: Moving toward a Sustainable Model." *Stanford Social Innovation Review,* Summer: 12–13.

Thornton, Patricia H. and William Ocasio. 2008. "Institutional logics." In Royston Greenwood, Christine Oliver, Roy Suddaby, and Kerstin Sahlin (eds), *The Sage Handbook of Organizational Institutionalism.* Los Angeles: Sage Publications: 91–129.

Weick, K. 1976. "Educational Organizations as Loosely Coupled Systems." *Administrative Science Quarterly* 21: 1–19

Wooten, Melissa E. and Andrew Hoffman. 2008. "Organizational Fields: Past, Present and Future of a Core Construct." In Royston Greenwood, Christine Oliver, Roy Suddaby, and Kerstin Sahlin (eds), *Handbook of Organizational Institutionalism.* London: Sage Publications: 130–147.

6

The Phenomenon of Social Businesses: Some Insights from Israel

Benjamin Gidron and Inbal Abbou

The past five years have seen a tremendous interest in market-driven social ventures, especially since the Nobel Peace Prize was awarded to Muhammad Yunus in 2006.Yunus, in his book (2008) analyzes primarily his efforts to eliminate poverty in Bangladesh through microlending, encouraging individuals, particularly women, to open their own businesses on the basis of small loans – a system that has existed in the West for a long time. Yet he also introduces the broader concept of building a "social business", namely a *business venture* with a *social (or environmental) goal*.[1] The concept of building an organization on the basis of two equally important pillars – the business and the social – is intriguing and presents major conceptual as well as practical and policy challenges.

The emerging literature on social enterprise basically places social businesses at the middle of a continuum, which finds at one end business entities that also engage in social activities ("primarily business") and on the other nonprofit entities that have a business venture as part of their operation ("primarily social"). Social businesses are placed in the center because these entities put equal value on achieving business results as well as on creating social impact. As a matter of fact they are established in order to achieve certain social goals or objectives, thus their *raison d"être* is their social mission, which they strive to achieve by the use of a business methodology. Unlike NPOs that use philanthropic funds to subsidize the budget in case of losses of their business venture, or business entities which may allocate a certain rate of their profits to social programs and which can be considered as philanthropy, social businesses do not use philanthropic resources; they rely on sales only. Furthermore, the business methodology expresses itself in the sale of products or services in the market for competitive prices, paying their workers regular salaries and taking economic risks. Unlike philanthropists, the investors of the business are entitled to receive back their investment, sometimes with a limited profit. However, the social orientation of the entity is also expressed in the fact that the profits are fed back into the enterprise in order to further the social goal of the entity, similarly to an NPO.

From a research perspective such entities pose a series of questions from at least three angles:

- **The business angle:** How does such an enterprise position itself in the context of the business world? How does it market and price its products/services? How does it finance its operations? What does it do with profits and losses?
- **The social angle:** What are the social goals of the entity and what are the strategies to reach them? What forms of evaluation exist in order to measure success/failure of the social goals? How does the social business entity compare with other nonsocial businesses in reaching similar goals with similar populations? What impact does working in a social business have on the worker and his or her family?
- **The organizational angle:** How is the entity governed, and how does the governance system deal with innate tensions? What kind of management models and managers does it use? What kinds of inter-organizational ties does it form with its environment? What criteria are used to select workers? To fire them?

In this chapter we will first define and describe the *social business* form of organization within the larger concept of *social enterprise* and analyze its unique features. We will then briefly present some key findings from a survey on market-driven social ventures conducted in Israel in 2011 and present a few examples of social businesses currently operating there. Finally we will deal with some major policy and management challenges that the social business paradigm presents.

Social enterprise and social business

The use of a business approach and activity within an organization with primarily social/environmental goals has received attention lately in a variety of contexts:

- In light of the 2008 world economic crisis, the decrease in philanthropic funds and the need to find creative solutions to the shortage in funding of third sector organizations.
- Similarly, long before 2008, the loss of government funds caused some NPOs to seize upon the idea of commercial revenue generation as a way to replace that loss (Crimmins and Keil, 1983; Salamon, 1997; Eikenberry and Kluver, 2004).
- There is a major effort, especially in countries with a *social economy* tradition, to use social enterprises, primarily consumer and producer cooperatives, in order to create employment opportunities for the hard-to-employ populations such as handicapped persons, ex-convicts,

women with low levels of education, homeless persons, etc. Such programs, sometimes also called Work Integration Social Enterprises (WISEs), address the difficult problems of social exclusion in the labor market (Spear and Bidet, 2005) and which exist in a large number of countries (Ho and Chan, 2010).

• Social enterprise became the domain for entrepreneurs and their supporters to introduce innovative ideas to create organizational frameworks that will benefit society and/or the environment around a new concept or technology and which will also be financially sustainable. While social and business entrepreneurs existed (separately) for a long time, the idea of combining, within the same enterprise, social *and* business orientations is new.

With all this thematic diversity and different points of departure it is not surprising that the literature on the subject lacks a uniform conceptual framework. Indeed, there are different research traditions and theoretical formulations that focus on different aspects of the phenomenon:

1. The literature analyzing the financial basis of NPOs relates to and sometimes compares business ventures and commercial activities within NPOs to other sources of income, namely, philanthropy and public sector grants/contracts. That literature analyzes the unique features of that source and its implications on the organization's dynamics. It focuses on issues such as: (1) whether the source of income is *related* or *unrelated* (to the mission of the organization), which in many countries has legal implications on tax exemptions on sales (James, 1998); (2) "crowding out" – implications of income from sales on other forms of income (Weisbrod, 1998; Young, 1998).
2. The literature on entrepreneurship views the phenomenon of social enterprise as a form of entrepreneurship and as such places special attention on its initial stages, namely the development of the idea, the plans, etc. It lacks a long view of the phenomenon in its steady state. It also focuses on the entrepreneurs – who they are and what motivates them – and not necessarily on managers, who will likely replace entrepreneurs at the next stage of the enterprise's development (Nicholls, 2006).
3. The social economy literature views the social enterprise phenomenon very often from the perspective of solidarity-based organizational forms typical to that framework, namely, consumer and producer cooperatives, and also from the opportunity for job creation (Defourny and Nyssens, 2006).
4. Social and environmental activities performed by business organizations are usually analyzed by the corporate social responsibility concept (Himmelstein, 1997).

Because of its newness, the academic literature on the unique form of social business, an organizational framework that puts equal weight on its social and business components, is not yet substantial and is composed mostly of case studies (Thompson *et al.*, 2000; Smallbone *et al.*, 2001; Thompson and Doherty, 2006; Alter, 2007). This is further complicated by the fact that the social business concept was developed by Yunus in Bangladesh where it evolved primarily around a general goal of alleviation of poverty and as such was "exported" to other developing countries. Thus far in the industrialized world it has developed with a different focus: it finds its expression primarily in employment schemes for a variety of populations, such as persons with retardation, people with mental or physical handicaps, youth in distress, ex-convicts and drug-addicts, etc. These populations have traditionally been directed to employment schemes in sheltered frameworks (of varying degrees); such frameworks see the target population as clients, not workers, and the work activity is basically a sort of rehabilitation, sometimes seen as training to acquire different life skills. The focus is not on standards of performance, and the expectations of the target population are accordingly, as is the pay, if any, and other work conditions, below the standards required of a business (such as minimum wages).

The development of social businesses as it is practiced in the Western world challenges that rehabilitation/client paradigm: it employs target populations in special frameworks fit for them (as opposed to regular firms that integrate a small number of persons with special needs in their staff). It treats them as workers, not clients, whereby on the one hand there are expectations of performance of them, but on the other they are treated and paid as regular workers, enjoy regular working conditions, can be promoted, etc. It is clearly a scheme that fits certain types of populations and not others, and therefore it is not in any position to compete or replace the existing rehabilitation/client paradigm.

The three organizational theories presented in the Introduction all focus on different configurations of external powers that impact on the organizational reality. Yet some of the issues mentioned above will also benefit from an analysis of the internal dynamics in these organizations. If one is to focus on the micro, organizational level, namely analyzing how these organizations act and develop, a conceptual framework that is proposed is that of hybrid organizations.

Hybridity

A hybrid organization is one that includes within its boundaries more than one (usually two) orientations or functions. These are by nature very different and sometimes negate each other. The reason they are included within the same organization has to do with the importance of both orientations to the mission of the organization (Hasenfeld and Gidron, 2005).

At the organizational level hybridity is not an easy concept to manage. Organizations tend to specialize and structure themselves along their main mission or orientation (Thomasson, 2009). This is reflected in the organizational components and processes. Thus, for example, organizations combining public and business orientations will have difficulties structuring their salary system, which, in the public sector, is based on a scale with fixed figures attached to each level, whereas in the business sector it is based on individual negotiations between the employer and employees. A hybrid organization combining those two orientations will face dozens of such cases where the different value systems, at the base of these organizations, lead to totally different organizational practices, which need to be dealt with. Similarly, an organization combining advocacy and service provision will find itself debating not only what portion of the budget should go to finance each of the two functions, but also strategic issues such as how to use government funding for the service delivery component and at the same time criticizing government policy toward the population served. The reason the two orientations or functions can be found within the same organization, rather than splitting the organization into two separate entities, has to do with their centrality to the mission of the organization. Thus, these organizations, which exist with an innate conflict, have to find some ground rules as to how to mediate between the two conflicting components (Bull, 2008).

Regarding the nature of hybrid organizations, there are actually two views on this issue: on the one hand there are those that claim there is no tension between the social and the business goals and that one needs to view them as one entity, as is expressed for example in the blended value concept in such organizations (Dees, 1998; Evers, 2001). On the other hand there are those who suggest there is an innate conflict in these organizations that focuses on the issue as to whether models of economic management, which fit business enterprises, also fit organizations with a social focus and with clear social goals (Anheier, 2003; Mendel, 2003; Cooney, 2006). As is shown below, it would seem that both views are correct and can be found in different entities.

The very type of such an organization built on the two competing paradigms raises the issue of sustainability of such an organizational structure (see Chapters 1 and 2). Can it be sustained? If so, under what conditions and around what kind of social issues and what kind of business ventures? We suggest that these issues need to be looked at from two angles: (1) the unique features of the organizational framework within which such activity can take place; and (2) the methods used in order to meet the social goals, or in other words the specific *social* mode(s) of intervention: what is the rationale and practice used in the process of integration of ex-convicts in society for example? After all, in the final analysis, the *raison d'être* of the entity is social and it needs to produce social returns.

Regarding the organizational framework, it is basically agreed that business activities are best performed within business organizations, where the institutional culture and ideology is geared toward profit maximization and competition. These values impact on the entire organization and its different subsystems, from personnel practices to marketing, etc. Furthermore, the legal-fiduciary obligations of such entities are to maximize profits for their owners/shareholders, so any deviations from these principles are likely to be met with objections. Social problems on the other hand are best dealt with in human service organizations, where the leading values and professional ideology are based on empathy and support, not competition. The organization is structured accordingly – it is not owned and governed by shareholders but by stakeholders, which is usually reflected in its board structure; decisions are made on the basis of the well-being of clients, not the amount of the dividend for the owners. The other subsystems function according to that fundamental logic. The hybrid structure needs to build bridging mechanisms between those two orientations and practices that need to be reflected in the way the organization is structured as well as in the way it is managed in order to allow the organization to achieve both its business and social objectives. The focus then is on the specific bridging mechanisms and practices as a unique feature in these entities.

The issue of the mode of *social* intervention practiced in such an entity is critical. The idea that the employment opportunity is in itself the helping mode does not distinguish it from any other sheltered entity. The issue at stake is whether a business environment, with its *competition imperative* and the need for *standards of performance* can help individuals with mental or physical handicaps or who are ex-convicts to integrate into society. And if so, how? Who can benefit from such an endeavor more than others?

Conventional thought suggests that organizations, as well as professions and modes of helping to deal with populations with disabilities, cannot be based on business logic, as such logic constitutes a trend to commodify them and treat them on the basis of their performance only and therefore create pressure that can be detrimental to the efforts to help them.

Such conventional thought is often questioned by people practicing challenging sports for example, which have tremendously helped individuals with handicaps over the past two to three decades. Such practices were never dared in the past because of fear of putting undue pressure on such persons. Yet, as we know by now, to see people with handicaps engage in a whole variety of challenging sports – parachuting, sailing, cycling, mountain climbing, etc. – activities that were not thought of as being suitable for them in the past, is no longer a rare sight. Engaging in such activities helps the individual gain self-confidence, which has tremendous impact on other aspects of his or her life. Obviously, the process of introducing the person to such activity and providing him or her with the confidence to start it, in light of an often low self-esteem and lack of confidence in the (failing) body, needs to be carefully planned and carried out (Davister *et al.*, 2004). The same rationale can be applied to the field of employment.

The literature on people with disabilities of the past 10–15 years introduces two diverging paradigms that are at the base of policies and practices in the field. Colin Barnes, a major researcher on these issues writes (2003):

> People with impairments [are] labeled "disabled" [and] viewed as not quite whole, not "normal", and incapable of participating in and contributing to the everyday life of the community. They are, therefore, in need of "care". In many countries this has resulted in the generation of a thriving and costly "disability" industry comprised of state institutions, private businesses, charities and voluntary organizations ... The end result is that disabled people's assumed inadequacy and dependence is assured and reinforced.

An alternative model to that "medical model" is the "social model", which looks at "economic, environmental and cultural barriers encountered by people viewed by others as having some form of impairment ... From this perspective, people with impairments are disabled by society's failure to accommodate their individual and collective needs within the mainstream of economic and cultural life".

Oorschot and Hvinden (2000, 294), discussing European disability policies, write about the "medical model" as well, stressing that it:

> places too much emphasis on individual limitations in functional ability as determined by medical conditions ... [This] led to a focus on individual shortcomings and the need for compensation, and that such a conceptualization disregards how aspects of the environment may reinforce the practical limitations arising from a particular bodily or psychological impairment ["the social model"]. The former conceptualization has been associated with segregated provisions, while the latter has been associated with notions of "mainstreaming", "equal opportunity" and "non-discrimination".

Thus, according to this view, the distinction between impairment, which is a condition of the body, and disability, which is a framework imposed by society, should lead to a different discourse, which should shift debates about disability from a biomedically dominated agenda to one that focuses on politics and citizenship, including employment policies (Hughes and Paterson, 1997, 325). An additional development of the "social model" is presented by Burchardt (2004) who relates it to the capabilities framework, which challenges a utilitarian basis for measuring value.

Barnes (2000) applies the "social model" of disability to the realm of work and maintains that when the right policy exists it is possible gainfully to employ large numbers of people with disabilities, as was the case during World War II in the UK, when a workforce was needed in light of the war effort and over half a million persons with disabilities were employed. This policy persisted after the war for a while until the government changed its priorities. The idea then is to fit the employment framework to the workers, not the other way around. An example given in this context is the policy toward mothers with small babies (ibid., 445–446). Roulstone (2004, 9) too suggests using the "social model" in planning employment policies toward people with disabilities and "shifting the focus squarely away from the functional limitations of impaired individuals and on to contemporary social organisations with a plethora of disabling barriers".

The "social model" of disability then, when applied to the realm of employment, provides a conceptual framework to fit real jobs to persons with a disability and treat them as regular workers. The process of "fitting" has to focus on the person's capabilities, not his or her impairment, which should be irrelevant for the particular job. Furthermore, a business environment, if it offers the person in focus a job that fits his or her abilities and skills, as is shown in the case studies below, can actually help the individual raise the level of performance and can be seen as a way to develop his or her potential. This needs to be a business venture based on an activity that is fit for the persons engaged in it on the basis of their innate skills, and practiced within an organizational context that is supportive, sensitive and caring.

A case in point is an international organization entitled Dialog in the Dark[2] – a museum that people enter in total darkness and have to use senses other than their sight to grasp the exhibits. The guides in the museum are all blind, as they are the ones who know best how to use these senses. From a business perspective the entrepreneur has found a niche where a business is built that helps handicapped persons around an activity in which they have a relative advantage, where their *disability* is turned into *capability*. Dialog in the Dark exists now in over 160 sites in 110 cities and 30 countries around the world. It is clearly a major tool in helping the blind. It does so by providing employment opportunities for blind persons, where they can use unique skills in which they excel, compensated fairly for their work and be appreciated for it. At the same time the museum is a most creative idea on how to raise awareness in society to the blind population, their special needs and their unique capacities. All this is done within a business framework, which has to be sustainable. The point to stress in this case and in successful social businesses in general is the fit between the type of work performed and the population that is employed –and –simultaneously helped. Under such conditions, the specific employees are the best fit for the job and, in the specific context, are no longer considered handicapped and could be treated as regular workers in any workplace. The outcome of such a venture is clearly a *blended value*, where the financial and the social aspects converge. In such a case there is very little need for bridging mechanisms between the two orientations as they are basically complementing each other.[3]

In the example given, the jobs these workers hold do not take away from the fact that they are blind, and outside the museum they have special needs that other people do not. Thus for example, if the state provides handicapped persons with a mobility allowance, it is totally unjustified for the state to "save" it because the person has found an appropriate place of employment. Furthermore, work as a guide in Dialog in the Dark does not fit all blind people – it requires a series of skills and capacities in addition to the basic condition of being blind. In other words, such creative solutions should not be looked at as a way to cut public budgets.

Enlarging the social business phenomenon requires first and foremost business creativity – of matching social problems and needs with a solution that can be turned into a business venture and be profitable. It evolves around using the unique features of a target population and turning those into an enterprise. It is very different from a general attempt to find job opportunities for a certain target population. If it is to be sustainable, it has to find the right niche where it has an advantage, given the population it employs. It has to develop a strategy on how to remain competitive, namely how to attract customers; in this context it raises the question as to whether to advertise the fact that it employs workers from a marginalized population. Finally, that structure also has to protect the rights of the (disabled) workers, so that under no circumstances are they abused.

The study

A survey into Israel's market-driven social ventures was conducted in 2011. It entailed two types of entities, each with a different legal form: business ventures within NPOs[4] and "social businesses", registered as regular business companies, which have a social mission that is part of their charter. In Israel there is no special legal form for such entities as is the case with community interest companies (CICs) in the UK or low profit limited liability companies (L3Cs)/B Corporations in the US. Thus, a businessperson who establishes a social business does so without any form of formal public support and actually needs to absorb all the extra costs pertaining to that form of organization. It is therefore not surprising that the phenomenon is new and small. Furthermore, in order to minimize risks some entrepreneurs prefer to establish a business venture within NPOs, as it enables such an entity to draw funds from philanthropic sources.

Before presenting the findings of the study we briefly present several short examples of Israeli social businesses, to provide the reader with an idea of the subject matter.

Social businesses: a few case studies

Ariel Netivim

Ariel Netivim Ltd is a social business – a branch of Ariel Netivim Group which is a private investment and holding company. The enterprise was established in 2009 and concentrates its business activities on job creation for people with disabilities. The firm achieves its goal by establishing businesses that primarily employ people with disabilities and by cooperating with businesses and/or nonprofit organizations for the creation of jobs for people with disabilities and providing them with tools for an independent career. It employs some 250 persons with handicaps, mostly in building maintenance activities. The social business was established by the owner of the investment and holding company after a successful career in the real estate domain. The enterprise has a board of directors composed of ten members, each representing a different aspect the enterprise needs – knowledge of specific disabilities, government policy, law and accountancy, etc. The charter of Ariel Netivim clearly states that all profits are fed back into the enterprise and that this proviso cannot be changed by a future board.

Call Yachol

Call Yachol is a social business, the first of its kind in the world, setting up call centers that are operated by and adapted for people with disabilities. Founded in 2008, Call Yachol has two centers and some 220 employees aged 20 to 65, almost all of them with some kind of disability (without cognitive impairment), and it is the largest employer of people with disabilities in the open market in Israel.

The call centers are adapted to the needs and the particular service approach of each client, meeting their business expectations without compromising standards. By creating a supportive working environment for their employees (a work environment combining technological solutions for a wide range of disabilities, flexible work hours and professional support staff) and employing a population with a higher than average level of job stability and motivation, who are willing to work for many years and are exceptionally loyal to the task and the client, the enterprise reduces the costs of personnel turnover for the client and offers a high level of professionalism, contributing to providing excellence in service provision. Call Yachol has contracts with leading business companies in Israel, such as a cellphone company, a bank and a credit card company, all of whom require high standards of performance to compete with other call centers. The customers are obviously aware of the nature of the workers and approve of them.

The founder of the enterprise is a CEO of an organizational consulting company, which has accompanied a large number of call centers over the past decade. As such, the consulting company acquired considerable experience in the field, which enabled it to develop a unique behavioral and administrative model fit for the population of Call Yachol (managers and employees) within a field in which it has appropriate know-how. One of the key organizational features of Call Yachol is the function of a "lioness", called by that name for her role of protecting her "cubs". That person is helping the workers individually in all matters not related to their work – from the need for a loan, to family tensions, or contact with government agencies, etc.

Liliyot

Liliyot is known in Tel Aviv as an excellent five-star restaurant. Yet it is a social business as it provides high school drop-outs with culinary training. The project provides opportunities for youths at risk to develop a career in the food services industry.

The restaurant has been owned since 2001 by Elem – a nonprofit organization treating youth at risk – and although it is located in a central location in Tel Aviv it was not well-managed and acquired losses in its operation. Collaboration with a social investor created the conditions for Liliyot Restaurant to be bought from Elem. A change in management ensued and the restaurant became profitable, while not abandoning its social mission. It trains and employs 15 young people who receive instruction, supervision and employment for a period of up to 18 months. The training provides the youngsters with a profession in high demand in the restaurant sector. The Liliyot restaurant and kitchen staff are chosen on the basis of their professionalism in culinary work but also on their abilities to develop meaningful relationships and be sensitive to the needs of the youth. In addition the staff includes a social worker, who supervises the process of integration of the youngsters in the world of work. The young people participating in the program are treated just like ordinary employees. They receive full payment for their labor in the restaurant, and they are expected to show the same commitment expected from ordinary employees.

Follow-up research of the program's graduates indicates significant improvement in participants' circumstances as a result of the training they received at Liliyot. Most of them became independent citizens, and half of them succeeded in finding placement in leading restaurants in Israel's culinary industry. The restaurant, which by now is a part of a series of five similar ones, are owned and supported by the Liliyot Group – a group of social action and business entrepreneurs. The charter of Liliyot clearly states that it is a social business with the goal of employing and training youths in distress and the governance structure includes a permanent representative of Elem – the nonprofit organization treating youth at risk – to ensure that.

Chokonoy

Chokonoy is a family owned enterprise specializing in the manufacture and marketing of pralines and other chocolate products. All the chocolate products are made of the finest quality ingredients. The enterprise was founded by the parents of a child who was mentally retarded in order to find him a decent workplace, which would allow him to use his abilities and skills to their full potential and at the same time provide other people with a similar condition an opportunity for self-fulfillment and a better life. The enterprise was founded in 2002 and employed at its height 15 workers. At a certain point it encountered financial and logistical difficulties, which forced the owners to close it and look for new investors. At the end of this year, after two years of reorganizing and after finding a silent partner who invested in purchasing new equipment, Chokonoy reopened at a new location.

Tulip Winery

Tulip Winery is a private enterprise founded in 2003, by a family who wanted to fulfill a special dream of theirs and establish a boutique winery that combines top quality wine production, as well as contributing to the community. The family chose to locate the winery next to a community settlement for people with special needs, which strives to allow the disabled community to develop and realize their potential. The village is inhabited by about 200 people, diverse in age, the nature of their disability, their adjustment difficulties, and their functioning and independence level.

The combination of the village's vision and the family's desire to make wine resulted in an exciting wine industry model that employs members of the village and provides them with a business platform that integrates them in the labor force, just like any other person. Tulip Winery includes the village members in the wine production process. It also promotes various joint activities with the village, such as the sale of handicrafts made by village members. The members that work in the winery take part in the harvest, bottling and packaging of the wines, and they assist in hosting at the winery's visitor center. Tulip Winery produces about 100,000 bottles of wine per year, sold in Israel and abroad.

Main findings of the study

We report here on a part of the study, namely a comparison of social businesses with business ventures within NPOs. The former entities, such as the examples given above, are legally registered as business companies; they all have some specific provisos in their charter or other formal documents that in our judgment justifies depicting them as a "social" business, such as employing a disenfranchised population as part of their mission, directing all or part of the profits to the social purpose of the entity, or including stakeholders on the board. The latter have been chosen out of a larger pool of business ventures within NPOs because they possessed a distinct business strategy which was clearly related to the NPOs overall mission, such as on organization that works with youth in distress that also has a business scheme employing them in order to help with their overall treatment.

The idea was to compare the two groups on the basis of their legal structure in order to gauge the expressions of the different organizational cultures. The study was based on a telephone interview with the manager of the enterprise, using a questionnaire which had both open and closed questions. There was reluctance on the part of some of the respondents to disclose detailed financial data.

Comparison between social businesses and business ventures within NPOs (*N* = 40)

A comparison on the basis of the legal status of the entities focused primarily on the ways they balanced the two types of goals, which seemed to be expressing themselves differently in social businesses as compared to NPOs with a business component. In order to clarify this issue on the basis of data in our study we limited the comparison to entities that met three criteria:

1. The entity employs workers belonging to a marginalized population (mentally or physically handicapped, economically deprived, etc.) in a production or service delivery capacity as a major activity;
2. In addition to the social goals of integrating that marginalized population in society the entity defines clear business goals and competes in the open market;
3. The entity pays at least minimum wages (and does not subsidize its wages).

Such criteria helped us eliminate social enterprises without a robust business base – those that engage in training do not compete in the market and do not pay real wages. This process resulted in the selection of 40 enterprises – 13 businesses and 27 NPOs.

We compared the two groups along two dimensions: organizational characteristics and financial aspects. The comparison revealed differences between the two types of enterprises regarding their organizational and financial characteristics.

Organizational characteristics

Goals. The two groups had practically *similar social goals*, such as "creating opportunities for employment and empowering the employees", "creating a rehabilitative framework", "to find frameworks to instill work habits", and in some cases also *similar business goals*, such as "to prove that employing handicapped persons could be profitable". But there were also clearly *different business goals*, which may explain the tendency to establish the enterprises within different legal structures. In the case of social businesses the goal was typically stated as "to reach high revenues and profits, growing sales, manufacturing products of the highest values and highest quality, making money". The business goals of business ventures within NPOs were much more modest: "to achieve financial balance, to cover our expenses".

Age. Most ventures were new, established after 2005. All social businesses were established after 2000, while a third of the business ventures within NPOs were established before 2000.

Types of products. Most of the social businesses are in the food and beverages industry: restaurants, coffee shops, preparing sandwiches and catering. NPOs can be found in food and beverages as well, but also in knitting, weaving and billboard advertising.

Initiator of the enterprise. Half of the enterprises were established by another organization. Social businesses were often established by NPOs, and business ventures within NPOs were established by both NPOs themselves and sometimes by public agencies (mainly local authorities).

Motivation for establishment. Among business ventures within NPOs there were some that stated the main motivation for their establishment as "to build a source of income for the parent organization". This motivation was not found among social businesses.

Financial aspects

Donations. Most of the NPOs (82 percent) reported receiving donations, whereas only 38 percent of the social businesses use this resource, mostly in the form of pro bono contributions of different professionals or in-kind donations (of furniture, computers, etc.).

Volunteers. A large majority of all social enterprises studied (80 percent) use volunteers in their organizations; social businesses tend to use this resource a little less than NPOs (70 and 85 percent respectively).

Income. Approximately half of the social businesses generate a yearly income of more than half a million shekels (roughly $145,000); only less than 10 percent of the NPOs reach that level of income.

Financial losses. Seventy percent of the NPOs declared they did not have financial losses, whereas only a third of the social businesses reported no losses.

Financial leverage. Social businesses tended to use financial loans from investors or financial institutions (banks, investment funds) more than NPOs: one-third of the social businesses reported using these tools to leverage their financial activities while less than 10 percent of the NPOs reported the same.

Wages. While all entities studied pay at least minimum wages to their employees, our survey found that half of the social businesses paid above minimum wages, whereas only a quarter of the NPOs reported above average minimum wages.

Discussion

Market-driven social ventures, which are only at the early stages, are as yet a small phenomenon in Israel. The organizations categorized as such are small (usually employing 10–25 individuals), most of them are new, having been established after 2000. The phenomenon revolves around different marginalized populations, in particular youth in distress and handicapped persons. The similar populations lead to similarity in social goals of the enterprises though the different legal frameworks used lead to different business goals and consequently also impact on the organizational, financial and business aspects of the enterprise. It is clear that social businesses, both because of legal restrictions and ideology, are more similar to regular businesses and so are actually more embedded in the business field and culture; and business ventures within NPOs seem to be extensions of their parent organization. The fact that no specific legal framework exists, as is the case in the US and the UK, that allows organizations with social objectives to distribute limited profits to owners is the major reason for the phenomenon to be small and based on initiatives of enlightened businesspersons as is shown in the case studies.

   In analyzing the case studies it seems there is an attempt to fit the task to the individual with his or her specific attributes and characteristics. In addition, there is a supporting managing system and sometimes a bridging mechanism between the business and social goals of the entity (such as the social worker at Liliyot restaurant or the "lioness" in Call Yachol) to ensure that the social objectives are protected. Furthermore, the fact that they are run as regular businesses provides their workers with opportunities for promotion and advancement. It would seem that the more there is a fit between the tasks and the individuals filling them, the more the likelihood of obtaining a *blended value* for outcome and the less the need to develop bridging mechanisms to reconcile differences between the social and the business orientations. Also, when analyzing the products/services these entities produce or deliver – they are engaged in producing for consumption of the general public – things one buys in a regular supermarket or needs when one has troubles with one's cellphone bill. This is significant in terms of changing the public's perceptions of and attitudes toward marginalized populations and their abilities.

Unique roles of social businesses

Given the developments concerning social businesses and the interests in them around the world, it would seem that a new type of organization is being developed, which at its current stage looks as a hybrid of two known types, though in the future, when better fits between tasks and workers may be found or developed, a new and unique type will evolve. Obviously such organizations will focus on a variety of social issues and problems. Yet, as this chapter (and current reality) focuses primarily on social businesses as loci of employment for hard-to-employ populations, the question arises as to their specific role vis-à-vis these populations and how they differ from other, less business-oriented schemes. It seems that a competitive organizational environment – provided its tasks fit the particular population and the entity is governed and managed by a supportive environment, similarly to the case of challenging sports for people with handicaps – can provide its workers with a framework to reach their potential abilities better.

Social businesses clearly represent a new and intriguing paradigm. From a business perspective it challenges a basic principle on which the business world is based, namely that the prime function of business is to maximize profits for its owners. From a helping/treatment perspective it raises the question as to whether help to marginalized populations cannot include components of challenge that are represented by the need to have performance standards, which in turn can raise the person's abilities and develop his or her potential.

Notes

1. According to Yunus, social business "operates for the benefit of addressing social needs that enable societies to function more efficiently. Social business provides a necessary framework for tackling social issues by combining business know-how with the desire to improve quality of life. Therefore instead of being self-focused *social business* is all about others" (http://www.grameencreativelab.com/a-concept-to-eradicate-poverty/the-concept.html).
2. See www.dialogue-in-the-dark.com/
3. This discussion and the "social model" pertain to people with physical and mental handicaps who are often labeled "disabled" – a category they carry for life. Other marginalized populations served by social businesses such as ex-convicts or youth in distress do not possess such "fixed" categories, and the issue of fitting a job for them is unrelated to their social problem.
4. These included only ventures within NPOs with a distinct *business* orientation, of selling a product/service made by the organization's clients or on their behalf; it did not include other forms of self-generated income, such as membership dues, renting the organization's facilities, fees for services, etc.

References

Alter, K. (2007) "Social Enterprise Typology", http://rinovations.edublogs.org/files/2008/07/setypology.pdf accessed 2 January 2012.
Anheier, H. K. (2003) "A Comparative Perspective of Structure and Change", in H. K. Anheier and A. Ben-Ner (ed.), *The Study of the Nonprofit Enterprise: Theories and Approaches.* Ney York: Kluwer Academic/Plenum Publishers.
Barnes, C. (2000) "A Working Social Model? Disability, Work and Disability Politics in the 21st Century." *Critical Social Policy* 20: 441–457.

Barnes, C. (2003) *Independent Living, Politics and Implications*, www.independentliving. org/docs6/barnes2003.html

Bull, M. (2008) "Challenging Tensions: Critical, Theoretical and Empirical Perspectives on Social Enterprise." *International Journal of Entrepreneurial Behaviour and Research* 14(5): 268–275.

Burchardt, T. (2004) "Capabilities and Disability: The Capabilities Framework and the Social Model of Disability." *Disability & Society*, 19(7): 735–751.

Cooney, K. (2006) "The Institutional and Technical Structuring of Nonprofit Hybrids: Organizations Caught between Two Fields?" *Voluntas* 17: 143–161.

Crimmins, J. C. and Keil, M. (1983) *Enterprise in the Nonprofit Sector*. New York: The Rockefeller Brothers Fund.

Davister, C., Defourny, J. and Grégoire, O. (2004) "Work Integration Social Enterprises in the European Union: An Overview of Existing Models", Working Papers Series, 04/04, Liège: EMES European Research Network.

Dees, G. (1998) "Enterprising Nonprofits: What Do You Do when Traditional Sources of Funding Fall Short?" *Harvard Business Review*, February, 55–67.

Defourny, J. and Nyssens, M. (2006) "Defining Social Enterprise", in M. Nyssens et. al. (eds), *Social Enterprises, at the Crossroads of Market, Public Policies and Civil Society*. Routledge, 3–26.

Eikenberry, A. M. and Kluver, J. D. (2004) "The Marketization of the Nonprofit Sector: Civil Society at Risk?" *Public Administration Review*, 64: 132–140.

Evers, A. (2001) "The Significance of Social Capital in the Multiple Goal and Resource Structure of Social Enterprises", in C. Borzaga and J. Defourny (eds), *The Emergence of Social Enterprise*, : Routledge, 296–311.

Hasenfeld, Y. and Gidron, B. (2005) "Understanding Multi-purpose Hybrid Voluntary Organizations: The Contributions of Theories on Civil Society, Social Movements and Non-profit Organizations." *Journal of Civil Society* 1(2): 97–112.

Himmelstein, J. L. (1997) *Looking Good and Doing Good*.: Indiana University Press.

Ho, A. P. and Chan, K. (2010) "The Social Impact of Work-integration Social Enterprise in Hong Kong." *International Social Work* 53(1): 33–45.

Hughes, B. and Paterson, K. (1997) "The Social Model of Disability and the Disappearing Body: Towards a Sociology of Impairment." *Disability & Society*, 12 (3): 325–340.

James, E. (1998) "Commercialization among Nonprofits: Objectives, Opportunities, and Constraints", in B. A. Weisbrod (ed.), *To Profit or not to Profit: The Commercial Transformation of the Nonprofit Sector*.: Cambridge University Press, 271–285.

Mendel, S. (2003) "The Ecology of Games between Public Policy and Private Action." *Nonprofit Management and Leadership* 13(3): 229–236.

Nicholls, A. (ed.) (2006) *Social Entrepreneurship*.: Oxford University Press.

Oorschot, W. van and Hvinden, B. (2000) "Introduction: Towards Convergence? Disability Policies in Europe." *European Journal of Social Security* 2(4): 293–302.

Roulstone, A. (2004) "Disability, Employment and the Social Model", in C. Barnes and G. Mercer (eds), *Disability Policy and Practice: Applying the Social Model*. Leeds: The Disability Press, 18–34.

Salamon, L. M. (1997) "The United States", in L. M. Salamon and H. K. Anheier (eds), *Defining the Nonprofit Sector: A Cross National Analysis*.: Manchester University Press.

Smallbone, D., Evans, M., Ekanem, I. and Butters, S. (2001) "Researching Social Enterprise: Final Report to the Small Business Service." Centre for Enterprise and Economic Development Research, Middlesex University Business School, Middlesex University, UK.

Spear, R. and Bidet, E. (2005) "Social Enterprise for Work Integration in 12 European Countries." *Annals of Public and Cooperative Economics* 76(2): 195–231.

Thomasson, A. (2009) "Exploring the Ambiguity of Hybrid Organizations: A Stakeholders Approach." *Financial Accountability & Management* 25(3): 353–365.

Thompson, J. and Doherty, B. (2006) "The Diverse World of Social Enterprise: A Collection of Social Enterprise Stories." *International Journal of Social Economics* 33: 361–375.

Thompson, J., Alvy, G., and Less, A. (2000) "Social Entrepreneurship: A New Look at the People and the Potential." *Management Decision* 38(5): 328–338.

Weisbrod, B. A. (1998) *To Profit or Not to Profit.* : Cambridge University Press.

Young, D. (1998) "Commercialism in Nonprofit Social Service Associations: Its Character, Significance, and Rationale." *Journal of Policy Analysis and Management* 17(2): 278–297.

Yunus, M. (2008) *A World without Poverty: Social Business and the Future of Capitalism.* New York: Public Affairs.

7
Social Enterprise in Mixed-Form Fields: Challenges and Prospects
Paul-Brian McInerney

The standard definition of a social enterprise is an organization that applies business-like structures and practices to produce social, as opposed to private, returns (Bielefeld, 2006; Dart, 2004b). Social enterprises blend values and practices from different institutional domains to produce new hybrid organizational forms (Battilana and Dorado, 2010; Cooney, 2006; Hasenfeld and Gidron, 2005). The evolution of hybrid organizational forms in institutionalized organizational fields presents theoretical challenges to scholars of organizations: Can such hybrids coexist alongside pure (legitimate) forms? Can they overcome legitimacy challenges to become the new taken-for-granted organizational form? How are hybrids innovative? How do they challenge incumbents in institutionalized organizational fields?

Despite a dearth of answers to these and other important theoretical questions, much of the research on social enterprise has focused on taxonomies (Roper and Cheney, 2005; Thompson, 2002; Weerawardena and Mort, 2006) or normative accounts of such organizations in action (Dees *et al.*, 2001, 2002; Emerson and Twersky, 1996). Scholars are just beginning to pay attention to the theoretical and practical implications of social enterprise as an organizational form. This chapter contributes to the growing body of literature that analyzes social enterprise as a specific institutional form. In it, I examine social enterprise as the blending of values, structures and practices across institutional domains to create a hybrid organizational form. I situate social enterprises in both their institutional domains and organizational fields, showing the symbolic and relational challenges these hybrid forms face as they attempt to gain legitimacy. The empirical materials for this chapter come from an ethnographic study of a social enterprise situated in the field of US nonprofit technology assistance providers.

The state of our knowledge about social enterprise

Many scholars have decried the commercialization of the nonprofit sector (Anheier and Toepler, 1998; Eikenberry and Kluver, 2004; James, 1998;

Salamon, 1999, 2003; Segal and Weisbrod, 1998; Weisbrod, 1998; Young, 1998). Yet, recent empirical analysis has called into question the "commercialization thesis", finding no evidence of an increase in the commercial revenue generated by nonprofit organizations (Child, 2010). Despite the questionable evidence of a large-scale trend toward commercialization in the voluntary sector, social enterprises raise theoretical and empirical questions regarding the influence of businesses and commercial ideas on nonprofit organizations. Even though the number of social enterprises in the US and abroad is growing rapidly (Austin *et al.*, 2006), their influence extends beyond their numbers. By bridging the institutional domains of the voluntary and business sectors, social enterprises are conduits for the transfer of ideas. As members of both organizational fields, they occupy the position of a structural fold, which is important for the generation of innovative ideas (Vedres and Stark, 2010).

Social enterprises have many different organizational structures, from freestanding organizations to subsidiaries or components of existing organizations. They also take various organizational forms: some are incorporated as "501(c)(3) nonprofit organizations", while others maintain for-profit status. Although many social enterprises are incorporated as nonprofit organizations, there are no conventions for organizational form. For example, Kiva and Grameen are both microcredit social enterprises. Kiva is nonprofit; Grameen is for-profit. However, both are subject to similar evaluative criteria: that is, whether the loans they make help to alleviate poverty, though one could argue that Grameen faces the additional evaluative burden of producing accountable profits. Social enterprises are designed to be self-sustaining. While nonprofit social enterprises can receive donations from individuals and foundations, such donations are often made based on the organization's potential sustainability. Among social enterprises, sustainability takes on specific meaning as fiscal sustainability, i.e. can the organization continue to meet its social mission while relying minimally (or not at all) on donative revenue, an institutional script adopted from the business sector? Within their system of values, social enterprises ought to generate all the revenues they need to achieve their social mission. However, many social enterprises operate in markets for social goods that make such a goal exceedingly difficult to achieve.

The diversity of structures, forms and size makes social enterprises difficult to classify and operationalize in realist terms. A more productive approach is to understand social enterprises in institutionalist terms, i.e. as hybrid organizations that combine market and social values that attempt to create and legitimize new institutional forms (Bielefeld, 2006; Borzaga and Defourny, 2001; Dart, 2004b). Social enterprises operate simultaneously across at least two institutional domains: the business and nonprofit sectors. As such, they assemble values from these seemingly incompatible worlds and must find ways to be accountable to each. Straddling two worlds as they do, social enterprises are challenged to appear legitimate in both institutional domains. This requires them to produce accounts that can be justified to parties on both sides of an ostensibly intractable chasm (McInerney, 2008; Stark, 2009). People from Wall Street and the social sector are likely to evaluate the organization's activities on different criteria. Social enterprises thus trade between social and market worlds, a social space that affords economic opportunity and innovation at the risk of losing moral legitimacy (Barth, 2000).

Social enterprises span institutional domains

Social enterprises struggle to establish legitimacy across multiple institutional domains (Battilana and Dorado, 2010), each of which have different evaluative criteria for what constitutes legitimacy. Suchman (1995, 574) defines legitimacy as "a generalized perception or assumption that the actions of an entity are desirable, proper, or appropriate within some socially constructed system of norms, values, beliefs, and definitions". Scholars identify multiple forms of legitimacy. Among such forms, moral legitimacy is the most problematic for social enterprise to establish. This is largely due to the social nature of nonprofit organizing. Nonprofit organizations are said to be driven by missions to provide social goods. To regulators, they must establish charitable worth in order to be granted tax-exempt status. To other nonprofit organizations, they must demonstrate allegiance to the ideals of volunteerism and charity in order to be accepted as legitimate members of the organizational field. Such legitimacy is more than symbolic; it is also necessary to access donative forms of revenue. Research has shown that nonprofit organizations that generate earned revenues may also see donative revenues decline (Guo, 2006). Such findings suggest foundations and other donors recognize certain organizational activities, such as volunteerism, as more legitimate in the nonprofit sector than others, such as earned revenue schemes.

Establishing moral legitimacy

Moral legitimacy concerns judgments about whether particular actors are "doing the right thing". It is closely related to cognitive notions of legitimacy, i.e. how organizations understand or make sense of their environments and themselves, to the degree that both draw on cultural understandings within fields. In other words, claims of moral legitimacy are about "doing the right thing"; claims of cognitive legitimacy are about "how things are done". "Right" ways of doing things, once institutionalized, become taken-for-granted as *the* way of doing things. As such, new organizations or organizations in new fields seeking legitimacy must establish moral legitimacy to be accepted as actors in the field. Subsequent cognitive legitimacy gives organizations a competitive advantage as they move toward being leaders in the field.

Moral legitimacy is based on judgments by other actors in the field (Ashforth and Gibbs, 1990; Suchman, 1995, 579). Negative judgments take the form of denunciation. Actors live simultaneously in multiple social worlds (Berger and Luckmann, 1966), which provide moral standpoints from which actors can make judgments, denouncing the actions of others or justifying their own actions (Boltanski and Thévenot 1991, 2006). Denunciation is the act of reaching across social worlds and applying the rules of legitimacy in one world to actions in another world. For example, social enterprises make moral claims based on their ability to generate earned revenue in the marketplace (Boltanski and Thévenot, 1999, 372). In doing so, they justify their work based on their ability to operate according to the moral logic of the market, justifying their behavior based on market forms of worth. On the other hand, social enterprises also make moral claims based on social goods that their organizations produce, e.g. what social problems their organizations help to solve. Here, the social enterprise justifies its work based on the moral logic of the social realm, i.e. producing accounts of social forms of worth. However, at the same time, nonprofit organizations or foundation actors can denounce the social enterprise for being too market-oriented or business-like. Depending on relationships among actors in the entrepreneur's field, such a denunciation can challenge the organization's moral legitimacy and ultimately the organization's access to key resources, such as financing or markets for social goods.

Justification is the basis of legitimation (Berger and Luckmann, 1966, 93). In order for something to be considered legitimate, it has to be justified. Legitimacy transforms subjective meanings, i.e. things considered true in some group, into objective meanings, i.e. knowledge taken for granted as true by everyone. In this way, the meanings of actions move from moral to cognitive forms of legitimacy on their way to being institutionalized as accepted practice. This is why it is so important for entrepreneurs, such as social enterprises, to defend successfully their organizational forms and practices within a given organizational field. Once such forms and practices are accepted as morally legitimate, they can be pressed into action as cognitively legitimate and ultimately institutionalized in the field.

Organizational fields and institutional domains

Competition over legitimacy occurs within the context of organizational fields (Ashforth and Gibbs, 1990). Organizational fields are "those organizations that, in the aggregate, constitute a recognized area of institutional life: key suppliers, resource and product consumers, regulatory agencies, and other organizations that produce similar services or products" (DiMaggio and Powell, 1991b, 64). DiMaggio and Powell (1991b, 65) continue, "fields only exist to the extent that they are institutionally defined". This means that organizational fields share a set of common meanings and understandings of what counts as legitimate and who counts as a legitimate member of the field according to the institutions of that field. "Field" is a relational concept expressing how actors facing the same set of constraints influence each other directly and indirectly (Martin, 2003). Organizations within fields "interact more frequently and fatefully with one another" (Scott, 1994, 208).

Institutions are "socially constructed, routine-reproduced (ceteris paribus), program or rule systems. They operate as relative fixtures of constraining environments and are accompanied by taken-for-granted accounts" (Jepperson, 1991, 149). Institutions govern behavior in everyday life. They help actors to manage uncertainty by giving meaning to resources and providing the dominant evaluative criteria by which people's performances, i.e. the legitimacy of their performances, are judged. Institutions provide the cognitive, normative and regulative pressures that influence the behavior of actors within fields (Friedland and Alford, 1991; Scott, 2008). Institutions emerge from successive interactions within fields (DiMaggio, 1991). At the same time, they shape future interactions. The result is the recursive process of structuration (Barley and Tolbert, 1997; DiMaggio and Powell, 1991a; Giddens, 1984). Therefore, legitimation processes at the intra- and inter-organizational levels can produce effects at the field level, which can, under the right circumstances, effect institutional change (Battilana, 2006; Battilana *et al.*, 2009; Boxenbaum and Battilana, 2005).

Yet, the process of institutionalization is contentious. Fields are "arenas of power" in which actors vie for legitimacy (Brint and Karabel, 1991). One form of contention is challenges to newcomers' legitimacy (Lampel and Meyer, 2008; McInerney, 2008). Social enterprises are challengers in markets for social goods, taking on incumbent forms, which are most often nonprofit organizations. The nonprofit sector, especially in the United States, has deeply entrenched institutional practices (DiMaggio and Anheier, 1990; Frumkin, 2002). Among them is a strong ambivalence regarding commercialization (Frumkin and Andre-Clark, 2000). While it is generally accepted practice to charge for services, nonprofit organizations are supposed to privilege "social values over financial values" (Kanter and Summers, 1987, 154). Therefore, social enterprises present theoretical puzzles over how challengers blend values across institutional domains to establish moral (and eventually cognitive) legitimacy in institutionalized fields.

In this chapter I examine the case of a social enterprise as it attempts to establish moral legitimacy by justifying its organizational form and practices in the field of nonprofit technology assistance providers. Social enterprises recombine practices and forms considered legitimate across multiple institutional domains. While innovative, such recombinations also render them vulnerable to legitimacy challenges from actors in any one domain.

For example, social enterprises may be seen as too commercial for actors in the nonprofit sector, yet not commercial enough for actors in the business sector. Such a position is problematic when the social enterprise considers itself accountable to both sides of a seemingly intractable chasm. In the next section, I describe the methods I used to conduct this study as well as the primary fieldwork site and the organizational field in which it is situated. The findings section explains how social enterprises generate and recombine market and social forms of worth through their modes of organizing and practices. The discussion and conclusion outlines the prospects for social enterprises in mixed-form fields.

Methods

The data for this chapter come from a multi-sited, field-level ethnography of nonprofit technology assistance providers in the US between May 2001 and November 2004. My primary field site was NPower NY, an entrepreneurial nonprofit in New York City. Fieldwork began only two months after the organization began working with clients, and continued for the first two and a half years that NPower NY operated. From this vantage, I was able to collect data about the organization from its very inception. Beyond NPower NY, I conducted fieldwork at additional Nonprofit Technology Assistance Providers (NTAPs) and events at which they convened throughout the US. Therefore, my ethnography afforded me the opportunity to see how demands from various organizations in the field were integrated into NPower NY as it developed, treating the organization itself as an ongoing process (Van de Ven and Huber, 1990).

The ethnography consisted of 15–20 hours per week of participant observation at NPower NY's office as well as additional observations at conferences, events and client sites. To gain access, I volunteered at NPower NY, helping the organization plan its workforce development program. In exchange, I was granted nearly unlimited access to the organization, its staff and its files. Observational data were recorded into field notebooks. Because I had my laptop at hand when at the office, I was often able to rewrite my jottings into full-fledged field notes almost immediately after recording them. This arrangement allowed me to keep accurate field notes, freeing me from problems associated with remembering the particulars of daily events, especially direct quotations. Ethnographic fieldwork extended to NPower's Seattle and National offices. I also attended key events related to NPower's partnerships, including NPower's "Summit", which convened key personnel from all NPower affiliates on the Microsoft Campus in Redmond, WA in October of 2002.

To supplement observational data, I conducted formal interviews, ranging from 40 minutes to two hours, with all of NPower NY's staff members, including two board members as well as key staff members from NPower

National, including the founder of the organization. Additional interviews were conducted with leaders of competing organizations, foundation program officers and representatives from corporate sponsors. In total, data from 57 formal interviews were analyzed for this chapter. Aside from formal interviews, I conducted countless informal interviews ranging from five-minute conversations around the water cooler to two-hour discussions on subway rides to visit clients or during after-hours gatherings at local bars and restaurants. All formal interviews were tape recorded (except for two respondents that refused to be recorded) and transcribed. To triangulate observation and interview data, I collected physical and electronic documents throughout my time in the field. Physical documents included memos, business plans, promotional materials, employee handbooks and manuals, board reports and other official organizational documents. Electronic documents I collected include emails, websites, memos, consulting records, tax forms and internal reports. Documents provide researchers with "official" representations of organizational processes and record how such processes develop over time (Hodder, 2000; Star, 1999).

Fieldnotes, interview transcripts and other documents were then coded according to emergent themes (Emerson *et al.*, 1995). Preliminary codes were recoded iteratively to make further sense of the data.

Primary research sites

NPower is a network of 13 nonprofit technology assistance providers located throughout the US. NTAPs are organizations or individuals that deliver information technology consulting and/or training services to nonprofit and grassroots organizations. Each NPower affiliate is independently incorporated as a 501(c)(3). The first NPower was founded in Seattle in 1999 with funding from Microsoft. NPower NY was founded two years later as part of a national expansion, also funded by Microsoft. Beginning with $600,000 in operating funds, the organization grew to over 20 full-time employees with a $2 million budget by the end of 2002, its second year of operation.

NPower NY began working out of donated office space located in the Gramercy Park neighborhood of Manhattan. When the lease expired on that space one year later, the organization moved to midtown Manhattan, where they occupied the entire floor of a six-storey office building. The location offered NPower NY managers and consultants easy access to the city's transit system, which allowed them to service clients throughout Manhattan and the outer boroughs. The newer office space was modeled on the high-tech start up aesthetic of their earlier offices. The walls were painted burnt orange. The main space featured an open office, with desks arranged in four rows along two five-foot high partitions. Managers were sequestered in offices along one of the outer walls of the building. Their offices featured permanent walls, which went 75 percent of the way to the ceiling. Only the executive manager had an office that was fully sealed off from the rest of the floor. Two classrooms were situated along the opposite side of the office. One was used as a training classroom for nonprofit clients. The other was for a program to teach low-income youths how to use computer technologies.

NPower NY has partnered with several for-profit corporations. Aside from its founding support from Microsoft, the organization secured collaborative relationships with several key technology and financial firms, including JP Morgan Chase, Accenture Consulting, Cisco, New Horizons and Dell. These partnerships provide material support, volunteers and staff, as well as technical support. Material support takes the forms of both cash and in-kind donations.

NPower and NPower NY are social enterprises to the degree they combine values and practices from the nonprofit and for-profit sectors to produce social goods. Incorporated as 501(c)(3)s, they have established their charitable worth to the Internal Revenue Service. NPower and NPower NY charge clients fees for their services. Their fees are subsidized by philanthropic support from nonprofit and corporate foundations as well as for-profit partners. Beyond material practices, they engage in symbolic practices representing the blending of values across sectors. For example, they refer to the organizations they assist as "clients"; employees that do on-site technical assistance with clients are called "consultants".

The NTAP field operates as a mixed-form market (Marwell and McInerney, 2005). Most NTAPs are freestanding nonprofit organizations or are programs of organizations that are incorporated as 501(c)(3) nonprofit organizations. However, many individual consultants also operate in the NTAP market. While not nonprofit in the technical sense of the term, these consultants call themselves "NPIs" or "nonprofit individuals". For-profit consulting firms work with nonprofit clients as well. In general, the market for technology services is a stratified market, meaning that, in general, certain types of organizations work with clients of different sizes (ibid., 23). Smaller nonprofit organizations are serviced by NPIs or smaller NTAPs. "Circuit Riding" is one common arrangement. "Circuit Riders" provide services to nonprofit and grassroots organizations, for which a third party (often a nonprofit foundation) pays (McInerney, 2007). Only the largest nonprofit organizations can afford the services of for-profit consulting firms. Among NTAPs, few identify expressly as social enterprises. Constituted by several organizational forms, subscribing to different justifications for legitimacy, the NTAP field provides an excellent field site with which to understand moral legitimacy challenges across institutional domains.

The organizational field in which NPower NY operated consisted of the following groups of organizations:

- **Donors:** NPower NY's primary philanthropic support comes from its corporate partners. However, the organization receives grants and other support from several nonprofit foundations, primarily the Robin Hood Foundation, which is known for its support of entrepreneurial nonprofits and programs. NPower NY receives additional support from Surdna and the Soros Foundation. For work related to the tragedy at the World Trade Center, NPower NY received funding from the September 11 Fund and support from the Red Cross.

• **Clients:** NPower NY works exclusively with nonreligious 501(c)(3) organizations. During my time in the field, clients included charter schools, after-school programs, theater and arts organizations, homeless shelters, hospitals and foundations. Most had medium to large budgets compared to the average nonprofit in New York City (as reported in Seley and Wolpert, 2002).

• **Other NTAPs:** At the time NPower NY started its operations, New York City was home to several well-established NTAPs, including the Fund for the City of New York, the Tech Foundation, the Low Income Networking and Communications (LINC) Project, and Media Jumpstart. These organizations justified their activities from different moral standpoints than NPower NY. Most judged their work based primarily on a civic order of worth, i.e. based on their ability to promote socially progressive outcomes through their work. For example, Media Jumpstart was a collectivist organization that worked exclusively with social justice groups. The LINC Project was a project of the Welfare Law Center and worked with economic justice groups. The Fund for the City of New York was itself a foundation with a longstanding technology assistance program for its grantees. While the Fund worked with many of the same organizations as NPower, it promoted an alternative technology platform, based on what it saw as the voluntary and collaborative ethos in the nonprofit sector.

Findings

As a mixed-form market, the NTAP field is subject to multiple and contradictory institutional demands. Circuit Riders and politically progressive NTAP groups consider themselves activists (McInerney, 2007). Legitimacy among activist groups is determined by contributions to social movements or in political realms. In contrast, NPower considers itself a consulting firm for nonprofit organizations (McInerney, 2008). NPower NY is deeply ensconced in New York City's mainstream nonprofit sector, but also subject to the institutional demands of for-profit partners, foundations and board members from the private sector. As such, its legitimacy is determined differently by these various groups. Among nonprofit organizations, its legitimacy depends on its ability to present itself as facing the same constraints as other nonprofit organizations, e.g. adhering to the nonprofit ethos of altruism and volunteerism (Clohesy, 2000; Jeavons, 1992). Among for-profit organizations, NPower NY's legitimacy depends on its ability to demonstrate fiscal sustainability and adhere to market principles. A leader a Media Jumpstart, a politically progressive Circuit Rider group, explained the perceived difference between their type of NTAP and NPower in political terms:

Any group that is politically not in line with social justice, we [at Media Jumpstart] just do not work with them ... Because we are not like NPower. We are not like groups that have a big public reputation as being an independent, neutral NTAP. There is one guy I met from NPower that said "we will work with the NRA [National Rifle Association]. We are here not to be ideological." Media Jumpstart is a political organization. It is explicitly so. There is no wavering or doubt. NPower is afraid that the NRA is going to say that NPower is a bunch of lefties and they do not want to work with us. If they say that about us, great. NPower also gets corporate funding and that is a whole different ballpark. (Personal interview, September 5, 2003)

The quote reflects the differential bases for moral legitimacy between Circuit Rider groups, which consider themselves activists, and NPower NY, which considers itself a nonprofit consulting enterprise. Legitimacy for activist Circuit Riders depends on their willingness to work with politically progressive groups (and conversely their rejection of reactionary groups). On the other hand NPower NY's moral legitimacy is based on market values, i.e. working with any group that is willing and able to pay for its services. Most of the people working for NPower NY consider themselves liberals on the political spectrum. For example, in a conversation with me the director of consulting expressed his ambivalence about the very same hypothetical call from the NRA. He explained that, personally, he would prefer not to work with politically conservative organizations, but understands that NPower NY must remain neutral and open to all secular nonprofit organizations (Field notes, December 20, 2001). Yet, political neutrality was part of NPower's model from its inception. As its founder explained the founding logic in an interview:

I have worked for years in direct [social] service delivery, doing domestic violence human services. They [organizations involved in direct social service delivery] are doing social change. It [Circuit Riders' exclusive relationship to social justice organizations] felt like this real judgmental thing. I think the hardest work is the doing. I think the agencies working on the ground, working with kids at risk, working with the elderly; they are doing the work of social change. They might not be advocating; they might not be lobbying; but they are doing the hard stuff. So, leading off with "we will only work with those doing social change", I just thought it was really patronizing quite honestly. (Personal interview, September 16, 2002)

As the founder alludes, NPower and NPower NY relied on the democracy of the market to provide clients: any nonprofit organization that was willing and able to pay for technology assistance services could get them from NPower. NPower's adoption of market principles arose from its early connections to for-profit companies like Microsoft, Starbucks and Cisco. They reached maturity with NPower NY's embracement of more diverse and intense corporate partnerships.

Enterprising foundations

NPower was started with funding from Microsoft. The organization solidified its partnership in 2000 when Microsoft funded a national expansion of NPower with $25 million ($10 million in cash and $15 million in software). A manager from Microsoft's community affairs department explained the expansion: "[Microsoft] would provide substantial capital funding, sort of like seed funding for three years, up to $250 [thousand] per year for three years, plus software, professional support services, connections to our local field offices for volunteers, or board members or whatever is appropriate for NPower. As long as the local community came together and matched the money"(Personal interview, June 6, 2002).

NPower NY was the first and arguably most successful affiliate created in that expansion. One of the conditions Microsoft set on its funding was for the start-up to identify matching funds from the local community. The people who founded NPower NY had existing relationships with large corporations in New York City. The organization began with board members from JP Morgan Chase Bank, Flatiron Partners (a venture capital firm) and Accenture (a multinational consulting firm). Such corporate partnerships made the people starting NPower NY particularly attractive to NPower and Microsoft. As the manager of community affairs from Microsoft explained, "in New York, heck, they already had the funders there. Their funding dwarfed what Microsoft was bringing. If someone asks you what has been the most successful start-up [among NPower affiliates], it was probably New York" (Personal interview, June 6, 2002). This also made NPower and Microsoft attractive to the founders of what would become NPower NY. As the executive director of NPower NY recalled in an interview, "I knew she [NPower's founder] was the real deal because she had a reputation out there in the community already, and she was starting this Microsoft partnership. It was already buzzing in the community that this Microsoft/NPower thing was in formation. In fact one of the people I talked to said that [the founder] was about to launch this partnership, so I knew right away that she was the real deal. She had Microsoft on her side" (Personal interview, August 30, 2001).

NPower NY had key advantages over many social enterprises in funding its start-up. Being incorporated as a 501(c)(3) meant that it could more easily garner donations from foundations. Key partnerships in the nonprofit sector also afforded it access to a pool of potential clients. For example, it attracted both funding and a portfolio of clients from the Robin Hood Foundation, a foundation modeled on social venture philanthropy. Furthermore, having a strong for-profit presence on the board meant NPower NY could more easily tap into networks of corporate funders. Research shows that corporations tend to donate more heavily in communities and cities in which their head-quarters are located (Useem, 1987). NPower NY's business and service provision model made it difficult to raise money from many nonprofit foundations beyond Robin Hood. As the director of development explained, "half the time they [foundation officers] do not even understand [technology]. People say they do not understand technology even though it is sitting on their desk and in their pockets" (Personal interview, April 10, 2003). However, corporate donors understood the importance of information technology for organizations and were willing to support such endeavors.

Like all social enterprises, NPower NY was situated in the precarious position of balancing the double-bottom lines of social and financial returns (Brinckerhoff, 2000). Its nonprofit status relieved some pressure to produce revenue much beyond expenditures. However, the organization remained accountable to organizations in multiple institutional domains, each with different evaluative criteria for determining legitimacy. On the one side, corporate partners and board members from the private sector expected NPower NY to generate enough earned revenue to be sustainable. From the corporate side, NPower NY was legitimate insofar as it adopted the rhetoric and practices of for-profit organizations. To be accountable in the for-profit institutional domain, the organization had to generate market forms of worth. On the other side, nonprofit organizations as clients, collaborators and competitors expected NPower NY to provide services that were affordable to various constituencies. To the nonprofit side, NPower NY was legitimate insofar as it expressed charitable ideals, such as low- or no-cost services. To be accountable to the nonprofit institutional domain, it had to generate social forms of worth. In the following sections, I show how NPower NY generates market and social forms of worth, while attempting to balance the two.

The market bases of moral legitimacy

The entrepreneurial spirit was a key part of NPower from its inception. At the NY affiliate, it was particularly fervent. A foundation officer from Robin Hood explained, "NPower NY raised their start-up capital prior to ever delivering a service, which is very unusual. Most [nonprofit organizations] start out of a storefront delivering services, and then go about back filling the need for money. I think what that has allowed NPower NY to do is to really be very conscious about how soon do they get out there, what do they promise, and not letting the delivery of services run ahead of their capitalization. So it is a little bit more like a business model" (Personal interview, January 27, 2004).

NPower NY took business models seriously. Board members, executive directors and staff of the organization often referred to NPower NY as a start-up in the early years of operation. Their approach to entrepreneurialism borrowed heavily from the rhetoric and style of New York's dot-com boom. Two of the founding board members had extensive experience in the venture capital world of New York's new media industrial district. One worked at JP Morgan Chase; the other for a venture capital firm called Flatiron Partners. I asked a board member whether he envisioned his role as a venture capitalist for NPower. "No question," he replied, "it is just that we are not going to take it public and cash out." He continued, "What I think is unique is that it [NPower NY] is run more and evaluated more as a venture nonprofit than many other nonprofits are" (Personal interview, May 16, 2003). Another board member told me:

> What we [NPower NY's board] did is we said let us fund this thing as if we were to fund a start-up. Let us cover one year's worth of operations before we have even launched. I think we got *some* traditional foundation money...But the money that came in from foundations and the money that came in from corporations was non-specific operating funds, which is really unique and very much like what a VC [venture capitalist] would do. When a VC puts money behind a company, he does not say "this for your marketing program". What he says is "this is for the business. Now, let us be very engaged and meet on a monthly basis and make sure that we are spending the money appropriately". (Personal interview, May 6, 2003)

While board members actively referred to the organization as a start-up and talked about applying venture capital models to NPower NY, they also understood that the organization's returns were social, i.e. going to help other organizations in the sector, rather than private. As one of the board members with venture capital experience explains,

> Without waxing too rhapsodic about what is going on [at NPower NY], I think that in some ways it is the best combination of the energy and enthusiasm you find in a start-up with the walk through walls commitment to a mission that you will find at the most altruistic of nonprofits...There are two kinds of people that go to the for-profit start-ups: there are the type that believe fervently in what they are doing, and it can be just a piece of software, but that what they are doing is going to change the world, and then there are the folks that believe that what they are doing is going to make them rich. NPower has plenty of the former, and none of the latter. (Personal interview, May 6, 2003)

The rhetoric of high-tech startup combined with nonprofit values was also expressed in organizational practices. While organized as a 501(c)(3) and working exclusively with other nonprofit organizations, NPower NY expressed a near-constant internal dialogue about how they could generate sustainable (earned) revenue. Many nonprofit organizations are concerned with sustainable revenues. With cuts in government funding and private foundation funding becoming increasingly competitive, nonprofit organizations are squeezed to find revenue sources. NPower NY did not receive government funding. All of their donations came from private sources: individual donors, private foundations, corporate foundations and corporate partnerships. To supplement their donations, the organization continually sought ways to generate new revenue and take better advantage of the revenue they had already generated.

Market values generate market forms of worth

Collaborating with for-profit consulting firms and venture capitalists profoundly shaped NPower NY's revenue model. In the beginning, the organization derived most of its revenue from fundraising. The executive director estimated as much as 75 percent of the revenue came from corporate and foundation grants in the first year of operation (Field notes, October 30, 2001). However, directives from the board, which was constituted by members of their for-profit partners, consistently sought to increase the amount of earned revenue the organization generated. One manager told the staff that the board expects NPower NY to generate 80 percent of its revenue from earned income by the end of their fourth year of operation (Field notes, January 21, 2003).

To increase earned income, NPower NY management worked closely with a board member from Accenture (a multinational consulting firm) to "standardize" and "streamline" the way consulting was done in the organization during this time (Field notes, May 7, 2002). Aside from efficiency gains, managers enacted two strategies to generate more earned revenue: increasing the number of billable hours consultants worked each week and the hourly rates they charged. To achieve the former, the director of consulting reconfigured consultants' schedules to attempt to increase billable hours from 20 to 24 hours per week. The goal was to continue increasing that number to 26 hours per week in three months (Field notes, March 25, 2003). To increase the hourly rates charged, the director of consulting was instructed to pursue actively more complex consulting engagements as well as to bill separately for "emergency" services, those falling outside standard contracted tasks. Much of consultants' time was spent working on basic installation and maintenance activities, e.g. setting computer networks or updating virus definitions on clients' servers. However, NPower NY could charge higher fees for more complex services, such as technology planning or website/database integration projects, especially for large nonprofit organizations, which had complicated computer networks and large budgets for technology.

As a result, NPower NY was able to increase its percentage of earned revenue over the course of my time in the field. Initially, it was operating at about 20 percent of earned income but moved toward 30 percent by the end of 2001. By the middle of 2002, the organization was moving closer to 45 percent with a goal of 50 percent by the end of 2003. In contrast, Media Jumpstart was able to achieve at best 20–25 percent of earned income during the same time span, according to a manager there.

The drive toward increasing earned revenue was predicated on a market order of worth, but justified otherwise on a civic order of worth. The executive manager explained NPower NY's business-like behavior:

> The bottom line is that in order to be an ongoing entity, we have to protect the bottom line. I think that is one of the mistakes that the other folks [NTAPs that closed recently] did not do was think enough about that. If you do not think enough about that, you can shut your doors in a couple of years if you do not watch out. We have got to be very aware of that. I think that we walk that line carefully and I do not ever think that it is mission *or* finances. It is both. In order to have the impacts you want to make, you have to understand how a really good solid grounding of both of those works. And they will interact with each other, but you cannot just think about doing good and not think about whether you are financially viable...all this money allows us to do things like free training weeks and to lower the prices on some of our services. I do not think they make that distinction, they just say all we do is talk about money all day. Well, the money is going to good stuff. If we make it, then we share that. It is not like it is going to the board of directors in the form of bonuses. That, I think people lose sight of, but I think it is important for us to never lose sight of that. (Personal interview, December 8, 2003)

Such a justification expressed the importance of a market order of worth to maintaining NPower NY's market legitimacy to its corporate partners and board members from the private sector. However, such justifications did not prevent competing NTAPs from denouncing NPower NY as "N-pire". Managers tried to ignore such denunciations as coming from the "social justice, social change crowd...[which is] just a different audience" (Field notes, May 1, 2003). Yet, the concern over such perceptions had to be addressed. As the executive director explained, "some of the folks out there say we are getting so bottom line oriented, where all we care about is the revenue, [that] we do not care about the mission anymore" (Personal interview, December 8, 2003).

NPower NY's relationship to corporate partners shaped the organization in profound ways, producing accounts that helped it establish moral legitimacy in the business institutional domain. However, these very same accounts also threatened to undermine its moral legitimacy in the nonprofit institutional domain.

Blending social and market values to generate multiple forms of worth

To combat the perception that it was too market-oriented, NPower NY blended social values with their business-like practices to generate social forms of worth. For example, it implemented a matrix fee structure based on the budget of the client and the level of difficulty of the engagement. The lower end of the fee structure charged nonprofits with smaller budget fees that were lower than market rates. These fees were subsidized by charging wealthier nonprofit organizations much higher rates. Additionally, the executive director and board strategized that larger nonprofits would also likely need more complex services, which would also come at a premium. The executive director explained the fee structure in a consultants' meeting:

> We are moving toward three tiers and three categories for consulting projects. This will be based on the skill sets necessary to get the work done. These are general guidelines for the pricing. Many projects will be priced differently in the future. The lowest level is actually lower than the present pricing; it includes most scheduled support and basic web design. The middle is a step up; it includes low-end networking and database as well as high-end scheduled support. The high level includes strategic planning and complex work – the work that requires higher level skills that we have to pay for. With work that cuts across these tiers, we will have to work out a blended rate. We also added a new category of nonprofit, those organizations with budgets greater than $10 million. (Field notes, April 8, 2003)

The matrix fee structure allowed NPower NY to blend social and market values simultaneously. Higher rates for more complex services, especially to larger nonprofits, generated revenues that could be used to subsidize services to smaller organizations or pro bono work, such as distributing and installing free anti-virus software on computers at nonprofit organizations throughout New York City. The revenue generation scheme allowed NPower NY to be socially accountable to the nonprofit sector (providing low-cost or pro bono services to small nonprofit organizations) while also being financially accountable to its for-profit partners (earning revenues by generating higher fees from serving larger nonprofits and delivering more complex services). The result was the integration of nonprofit and for-profit values.

The result blends market and social principles: making money at one end of the matrix means the organization can continue to provide pro bono or inexpensive services at the other end of the matrix. This blending of justificatory principles represents an entrepreneurial strategy of keeping multiple moral logics in play (Stark 1996, 2009). In doing so, NPower NY responds to denunciations from multiple moral standpoints simultaneously. To competing, politically progressive NTAPs, the organization claims to provide an important social good, e.g. "free training weeks" and reduced prices for technology services. To its business partners and donors, the organization claims to be financially responsible with their donations.

Social values generate social forms of social worth

The consulting and training departments at NPower NY generated revenue and therefore reflected the organization's commitment to market values. To generate purely social forms of worth, it created a charitable program as well. Called Technology Service Corps (TSC), the program "trains talented New York City youth, age 18 to 25, from low-income communities on networking, computer basics, and web development skills and places them in available nonprofit staff positions as junior information technology administrators" (Npower – NY, 2002, 4). The program is small (serving eight to ten students at a time) and intensive (students train full-time over an eight-week period and work as interns at nonprofit organizations for another four weeks afterward).

TSC was completely funded by donations; it did not generate revenue for NPower NY. Foundations provided grant support for the program, making it, as one manager explained, "the only department that we have a restricted grant for" (Personal interview, June 19, 2003). Yet, the program was expensive to run, especially for the number of students they served. Two full-time staff members oversaw the teaching and training and one director worked exclusively to assemble the components of the program and maintain it. The program's expense per student made it difficult for the development department to solicit donations from foundations. TSC draws resources from NPower NY's general operating funds. Yet, in a board meeting, members found a silver lining in that: losing money on TSC meant they could charge closer to market rates for consulting services without jeopardizing their tax exempt status (Field notes, December 5, 2002).

Throughout my time in the field, NPower NY struggled internally with two aspects of TSC. First, working with students from low-income backgrounds created social work problems that the technology-oriented staff at NPower NY was ill-equipped to manage. This problem was generally limited to staff that had hands-on contact with the students of the TSC program. At times, TSC staff were called on to help students complete applications for food stamps or find temporary housing. This strained the time and resources of staff. It also contributed to a second problem: since TSC relied exclusively on donations and did not generate any revenue, staff continually struggled to integrate with the rest of the organization. Despite being part of NPower NY's original business plan, in practice TSC did not fit in with consulting and training as directors and board members envisioned. Aside from the social work aspects of the program, TSC drew resources away from consulting and training. To business-minded directors and board members, TSC diverted funds that could be invested elsewhere in the organization to generate more revenues. During my time in the field, directors and board members floated various schemes to help TSC generate revenues. For example, one idea was to send TSC graduates into the field as junior consultants, charging lower fees for their services. This plan was abandoned when directors realized the graduates, while technically proficient, lacked many of the customer service skills NPower NY demands of its consultants.

Despite the problems with the program's implementation, the directors and board members considered TSC successful, particularly as it generated goodwill for the organization. Working with low-income youths provided members of the NTAP field with proof that NPower NY was legitimately nonprofit. TSC as a purely charitable endeavor produced social forms of worth. The executive director explained at a TSC event, "consulting and training are the 'bread and butter', but TSC is the 'heart and soul' [of NPower NY]" (Field notes, January 21, 2003). Aside from foundations that rewarded NPower NY with restricted grants for the program, other actors in the NTAP field responded positively to TSC. Several NTAPs, including the LINC Project, took on TSC students as interns. TSC allowed NPower NY to be socially accountable to foundations and other actors that might evaluate their moral legitimacy from the standpoint of a nonprofit institutional domain.

Discussion

NPower NY leans toward the business and market oriented side of social enterprise. The organization seeks and receives much of its moral legitimacy in that institutional domain. Moral legitimacy in the business institutional domain affords the organization access to corporate partnerships as well as the material and symbolic resources such relationships provide. As I have shown, the basis for NPower NY's moral legitimacy in the business sector is based on the organization's ability to produce market forms of worth through revenue generation schemes, such as increasing earned revenue through enhanced efficiencies ("streamlining"). Producing market forms of worth demonstrates a commitment to fiscal sustainability to resource holders, such as corporate partners and board members from the business sector.

Yet, gaining moral legitimacy among businesses risks undermining NPower NY's moral legitimacy in the nonprofit institutional domain, particularly among activist NTAPs in the organizational field. The latter have reason to attack NPower NY's moral legitimacy in the nonprofit institutional domain. By establishing moral legitimacy, the organization also establishes the cognitive legitimacy of its enterprising model of technology assistance, which threatens the material and symbolic existence of politically progressive NTAPs like the Circuit Riders (McInerney, 2009). The result is a contentious organizational field in which NPower NY and the Circuit Riders vie for legitimacy. To maintain moral legitimacy in the nonprofit institutional domain, NPower NY generates blended and purely social forms of worth. For example, the organization tempers its commercial impulses with a matrix fee structure and provides direct social services with its workforce development program.

NPower NY grew quickly in terms of budget and staff size due to the entrepreneurial strategy of combining multiple orders of worth to appeal to actors across institutional domains. Their strategy allowed actors from market and nonprofit institutional domains to hold the organization accountable to different evaluative principles, which constituted different justifications for moral legitimacy. Yet, the organization's success depended on their access to powerful actors in the market sector, as well as institutional shifts taking place across the nonprofit sector toward greater acceptance of market values (Dart 2004a, 2004b; McInerney, 2008; Young, 2003).

Conclusion

Different forms of worth provide the evaluative bases for different claims of legitimacy. Market forms of worth appeal to corporate partners and board members from the private sector. They establish the moral legitimacy of NPower NY in the market institutional domain. Social forms of worth appeal to nonprofit clients, collaborators and foundations. They establish the moral legitimacy of NPower NY in the nonprofit institutional domain. Hybrid practices, like the matrix fee structure, generate multiple forms of worth simultaneously to convey a multivalent story. The result is an entrepreneurial strategy, which allows organizations to justify their behavior to multiple constituencies (Thévenot, 2001). As Stark (2005, 5) explains, *"entrepreneurship is the ability to keep multiple orders of worth in play and to exploit the resulting overlap"*. As hybrid organizational forms, social enterprises will be successful to the degree they blend multiple forms of worth to demonstrate legitimacy in multiple institutional domains. Yet, such strategies place the organization in the unenviable position of having to produce constantly multiple accounts of worth to justify their legitimacy across institutional domains.

References

Anheier, Helmut K. and Stefan Toepler. 1998. "Commerce and the Muse: Are Art Museums Becoming Commercial?" In *To Profit or Not to Profit: The Commercial Transformation of the Nonprofit Sector.*, edited by B. A. Weisbrod. New York: Cambridge University Press, pp. 233–248.

Ashforth, Blake E. and Barrie W. Gibbs. 1990. "The Double-Edge of Organizational Legitimation." *Organization Science* 1: 177–194.

Austin, James E., Howard H. Stevenson, and Wei-Skillern Jane. 2006. "Social and Commercial Entrepreneurship: Same, Different, or Both?" *Entrepreneurship: Theory and Practice* 30: 1–22.

Barley, Stephen R. and Pamela S. Tolbert. 1997. "Institutionalization and Structuration: Studying the Links between Action and Institution." *Organization Studies* 18: 93–117.

Barth, Fredrik. 2000. "Economic Spheres in Darfur." In *Entrepreneurship: The Social Science View*, edited by R. Swedberg. New York: Oxford University Press, pp. 139–160.

Battilana, Julie. 2006. "Agency and Institution: The Enabling Role of Individuals' Social Position." *Organization* 13: 653–676.

Battilana, Julie and Silvia Dorado. 2010. "Building Sustainable Hybrid Organizations: The Case of Commercial Microfinance Organizations." *Academy of Management Journal* 53:1419–1440.

Battilana, Julie, Bernard Leca, and Eva Boxenbaum. 2009. "How Actors Change Institutions: Towards a Theory of Institutional Entrepreneurship." *Academy of Management Annals* 3: 65–107.

Berger, Peter L. and Thomas Luckmann. 1966. *The Social Construction of Reality: A Treatise in the Sociology of Knowledge*. New York: Anchor Books.

Bielefeld, Wolfgang. 2006. "Issues in Social Enterprise and Social Entrepreneurship." *Journal of Public Affairs Education* 15: 69–86.

Boltanski, Luc and Laurent Thévenot. 1991. *De la Justification*. Paris: Gallimard.

Boltanski, Luc and Laurent Thévenot. 2006. *On Justification: Economies of Worth*, tr. C. Porter. Princeton: Princeton University Press.

Borzaga, Carlo and Jacques Defourny. 2001. *The Emergence of Social Enterprise*. London and New York: Routledge.

Boxenbaum, Eva and Julie Battilana. 2005. "Importation as Innovation: Transposing Managerial Practices Across Fields." *Strategic Organization* 3: 355–383.

Brinckerhoff, Peter C. 2000. *Social Entrepreneurship : The Art of Mission-Based Innovation*. New York: John Wiley.

Brint, Steven and Jerome Karabel. 1991. "Institutional Origins and Transformations: The Case of American Community Colleges." In *The New Institutionalism in Organizational Analysis*, edited by W. W. Powell and P. DiMaggio. Chicago: University of Chicago Press, pp. 311–336.

Child, Curtis. 2010. "Whither the Turn? The Ambiguous Nature of Nonprofits' Commercial Revenue." *Social Forces* 89: 145–162.

Clohesy, William W. 2000. "Altruism and the Endurance of the Good." *Voluntas* 11: 237–253.

Cooney, Kate. 2006. "The Institutional and Technical Structuring of Nonprofit Ventures: Case Study of a Hybrid Organization Caught Between Two Fields." *Voluntas* 17: 143–161.

Dart, Raymond. 2004a. "Being 'Business-Like' in a Nonprofit Organization: A Grounded and Inductive Typology." *Nonprofit and Voluntary Sector Quarterly* 33:290–310.

Dart, Raymond. 2004b. "The Legitimacy of Social Enterprise." *Nonprofit Management and Leadership* 4: 411–424.

Dees, J. Gregory, Peter Economy, Jed Emerson, and NetLibrary Inc. 2001. *Enterprising Nonprofits a Toolkit for Social Entrepreneurs*. New York: Wiley.

Dees, J. Gregory, Jed Emerson, and Peter Economy. 2002. *Strategic Tools for Social Entrepreneurs : Enhancing the Performance of Your Enterprising Nonprofit*. New York: Wiley.

DiMaggio, Paul. 1991. "Constructing An Organizational Field as a Professional Project: u.s. Art Museums, 1920–1940." In *The New Institutionalism in Organizational Analysis*, edited by W. W. Powell and P. DiMaggio. Chicago: University of Chicago Press, p. 267–292.

DiMaggio, Paul J. and Helmut Anheier. 1990. "The Sociology of Nonprofit Organizations and Sectors." *Annual Review of Sociology* 16:137–159.

DiMaggio, Paul and Walter W. Powell. 1991a. "Introduction." In *The New Institutionalism in Organizational Analysis*, edited by W. W. Powell and P. DiMaggio. Chicago: University of Chicago Press, pp. 1–38.

DiMaggio, Paul and Walter W. Powell. 1991b. "The Iron Cage Revisited: Institutional Isomorphism and Collective Rationality." In *The New Institutionalism in Organizational Analysis*, edited by W. W. Powell and P. DiMaggio. Chicago: University of Chicago Press, pp. 63–82.

Eikenberry, Angela M. and Jodie Drapal Kluver. 2004. "The Marketization of the Nonprofit Sector: Civil Society at Risk?" *Public Administration Review* 64: 132–140.

Emerson, Jed and F. Twersky. 1996. *New Social Entrepreneurs: The Success, Challenge, and Lessons of Non-profit Enterprise Creation*. San Francisco: Roberts Foundation.

Emerson, Robert M., Rachel I. Fretz, and Linda L. Shaw. 1995. *Writing Ethnographic Fieldnotes*. Chicago: University of Chicago Press.

Friedland, Roger and Robert R. Alford. 1991. "Bringing Society Back In: Symbols, Practices, and Institutional Contradictions." In *The New Institutionalism in Organizational Analysis*, edited by W. W. Powell and P. DiMaggio. Chicago: University of Chicago Press, pp. 232–263.

Frumkin, Peter. 2002. *On Being Nonprofit : A Conceptual and Policy Primer*. Cambridge, MA: Harvard University Press.

Frumkin, Peter and Alice Andre-Clark. 2000. "When Missions, Markets, and Politics Collide: Values and Strategy in the Nonprofit Human Services." *Nonprofit and Voluntary Sector Quarterly* 29:141–163.

Giddens, Anthony. 1984. *The Constitution of Society: Outline of the Theory of Structuration*. Cambridge: Polity Press.

Guo, Baorong. 2006. "Charity for Profit? Exploring Factors Associated with the Commercialization of Human Service Nonprofits." *Nonprofit and Voluntary Sector Quarterly* 35: 123–138.

Hasenfeld, Yeheskel and Benjamin Gidron. 2005. "Understanding Multi-purpose Hybrid Voluntary Organizations: The Contributions of Theories of Civil Society, Social Movements, and Non-profit Organizations." *Journal of Civil Society* 1: 97–112.

Hodder, Ian. 2000. "The Interpretation of Documents and Material Culture." In *The Handbook of Qualitative Research*, edited by N. K. Denzin and Y. S. Lincoln. Thousand Oaks: Sage Publications, pp. 703–715.

James, Estelle. 1998. "Commercialism Among Nonprofits: Objectives, Opportunities, and Constraints." In *To Profit or Not to Profit: The Commercial Transformation of the Nonprofit Sector*, edited by B. A. Weisbrod. New York: Cambridge University Press, pp. 271–286.

Jeavons, Thomas H. 1992. "When the Management Is the Message: Relating Values to Management Practice in Nonprofit Organizations." *Nonprofit Management and Leadership* 2: 403–417.

Jepperson, Ronald L. 1991. "Institutions, Institutional Effects, and Institutionalization." In *The New Institutionalism in Organizational Analysis*, edited by W. W. Powell and P. DiMaggio. Chicago: University of Chicago Press, Pp. 143–163.

Kanter, Rosa Beth Moss and David V. Summers. 1987. "Doing Well while Doing Good: Dilemmas of Performance Measurement in Nonprofit Organizations and the Need for a Multiple-Constituency Approach." In *The Nonprofit Sector: A Research Handbook*, edited by W. W. Powell. New Haven: Yale University Press, pp. 154–166.

Lampel, Joseph and Alan D. Meyer. 2008. "Field-Configuring Events as Structuring Mechanisms: How Conferences, Ceremonies, and Trade Shows Constitute New Technologies, Industries, and Markets." *Journal of Management Studies* 45: 1025–1035.

Martin, John Levi. 2003. "What is Field Theory?" *American Journal of Sociology* 109: 1–49.

Marwell, Nicole P. and Paul-Brian McInerney. 2005. "The Nonprofit/For-Profit Continuum: Theorizing the Dynamics of Mixed-Form Markets." *Nonprofit and Voluntary Sector Quarterly* 34: 7–28.

McInerney, Paul-Brian. 2007. "Geeks for Good: Technology Evangelism and the Role of Circuit Riders in IT Adoption among Nonprofits." In *Nonprofits and Technology: Emerging Research for Usable Knowledge*, edited by M. Cortes and K. M. Rafter. Chicago: Lyceum, pp. 148–162.

McInerney, Paul-Brian. 2008. "Showdown at Kykuit: Field-Configuring Events as Loci for Conventionalizing Accounts." *Journal of Management Studies* 45: 1089–1116.

McInerney, Paul-Brian. 2009. "Technology Movements and the Politics of Free/Open Source Software." *Science, Technology, and Human Values* 34: 206–233.

Npower NY. 2002. "NPower NY 2002 Annual Report." New York City.

Roper, Juliet and George Cheney. 2005. "Leadership, Learning, and Human Resource Management: The Meanings of Social Entrepreneurship Today." *Corporate Governance* 5: 95–104.

Salamon, Lester M. 1999. *America's Nonprofit Sector: A Primer*. New York: The Foundation Center.

Salamon, Lester M. 2003. *The Resilient Sector: The State of Nonprofit America*. Washington, DC: Brookings Institution Press.

Scott, W. Richard. 1994. "Conceptualizing Organizational Fields: Linking Organizations and Societal Systems." In *Systemrationalitat und Partialinteresse* (System Rationality and Partial Interests), edited by H.-U. Derlien, U. Gerhardt, and F. W. Scharpf. Baden-Baden: Nomos Verlagsgesellschaft, pp. 203–221.

Scott, W. Richard. 2008. *Institutions and Organizations: Ideas and Interests*. Los Angeles: Sage.

Segal, Lewis M. and Burton A. Weisbrod. 1998. "Interdependence of Commercial and Donative Revenues." In *To Profit or Not to Profit: The Commercial Transformation of the Nonprofit Sector*, edited by B. A. Weisbrod. New York: Cambridge University Press, pp. 105–128.

Seley, John E. and Julian Wolpert. 2002. "New York City's Nonprofit Sector." The New York City Nonprofits Project, New York.

Star, Susan Leigh. 1999. "The Ethnography of Infrastructure." *American Behavioral Scientist* 43: 377–391.

Stark, David. 1996. "Recombinant Property in East European Capitalism." *American Journal of Sociology* 101: 993–1028.

Stark, David. 2005. "For a Sociology of Worth." Center on Organizational Innovation, Working Paper, New York.

Stark, David. 2009. *The Sense of Dissonance: Accounts of Worth in Economic Life.* Princeton: Princeton University Press.

Suchman, Mark. 1995. "Managing Legitimacy: Strategic and Institutional Approaches." *Academy of Management Review* 20: 571–610.

Thévenot, Laurent. 2001. "Organized Complexity: Conventions of Coordination and the Composition of Economic Arrangements." *European Journal of Social Theory* 4: 405–425.

Thompson, John L. 2002. "The World of the Social Entrepreneur." *The International Journal of Public Sector Management* 15: 412–432.

Useem, Michael. 1987. "Corporate Philanthropy." In *The Nonprofit Sector: A Research Handbook*, edited by W. W. Powell. New Haven: Yale University Press, pp. 340–360.

Van de Ven, Andrew H. and George P. Huber. 1990. "Longitudinal Field Research Methods for Studying Processes of Organizational Change." *Organization Science* 1: 213–219.

Vedres, Balazs and David Stark. 2010. "Structural Folds: Generative Disruption in Overlapping Groups." *American Journal of Sociology* 115: 1150–1190.

Weerawardena, Jay and Gillian Sullivan Mort. 2006. "Investigating Social Entrepreneurship: A Multidimensional Model." *Journal of World Business* 41: 21–25.

Weisbrod, Burton A. 1998. "The Nonprofit Mission and Its Financing: Growing Links between Nonprofits and the Rest of the Economy." In *To Profit or Not to Profit: The Commercial Transformation of the Nonprofit Sector*, edited by B. A. Weisbrod. New York: Cambridge University Press, pp. 1–24.

Young, Dennis R. 1998. "Commercialism in Nonprofit Social Service Associations: Its Character, Significance, and Rationale." In *To Profit or Not to Profit: The Commercial Transformation of the Nonprofit Sector*, edited by B. A. Weisbrod. New York: Cambridge University Press, pp. 195–216.

Young, Dennis R. 2003. "New Trends in the US Non-profit Sector: Towards Market Integration." In Organisation for Economic Co-operation and Development (OECD) (ed.), *The Non-profit Sector in a Changing Economy*. Paris: OECD, pp. 61–77.

8
Chasing the Double-Bottom Line: Fair Trade and the Elusive Win–Win

Curtis Child

Social enterprises embody a problematic proposition. They are premised on the idea that it is possible to create simultaneously social and economic value in a direct, explicit way, yet it would seem that each of these goals is in some amount in consequential tension with the other. The argument of social enterprise is nevertheless that one outcome – financial or social returns – need not be seen as the eventual by-product of focusing on the other, but rather that both can be productively pursued in an immediate sense. Scholars have only started to examine in detail *how* social enterprises accomplish this delicate balancing act.

The literature on social enterprise and social purpose businesses has been primarily concerned with describing the trend broadly (Cooney and Shanks, 2010), contemplating its legal ramifications (Taylor, 2010), advocating for its expansion (Prahalad, 2004; Yunus, 2008; Yunus and Weber, 2010) and providing inspiring accounts as well as how-to or best-practice instructions for aspiring social entrepreneurs (Bornstein, 2004; Lynch and Walls, 2009). Some work has been more critical (e.g. Edwards, 2008). But, with few exceptions (such as Cooney, 2006), the literature has failed to problematize adequately social enterprise, thus overlooking its sometimes contradictory nature while broadcasting its perceived benefits.

If we approach social enterprise with a critical eye – as something that must be *accomplished* rather than something that just *is* – then certain questions immediately become evident. The one I reflect on in this chapter is: How do social enterprises balance their dual commitments to prosocial and financial goals? We cannot answer this question until we first understand the ambiguous institutional terrain on which social enterprises operate, so I propose a schema for thinking about the matrix of options available to social enterprises as well as their variable consequences. I then discuss how well commonsense expectations derived from the schema reflect reality, using the fair trade industry as a reference point. Doing so highlights some unexpected results. For example, it turns out that being able to act in ways that increase the likelihood of maximizing social *and* financial returns – the Holy Grail of social enterprise – is actually more challenging than it might seen from a distance, and fair trade businesses will often be required to forego one goal while in pursuit of the other. Although most observers would not be surprised to learn that businesses will favor financial commitments over social ones, it is perhaps more difficult to understand the circumstances under which such ventures would pursue prosocial ends if they interfered with revenue potential – especially considering the market pressures under which for-profit enterprises operate. I use the case of Coastal Coffees to illustrate not only the inherent complexity of social enterprise generally but in order to provide one explanation for why, if market pressures exert such a compelling force on for-profit social enterprises, these organizations might be willing to hold them in check. Data collected during a three-year investigation of two social enterprise industries – fair trade and socially responsible investing – suggest that there is not a simple answer to why businesses would pursue social goals even if a financial calculus would compel them to do otherwise. There are a variety of mechanisms that serve to keep organizations focused on their social missions, and I focus on one that is evident in the fair trade industry – namely, the effect that first-hand encounters with the communities impacted by their business decisions can have on social business practitioners.

Background and data

The empirical context for this chapter is the fair trade industry. According to FINE (Krier, 2008, 23), an international network of fair trade organizations, "fair trade" is

> a trading partnership, based on dialogue, transparency and respect, that seeks greater equity in international trade. It contributes to sustainable development by offering better trading conditions to, and securing the rights of, marginalized producers and workers – especially in the South. Fair Trade organizations (backed by consumers) are actively engaged in supporting producers, in awareness raising and in campaigning for changes in the rules and practices of conventional international trade.

Fair trade businesses, therefore, are social enterprises par excellence. As for-profit ventures, they are committed to financial returns, yet as participants to the fair trade movement, they also have decidedly prosocial ambitions. They operate in the for-profit marketplace, but they do so in unconventional ways by actively pursuing social goals alongside monetary ones. For this reason, they are ideal sites to examine the complexities of this particular organizational form.

As a movement, the history of fair trade reaches back to at least the 1940s and 1950s, when European groups such as Oxfam UK and Fair Trade Original (a Dutch organization) began importing and retailing goods produced by artisans from the global South with the explicit goal of supporting economic and community development (see Fridell, 2007). In the 1950s and 1960s, US groups such as the Mennonite's Central Committee and the Church of the Brethren likewise began supporting the fair trade cause (eventually evolving into Ten Thousand Villages and SERRV, respectively). Other organizations, such as Equal Exchange in the early 1980s, followed suit.

The fair trade movement grew considerably over the next 30 years. By 2008, Fair Trade USA (formerly TransFair USA), a US-based fair trade certification initiative, boasted that it was responsible for tracking the supply chains between more than 800 US companies and the 1.5 million farmers from whom they source, auditing in the process more than 40,000 interactions between producers, importers and manufacturers (TransFair USA, 2010). In 2010, Fair Trade USA imported nearly 110 million pounds of fair trade certified coffee, along with 51 million pounds of produce, 18 million pounds of sugar, 4 million pounds of cocoa and nearly 10 million flower stems, as well as millions of pounds of tea, grain, spice, honey and wine (Fair Trade USA, 2010). Total retail sales for the year were $1.2 billion (TransFair USA, 2010). As much as they demonstrate the tremendous growth of the movement, these figures actually underestimate the scope of the fair trade market, since they do not include the sales of goods for which no certification exists, such as handicrafts and textiles. Nor do they represent fair trade transactions that are monitored by other certification initiatives, such as the Fair for Life Social & FairTrade Certification Programme (a certification initiative that has recently been growing in popularity), Utz Certified, the Rainforest Alliance, and others.

As part of a larger study, I conducted 40 semi-structured interviews with members of 30 fair trade businesses between 2009 and 2011, supplemented with participation and observations (including numerous informal interviews) at industry conferences and other events. Because of space limitations, I have drawn selectively on these data (but see Child, 2011 for more detail).

Conceptualizing social enterprise outcomes

Conceptually, we can think of social enterprises as pursuing two goals: social returns and financial returns (see Figure 8.1). From this perspective, practitioners make decisions that can have four ideal-typical outcomes – the most desired one being the so-called win-win outcome that increases the likelihood of maximizing both prosocial and economic returns. When faced with such a possibility, the obvious choice is to pursue it. A second possibility is that a decision leads the company to diminish the likelihood of maximizing social and economic returns. In this case, the organization would unproblematically avoid the situation. A third (and fourth) scenario

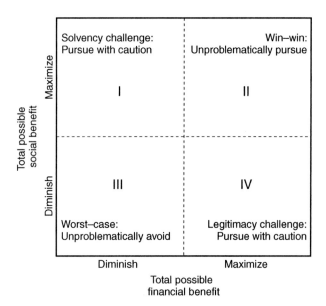

Figure 8.1 Ideal-typical outcomes for social enterprise decisions

is that one goal must be tempered in favor of the other. On the one hand, a decision could increase the likelihood of maximizing social benefit while decreasing the likelihood of maximizing financial returns. Or, a decision could increase the prospects of maximizing financial benefit but diminish the chances of maximizing social returns.

Decisions that locate an organization within quadrants I or IV have particularly interesting implications. First, a social enterprise that consistently favors its social goals over its financial ones risks insolvency. Although the likelihood of achieving the prosocial mission increases, its financial prospects diminish. This is especially an issue for *for-profit* ventures, which are subject to the full force of market dynamics that cannot typically be cushioned through the receipt of philanthropic support in the same way that nonprofits can. Consistently favoring financial goals at the expense of social ones makes it more likely that the enterprise will remain solvent, but it does present the organization with a potential legitimacy problem. If relevant stakeholders perceive the venture as focused more on earning revenues than providing a social benefit, then their support for it will likely wane and its credibility will suffer.

Based on a logical reading of Figure 8.1, what empirical patterns might we expect to find among actual social enterprise ventures? Two choices are clear: avoid quadrant III and pursue quadrant II. One might assume that businesses would never (or at least rarely) pursue social mission over economic concerns (quadrant I) because the risks to the business's financial health – what I have labeled the solvency challenge – would be too great. Social enterprises might, however, make decisions that locate them in quadrant IV if they can devise ways to deal with the attendant legitimacy challenge, which they *can* do by taking advantage of the abundant rhetorical resources that are available to them. Spurred by the corporate social responsibility movement, a constellation of justifications and tropes have been used to frame virtually any business-oriented activity as prosocial. In the language of Figure 8.1, discursive resources are available to organizations that, if used, can help them to deal with credibility problems (quadrant IV) by framing decisions and their outcomes as actually consistent with quadrant II. That is, even decisions that clearly favor economic benefit over social mission can be framed and marketed as "win–win".

How well does reality match these expectations? My research on for-profit social enterprises suggests that this commonsense reading of the optimal decision-choices for social entrepreneurs does not entirely capture what is happening in the fair trade industry. One of the most obvious ways that expectations derived from Figure 8.1 fail to match reality has to do with quadrant II. Although social enterprises aspire to accomplish two goals, in practice market pressures and prosocial ones pull organizations in different directions. Despite the "doing well by doing good" rhetoric that often accompanies such initiatives, social enterprises must frequently make compromises. An importer of fair trade goods, for example, could be personally committed to the ideals of the fair trade mission but may actually find it easier to work with well-established exporting cooperatives rather than other communities that would likely benefit more from the exchange relationship. From a distance, working with *any* fair trade cooperative would seem to provide evidence of successfully pursuing a social mission, but when one examines the situation more closely it becomes clear that a degree of the prosocial goal has been sacrificed in favor of financial considerations. Although there may be a net social and financial benefit, this does not obviate the fact that the pursuit of one objective can limit the degree to which the other could be obtained. Hidden tradeoffs like these are common among the social enterprise ventures I studied.

Of course, as suggested above, practitioners will often represent their efforts as consistent with the likelihood of maximizing social and financial goals, and for this reason it is important to understand quadrant II. Making decisions that locate the organization within the quadrant means that it can stay financially profitable and at least outwardly committed to the business's social mission.

Insofar as quadrant I is concerned, there is some evidence to support the idea that social entrepreneurs avoid making decisions that favor social mission over financial security. Practitioners I interviewed spoke with clarity about the necessity of paying attention to market forces. And although they often seemed genuinely committed to their business's" prosocial goals, they were not starry-eyed about the realities of operating in the for-profit world. As one fair trader put it, "the market does a real good job of enforcing discipline that we're on our toes on the business side". Even so, practitioners did not altogether shy away from decisions that advanced a social goal while forfeiting the possibility of increased financial returns. In fact, they clearly pursued prosocial goals at times when there were no clear financial incentives for doing so. This is a remarkable observation, which I return to below, since it contradicts behavior that we might otherwise expect from for-profit ventures.

Thus, even though social entrepreneurs promote their efforts as win–win by suggesting that they can increase the likelihood of maximizing financial returns while at the same time maximizing their benefit to society, I have suggested that true win–win scenarios are difficult to come by. Forced from quadrant II, market forces should push organizations into regularly making decisions consistent with quadrant IV. Yet interestingly, data suggest that while some do so, some also make decisions that defy a market rationality by favoring social mission over financial benefit. In the following section, I use the case of Coastal Coffees to illustrate the complicated nature of supposed win–win scenarios and to shed empirical light on how for-profit social enterprise ventures keep their financial ambitions in check in light of the pressures they are under. Doing so ultimately provides insight into how social enterprises balance their dual commitments.

The case of Coastal Coffees

Coastal Coffees is a family-run, independent business that was established in the 1970s. (The name of the company, the names of the people involved and other identifying information has been changed in accordance with a commitment to anonymity.) Employing roughly 60 people, it imports and roasts green coffee beans from around the world, which it sells under the Coastal Coffees brand as well as a private label. It also operates multiple coffee shops or bars in a mid-sized, progressive, East Coast city. Oliver and Sophie Harper founded the business, but it is now run primarily by their daughter, Kristen.

Although a specialty coffee business, Coastal Coffees did not initially carry fair trade offerings – and had not even interacted much with farmers – until the mid-1990s, when the Harper family went on a coffee-buying trip to Central America. At that point, there was not a robust market for fair trade coffee, and Fair Trade USA (formerly TransFair USA) – now a significant certifier and promoter of fair trade coffee – was no more than a few employees in basement cubicles. Kristen was young at the time of the trip, but her parents had spent decades in the coffee industry. Even so, this was, in her words, "one of the first experiences they had really witnessing coffee production firsthand", and the result was "very eye opening".

For reasons explained in greater detail below, Coastal Coffees started purchasing fair trade coffee shortly after the aforementioned coffee-buying trip. Signing on with the nascent fair trade movement, Kristen explained, "was a natural conclusion" in light of her family's recent experience. They had seen impoverished farmers in need of willing buyers, and they thought that the East Coast community in which they primarily operated would be excited about the idea of fair trade coffee. Adopting the mantra of social enterprise, Kristen said of the decision to start purchasing fair trade coffee: "it was a win–win. We're small roasters, we get to do more for the farmers, and we get to market ourselves as being socially conscious as opposed to the Big Green Giant across the street."

Based on Kristen's account, at one level it is clear that supporting fair trade was unproblematic for the company. Coastal Coffees could "do well by doing good", and the way forward was clear. In reality, however, the story was more complicated. Although it brands itself as committed to fair trade ideals and employees boast of their pioneering role in the fair trade move-ment, Coastal Coffees was – and remains – unwilling to let go of conven-tional (i.e. non-fair-trade) lines of coffee and thus fails to embrace fully the movement's ideals. (Many other fair trade coffee companies, by way of contrast, have chosen to source, roast and/or sell only fairly traded beans. Being a "one hundred percenter" has, in turn, become something of an authenticity test to enthusiasts and supporters.)

When I asked what keeps her company from being completely committed to fair trade, Kristen was quick to mention financial constraints:

> What prevents us from going 100 percent fair trade is, more than anything, price sensitivity with some of our major customers. Now that fair trade has gone mainstream, they are interested in carrying one or two fair trade coffees, but they will never be interested in carrying 100 percent fair trade. They feel that consumer demand has reached – I don't want to say that it's not still growing – but there's an equilibrium now ... If you offer at least one fair trade coffee (Starbucks has one fair trade coffee; Walmart has fair trade coffee now), then that's sort of good enough. So, because we have customers who buy a large volume of our coffee as far as our volume is concerned, if we just converted to 100 percent fair trade, then we would either have to take a huge hit on margin or they would probably not want to carry our coffee.

In terms of Figure 8.1, the decision to forego an opportunity to increase its commitment to fair trade in order to ensure better financial returns would locate Coastal Coffees in quadrant IV. Fair trade was, after all, "a really valuable marketing tool for us," Kristen explained, and the business was unwilling to pursue further potential prosocial returns if that meant undermining its financial prospects. Using the discursive tools available – the "win–win" language and fair trade friendly marketing – to represent itself as unproblematically increasing the likelihood of maximizing both social and financial goals, Coastal Coffees sought, apparently quite successfully, to avoid the legitimacy challenge that might ensue.

Up to this point, the reading of Coastal Coffees has been consistent with an economics-centered view of social enterprise. It is an account of an organization being fundamentally driven by market dynamics that nevertheless has the public relations savvy to frame its actions as prosocial. Yet there is still more to the story. Despite her candid concession that Coastal Coffee's involvement in fair trade could be a useful marketing tool, Kristen insisted that the impetus for purchasing fair trade coffee was less about financial gain and more about moral commitment:

> Fair Trade was the right thing to do so we did it. And the goal was to grow it and make it more part of our company and, you know, I think that it was also potentially a marketing strategy for us. But that was so far down on the list of reasons to do it that it really isn't measurable in terms of how well did it deliver on that potential. 'Cause we were more like, "this is the right thing to do, and we've got to be leaders in this". It was a moral commitment, not a business strategy.

Financial benefit, according to Kristen, was decidedly not the prime motivator:

> Our primary reason as a company for doing anything involving fair trade was ethical. I mean, I said it became a marketing tool for us, and there was this idea that "hey, we're going to differentiate ourselves around our commitment to social responsibility". But there was no imperative in the industry to get involved in Fair Trade. We were one of the first people to get involved.

Statements such as these hint at extra-financial motivations and become more believable once it is clear that, for a number of reasons, opening up their offerings to include fair trade coffee was *not* clearly advantageous to Coastal Coffees from a business standpoint. First, because the movement was not well-established at the time, there was not a ready-made market for fair trade coffee, nor was there a clear way to capitalize on its fair trade involvement. In Kristen's words, "we were going out on a limb". There were few models to follow of how to turn fair trade into a compelling marketing strategy, which was particularly a challenge considering that fair trade coffee, especially in its early years, was criticized for lacking the flavor profile that other specialty coffees could provide. Things improved considerably in the ensuing years, but fair trade coffee was not initially known for its quality, which could make for a tough sell. Second, the local community was initially skeptical of Coastal Coffee's claims that money from fair trade coffee sales would actually make it back to farming communities. Even if it did accept fair trade in terms of its humanitarian aims, the progressive community that was the main consumer base for Coastal Coffees was concerned with the viability of the model. Because TransFair, the certification initiative, was still so new, it was not instantly credible. Third, as fair trade did become more common and better recognized, whatever marketing edge it may have initially provided was eroded. Moreover, Coastal Coffees became an active participant in the budding fair trade movement and, defying market incentives, advised other businesses on best-practices for marketing and selling fair trade coffees. For these reasons, moving in the direction of fair trade did not clearly promise financial benefit.

If dealing in fair trade coffees introduced risk and had, at times, ambiguous benefits, why did Coastal Coffees maintain its commitment? For Kristen, there was a clear connection between Coastal Coffee's involvement in fair trade and her family's experience of interacting directly with farming communities. As noted above, their initial interest in fair trade came as a result of a family trip to Central America. Later, her mother made a second trip, the effect of which Kristen described to me:

> That was the first experience for my mom of really getting out of the United States to someplace other than Europe and seeing people that live in extreme poverty – and realizing that the coffee that she sells everyday is grown by these people. That was life changing for her. And by the end of the year, we were all down there ... And she just felt like she, you know, she had to get my dad and myself on board with this because it was a mission for her.

In reflecting on her own experience visiting with coffee farmers, Kristen explained that moving Coastal Coffees in the direction of fair trade was not a tough sell because it involved what she described as a "personal transformation". "I became a different person," she said, after meeting with farmers. "It [was] hard to actually witness the suffering of other human beings and not feel some responsibility to be involved in improving the situation." Statements such as these suggest that Coastal Coffee's involvement in fair trade coffee should be understood as much through a social and moral lens as through a narrow economic one. Viewing its decisions as driven primarily by business considerations does not do justice to the complexity of the situation, let alone Kristen's first-hand account. The influences were multifaceted and point in many ways to other-oriented motivations that directed the company.

In terms of Figure 8.1, Coastal Coffees was willing and able to make decisions that placed them in quadrant I, where it could increase the likelihood of social returns even though economic benefits were less clear. It was willing, at times, to act contrary to market pressures because of the direct experiences members of the company had had with the people who were impacted by their business decisions. Importantly, the effect of these direct encounters were more than cerebral and emotional. Indeed, they led the company to alter its actual business practices. These observations point to the impact that such encounters can have.

Discussion and conclusion

The case of Coastal Coffees serves two purposes. First, it illustrates how social enterprise can be a complicated endeavor despite slogans and advertising campaigns to the contrary. Decisions that, at a distance, might appear to have win–win outcomes necessarily involve tradeoffs when inspected closely. Second, the case of Coastal Coffees illustrates one reason why a for-profit social enterprise might be willing to act against its financial interests. Calling again upon Figure 8.1, the case provides a clue as to why such businesses do not operate only in quadrants II and IV, although this is where much of conventional wisdom would place them.

During the course of my fieldwork, it became clear that social enterprises were willing and able to act against market pressures for a variety of reasons. I have not considered all of these reasons here but have focused on one that was particular to the fair trade industry and that raises interesting questions about the *accomplishment* of social enterprise – at least how they might be expected to pay due attention to their financial goals as well as their prosocial ones. In using the case of Coastal Coffees, I have aimed to add flesh to the idea that meaningful encounters with others who are impacted by a business's decisions can cause members of that business to alter conventional market-oriented activity. Other men and women I studied shared experiences similar to the Harpers', although space limitations do not allow me to record them here.

The specific kinds of encounters highlighted here are those that bring together individuals who are part of the same social and economic network – for example, actors at opposite ends of the supply chain – in ways that, under conventional business practice, would not typically take place. Relationships like these are especially likely to develop in the fair trade industry, where direct interactions are encouraged: traders interact with producing communities from developing nations for economic reasons – to exchange money for goods, to settle on contracts, to monitor production facilities and processes, for training purposes, and so on. Such encounters are notable because they put businessmen and women into direct contact with the very people who are impacted by their decisions. As images of poverty or need weighed upon business practitioners, or as business associations evolved into meaningful friendships, it became difficult for some of the US-based importers whom I interviewed to think of interacting with farmers and artisans in a business-as-usual manner. Such encounters created a kind of blockade against market pressures.

Of course, not all interactions with others motivate prosocial outcomes, so it is important to qualify what we can and cannot say based on these evidences. To conclude that placing members of a financial network into direct contact with each other will alter the way they do business with each other is too simple a recipe. Other factors are at play, and scholars of social enterprise would do well to study them. My own research, for example, suggests that many people come to their work in social enterprise primed to be motivated by meaningful encounters with others. That is, there is a certain selection effect at work. Yet selection is not the only mechanism operable, as the case of Coastal Coffees illustrates. The Harpers were in the coffee business for decades before they developed an interest in fair trade. Their encounters with farmers impacted on them in such a way as to motivate moving the business in a more prosocial direction, even when the financial returns were not clear. Encounters like those that they experienced, therefore, can have a kind of *treatment* effect that works independently of selection effects.

There are other conditions as well that likely play a part in creating the outcomes illustrated in the case of Coastal Coffees. For example US-based traders perceived their efforts as noble, thus allowing them to enact their own caring self-images. They also had a sense of efficacy in that they believed that their other-oriented actions could and would make a meaningful difference. Because the size of fair trade organizations tend to be small, the practitioners I studied also had significant freedom to shape the direction of the companies that they led. All of these considerations, and no doubt others (such as the industry setting), could be further examined in order to understand the workings of and pressures on social enterprises.

In summary, research on the fair trade industry, including this case study of Coastal Coffees, highlights the complicated and sometimes contradictory nature of these ventures. The point in suggesting that it is a flawed or paradoxical proposition is not to argue that social enterprise has no place in the organizational landscape but rather to open the door wider for thoughtful scholarship. With important exceptions, what writing has been done on social enterprise tends to be anecdotal, sympathetic and boosterish. By starting from the premise that win–win outcomes are plentiful, we close the door to the range of possible outcomes, some of which may be less than optimal. Considering the problematic nature of social enterprise may be discomfiting for practitioners and academics who are hopeful about its possibilities, yet such scholarship allows not only dialogue about the unique challenges to social enterprises but how they might constructively be addressed.

Are there lessons here for practitioners and scholars? Certainly. For practitioners (and their stakeholders) who are concerned about mission drift
in the face of considerable financial pressures, the argument suggests that
putting employees into direct contact with the consequences of their efforts
can provide incentives to keep them committed to the organization's prosocial goals. One particularly successful fair trade company that I studied,
for example, regularly sends all new employees to producing communities.
Doing so, a board member explained to me, helps employees – even account-
ants and marketing agents, whose work would otherwise be removed from
the farmers' lives – to recognize the larger value of what they are doing.
Yet putting employees in contact with the consequences of their work will
certainly not work in every situation, and this is where scholars could make
a useful contribution. More work could be done to understand the conditions under which the outcomes described in the case of Coastal Coffees
(and other organizations) obtain. This could fruitfully involve close analysis
of a case in which face-to-face encounters occur but a prosocial outcome
does not result.

It is because win–win situations are in short supply and lose–lose situations are unambiguously avoided that, theoretically speaking, social
enterprise can be considered a fundamentally problematic proposition.
Realistically, social entrepreneurs are left to decide where and how their
decisions should be distributed across quadrants I and IV, both of which
introduce unique challenges to the potential longevity of the venture. This
is the difficult material and normative environment in which social enterprises must operate. The conceptual schema in Figure 8.1 and the case of
Coastal Coffees ultimately shed light on how social enterprises navigate this
terrain and balance their commitments. I have problematized social enterprises conceptually, provided a way to think about their competing goals
and offered one perspective on how such ventures might negotiate their
differential demands.

References

Bornstein, David. 2004. *How to Change the World: Social Entrepreneurship and the Power of New Ideas.* New York: Oxford University Press.
Child, Curtis. 2011. "Social Enterprise and the Problem of Competing Logics: Profits and Prosocial Missions in the Fair Trade and Socially Responsible Investing Industries."
Cooney, Kate. 2006. "The Institutional and Technical Structuring of Nonprofit Ventures: Case Study of a U.S. Hybrid Organization Caught Between Two Fields." *Voluntas* 17: 143–161.
Cooney, Kate and Trina R. Williams Shanks. 2010. "New Approaches to Old Problems: Market-Based Strategies for Poverty Alleviation." *Social Service Review* 84: 29–55.
Edwards, Michael. 2008. *Just Another Emperor? The Myths and Realities of Philanthrocapitalism.* Demos: A Network for Ideas and Action; The Young Foundation.

Fair Trade USA. 2010. *2010 Almanac*, www.transfairusa.org/resource-library/downloads

Fridell, Gavin. 2007. *Fair Trade Coffee: The Prospects and Pitfalls of Market-driven Social Justice*. Toronto: University of Toronto Press.

Krier, Jean-Marle. 2008. "New Facts and Figures from an Ongoing Success Story: A Report on Fair Trade in 33 Consumer Countries," The Dutch Association of Worldshops, www.wfto.com/index.php?option=com_docman&task=doc_download&gid=1110&&Itemid=109

Lynch, Kevin and Julius Walls. 2009. *Mission Inc.: The Practitioners Guide to Social Enterprise*. San Francisco: Berrett-Koehler Publishers.

Prahalad, C. K. 2004. *The Fortune at the Bottom of the Pyramid: Eradicating Poverty Through Profits*. Upper Saddle River: Wharton School Publishing.

Taylor, Celia R. 2010. "Carpe Crisis: Capitalizing on the Breakdown of Capitalism to Consider the Creation of Social Businesses." *New York Law School Law Review* 54: 743–771.

TransFair USA. 2010. *Annual Report 2009*, www.transfairusa.org/resource-library/financial-information

Yunus, Muhammad. 2008. *Creating a World Without Poverty: Social Business and the Future of Capitalism*. New York: PublicAffairs.

Yunus, Muhammad and Karl Weber. 2010. *Building Social Business: The New Kind of Capitalism that Serves Humanity's Most Pressing Needs*. New York: Public Affairs.

9
Mission Control: Examining the Institutionalization of New Legal Forms of Social Enterprise in Different Strategic Action Fields

Kate Cooney

During the first decade of the 21st century, new legal forms for socially motivated business enterprises have emerged in the UK and in the US creating new options for businesses active in social enterprise activities. In this chapter I examine three efforts to create new platforms for social business: the community interest company or CIC (UK), the low profit limited liability company or L3C (US) and the B Corporation (US) through the lens of social movement theory, exploring the efforts to institutionalize these new legal forms as social movements occurring in different strategic fields of action (Fligstein and McAdam, 2011). Building on recent efforts to bridge social movement analysis with organizational theory (Davis *et al.*, 2005), this chapter includes a stakeholder analysis of each new model to sharpen the comparative focus of the investigation of the early efforts to institutionalize these new legal forms for social enterprise. Such an approach assumes that the institutionalization process is shaped both by specific characteristics of organizational form and by the larger environmental conditions surrounding the efforts to codify new legal forms and promote their use.

After an overview of the limitations attributed to the pure for-profit and traditional nonprofit organizational forms for advancing the blended value goals of social enterprise, I explore the specifics of each new legal form and the broader collective action surrounding their establishment.

New legal forms as corrections to pure for-profit and nonprofit approaches

The social business trend in the US and Western Europe has emerged from business, government and civil society sectors, producing a group of organizations operating at the borders of the nonprofit, government and market sectors that share a similar drive toward hybridity but that retain distinctive motivating influences rooted in their sector of origin (Spear *et al.*, 2007).

From the business sector, corporate social business projects engaged in corporate social responsibility attach social goals to business models that are otherwise structured by profit maximizing incentives (Marquis *et al.*, 2007), while in other cases, such as fair trade or microenterprise, new firms capitalizing on the consumer markets created by social and environmental movements have emerged with more blended templates for using core business functions for social ends. Nonprofit organizations, influenced by widespread veneration of business approaches to social problems inculcated throughout the 1990s and 2000s (Cooney and Williams Shanks, 2010), increasingly adopt earned income ventures into their service repertoires both to diversify revenues and to develop innovative approaches to meeting mission goals (Dees and Anderson, 2003; Foster and Bradach, 2005; Young and Salamon, 2002). Such efforts have also been embraced by public actors, whom in an effort to leverage public dollars and shrink the size of government have developed initiatives to bolster social enterprise activity from both private business and the nonprofit sectors in order to tackle entrenched social problems by funding "whatever works" (Ball, 2010; Korosec and Berman, 2006).

Although these hybrid approaches blending commercial and social goals vary by the primary sector from which the innovation emanates (for-profit or nonprofit) (Spear *et al.*, 2007), all endeavor to integrate social and business logics through innovations in organizational forms historically constructed to harness either one or the other (Neck *et al.*, 2009). For traditional business organizations pursuing social goals, the embrace of dual value creation can be constrained by the contemporary norm that shareholder profit maximization functions as the primary organizing purpose for business endeavors. To this end, a considerable amount of the research on corporate social responsibility attempts to quantify the benefits to the bottom line that result from socially oriented activities to legitimate these activities in terms of financial returns and alleviate concerns regarding risks to these returns that social goals may pose (Margolis and Walsh, 2003; Orlistzky *et al.*, 2003). Even for profitable social business models, such as Ben & Jerry's, in the aftermath of their sale to Unilever, the specter that bottom line focused investors can exercise their shareholder rights to profit and act on self-interest when stocks do not perform financially in social business models became a highly publicized threat (Katz and Page, 2010; Moneybox, 2000).

On the other hand, nonprofits, which are organized formally to fulfill social mission goals, face constraints in raising capital for social business endeavors that can lead to risks to mission that include: the potential shift toward serving more advantaged (paying) client populations (Salamon, 1993); the reduction of investment in programs that are not profitable (Weisbrod, 2004); the movement away from fostering community ties as business networks are nurtured (Eikenberry and Kluver, 2004); a drain on the general operating funds overtime (Foster and Bradach, 2005; Tuckman, 1998; Weisbrod, 2004).

The three new legal forms for socially motivated business enterprises that have emerged in the UK and in the US in recent years are explicitly designed to more readily support a blending of business and social goals. The new social business forms each attempt in different ways to address the two big constraints to social business hybrid activity from either the traditional business or nonprofit form, namely, the narrow conception of stakeholder rights in traditional for-profits and the constraints on attracting capital in traditional nonprofits. A primary question for governments investing in these initiatives, for public or civil society actors considering launching a social business enterprise, and for communities and clients consuming products or receiving services from hybrid social businesses, is: how do these new legal forms structure social business enterprise vehicles, which claim to elevate social goals? And how do they do this in such a way that social mission is truly in the driver's seat (Alter, 2006; Bode *et al.*, 2006; Dart, 2004; Foster and Bradach, 2005)?

The analysis flows from two hypotheses that inform the framework for analysis: (1) that formally legitimizing and codifying a broader set of stakeholder rights in social business models is a key mechanism for achieving mission control in social business models blending social and commercial goals; (2) that the political opportunities, mobilizing structures and framing processes surrounding the efforts to institutionalize these new forms will interact with the level specifics of the organizational form in such a way that will constrain or enable the institutionalization of these new legal forms.

After presenting the theoretical lens guiding the analyses, this chapter proceeds with a multiple case study analysis of the efforts to institutionalize CICs, L3Cs and B Corps.

Stakeholder theory, social movement theory and social enterprise models

Stakeholder theory expands the conception of the firm beyond that of a profit-maximizing organization concerned primarily with shareholder wealth to one of an organization balancing multiple stakeholder interests (Freeman, 1984; Phillips *et al.*, 2003). Stakeholders can be defined narrowly, as a group beyond shareholders but confined to those who have financial interests in the organization (Orts and Strudler, 2009) such as employees and suppliers or broadly as "any group or individual who can affect or is affected by the achievement of the organization's purpose" (Freeman, 1984, 53) including social stakeholders like the community and the environment (also referred to as "silent stakeholders' *pace* Simmons, 2004). At its heart, stakeholder theory contains a normative thrust – namely that "stakeholders are identified by their interests in the corporation, whether the corporation has any corresponding functional interest in them" and that "the interests of all stakeholders are of intrinsic value" (Donaldson and Preston, 1995, 67).

Still, a central critique of stakeholder theory is the vague and overly broad nature of the concept that can serve to render it almost meaningless (Orts and Strudler, 2009).

In recent years, stakeholder theory has been reinvigorated by social movement scholars examining field level efforts to induce change in corporate (or other types of organizations') behavior (Davis *et al.*, 2005; King, 2008; Maguire and Phillips, 2010). At the heart of this more recent scholarship in stakeholder theory is the question of who matters to the firm and how they come to be constructed as salient stakeholders (Mitchell *et al.*, 1997). Although proponents of stakeholder management put forth that "corporations should attempt to distribute the benefits of their activities as equitably as possible among stakeholders, in light of their respective contributions, costs, and risks" (Sloan Colloquy, 488, cited in Phillips *et al.*, 2003), in reality managers may respond more vigorously to more powerful stakeholders, to those with higher levels of legitimacy and to those with more urgent claims (Mitchell *et al.*, 1997). According to Mitchell *et al.*'s (1997) model of stakeholder influence, "highly salient" stakeholders possess power, legitimacy and urgency for their claim, although those stakeholders with two out of the three endowments can possess the "moderate" levels of salience necessary to exert influence. Many socially oriented businesses draw on stakeholder theory to justify their strategic attention to a broader set of social goals rather than a narrower focus on financial performance (Wheeler and Sillanpää, 1998). New legal forms of social business can be seen as organizations experimenting with a more formal integration of socially motivated stakeholders into the legal structure of the organization, thereby increasing their salience through adjustments to organizational structure.

Taking the view that endeavors to establish new legal forms for social enterprise are at their core institutional change efforts, even with new legal language empowering a broader set of stakeholders to hold a company or corporation accountable to social as well as financial goals, the success of these new forms may depend to some degree on the relations in which they are embedded (King, 2008). To that end, I draw on social movement theory concepts to compare conditions for institutional change across the three cases at the field level. Examining both the organizational form and the field level conditions surrounding the establishment of each form utilizes a multilevel analysis and builds on the scholarly work at the intersection of social movement and organizational theory (Davis *et al.*, 2005).

Institutional change, that is, efforts to change the rules of the game, according to social movement theory can be compared according to three factors: availability of mobilizing structures, nature of political opportunities, and framing processes surrounding the change efforts (McAdam *et al.*, 1996). Defined as "mechanisms that pool individual inputs" (King, 2008, 27), mobilizing structures are most often conceptualized as formal organizations or interpersonal networks that facilitate both collective action by harnessing resources and the emergence of a collective identity. Political opportunities refer to the opportunities and constraints in the landscape in which the social movement is embedded. Both mobilizing structures and political opportunities are said to develop from framing processes, defined as "strategic use of shared meanings and definitions to invoke claims on individuals' identity and cultural sense of responsibility to a cause" (ibid., 31).

The first part of the analysis presented below compares the three new legal forms for social enterprise on the basis of the degree to which they achieve the three key components of stakeholder salience outlined by Mitchell *et al.*, namely: power, legitimacy and urgency. As the analysis will show, while all three approaches to social business provide more legitimacy and in some cases power for socially motivated stakeholders, a close assessment of the legal text for each indicates that the firm level rights for secondary stakeholders vary substantially across forms. Next, I investigate the institutionalization projects surrounding the establishment of these three new social business models as collective efforts facilitated by mobilizing structures, political opportunities and framing processes. I argue that to understand fully the early institutionalization efforts of each new legal form, both the firm level characteristics and the conditions in the broader environment (what sociologists Fligstein and McAdam, 2011 refer to as the strategic action field). In the US case, there is evidence that at the early stages of efforts to legalize these new social business forms, firm level characteristics serve to hinder (in the L3C instance) or enhance (true for the B Corp) field level institutionalization efforts. By contrast, in the UK, while early field level institutionalization efforts were facilitated by government support, the strong association of the initiative with the Labour Party and their newer role in National Health Service reform create ongoing legitimacy issues for CIC organizations under current Conservative Party rule.

Methodology

Data were collected on each of the three legal forms.

- *LC3s*: Text of legislation or proposed legislation establishing L3Cs across several US states were obtained through web searches. The database of Vermont L3Cs was retrieved from the Vermont Secretary of State website and further refined through web searches with the aim of collecting specific data on the nature of the social business endeavor for each firm listed. Literature reviews on L3Cs were also conducted and content from the official website for L3C education and advocacy were examined.
- *B Corps*: Recommended legal text for establishing B Corps and the B Corps standards were downloaded from the B Lab website. Literature reviews and web searches on B Corps and website reviews of a selection of businesses

achieving the B Corps seal were conducted. For further elucidation of the difference between structural forms, text and materials from Criterion Ventures Structure Lab workshop on US based legal structures for social business were consulted.

- *CICs*: The text of the legislation establishing CICs was obtained. The researcher had access to survey outcomes conducted by Social Enterprise Coalition UK and the CIC Association (CIC ASS). Information interviews were conducted over the summer of 2010 with a representative from the Social Enterprise Coalition UK and CIC ASS.

Data on each social business form were first examined as three independent cases. Case descriptions were produced summarizing the historical development of the effort leading to the establishment of each new legal form and the specific characteristics of each legal structure. Second, cross-case analyses were conducted according to the framework for stakeholder saliency developed by Mitchell *et al.* (1997) to investigate the degree to which each new legal structure produces high levels of saliency for secondary stakeholders by coding the legal text for each new social enterprise model according to the three categories of stakeholder saliency: power, legitimacy and urgency. Finally, the cases underwent a second cross-case analysis utilizing a social movement theory lens to examine the mobilizing structures, political opportunities and framing processes surrounding the early institutionalization efforts of the three focal legal forms for social business.

What follows, after a brief overview of the three new organizational forms, is a multiple case comparison of three new legal forms for social businesses through the lens of stakeholder and social movement theories.

Overview of the new social enterprise forms

The CIC

The CIC was established by the UK in 2005 under the Companies (Audit, Investigations and Community Enterprise) Act of 2004 to allow a company to ensure that their assets are dedicated to public benefit without taking on charitable status in the UK. They are intended to provide a "simple, clear way of locking assets to a public benefit" while concurrently meeting the "need for a transparent, flexible model, clearly designed and easily recognized" (The Regulator of Community Interest Companies, 2009, 4). A CIC differs from a charity in that charities are more heavily regulated, must be organized exclusively around a charitable purpose,[1] whereas CICs are more lightly regulated and can be arranged around any purpose as long as their activities are carried out for public benefit. Charities enjoy certain tax advantages that CICs do not enjoy though CICs are free to "operate more commercially than charities" by, for example, paying out dividends to shareholders (ibid., 5).

Further, the community benefit threshold for CICs is less stringent than the charitable purpose test for charities.

The key feature of the CIC is the asset-lock, which functions as one of the central mechanisms through which public benefits are safeguarded. The asset-lock prevents assets (e.g. profits or other surpluses, land, buildings, etc.) held by a CIC from being transferred to another owner unless one of the following conditions are met: the asset is sold for full market value so as to retain the value for the CIC, the asset can be transferred for below market value if it is transferred to another asset-locked body (another CIC, a charity or an Industrial and Providence Society benefit company, the UK form for co-ops), the asset can be transferred to another asset-locked body with consent from the regulator, or the asset is transferred for the "benefit of the community" in some other way (ibid., 9).

The profit motive is constrained through caps on profit distribution as well. For example, CICs that incorporate as companies limited by shares issue investor shares, but dividends on these shares are capped at a rate set by the Regulator "in a way that balances the need to encourage investment with the primary purpose of community interest" (ibid., 11). There is an additional stipulation, in place since the originating 2005 legislation, that the amount of profit distributed be limited to 35 percent of distributable profits. These are maximum limits, and CICs are not required to meet them. Finally, to protect the asset-lock upon CIC dissolution or charity conversion, the surplus assets must be transferred "in a way which ensures that they continue to be retained for community interest or charitable purposes rather than distributed to investors."

The L3C

The L3C is a new legal form available to social businesses in the United States. The first L3C-related legislation was passed in Vermont in 2008 as an addendum to the general limited liability act. Since 2008 legislation modeled on the Vermont addendum has been passed in nine states and two American Indian Tribes, with several more states in the process of introducing legislation (Americans for Community Development, 2011). Built on the legal structure of a traditional limited liability corporation, which "may be organized and operated for any lawful business purpose", an L3C must additionally meet three criteria: (1) it must "significantly further the accomplishment of one or more charitable or educational purposes" and "would not have been formed but for its relationship to the accomplishment of such purposes"; (2) "no significant purpose of the company is the production of income or the appreciation of property (although the company is permitted to earn profit)"; and (3) it must not be organized "to accomplish any political or legislative purpose" (Social Enterprise, 2009). These three criteria must be specified in the L3C's organizing documents.

The legal language of the L3C addendum consciously mirrors the IRS requirements for foundation program related investment (PRI). Foundation PRI allows foundations to make loans or investments at below market rates to for-profit organizations as long as the organizations are predominantly mission oriented. Foundation PRIs are viewed by some as an under-utilized source of patient capital for social businesses due to the hesitancy of foundations to risk large fines if the IRS does not recognize a PRI project as "adequately charitable" (Zouhali-Worrall, 2010). Robert Lang, the CEO of the Mary Elizabeth and Gordon B. Mannweiler Foundation and central architect of the L3C legal form, "envisions the [L3C] business structure as a preapproved mechanism for PRI investment" (ibid.).

To form an L3C, a company files Articles of Organization with the appropriate state regulatory body in a state where the L3C has been established as an alternative form of a limited liability company. An L3C can register to do business throughout the United States by registering as a foreign entity doing business in another state. L3C proponents claim that the L3C structure not only facilitates PRI from foundations but also helps attract other forms of investment by pooling risk in different tranches. The L3C legal form aims to facilitate layered investing (all known as tranching). Accordingly, the key is to use "low-cost foundation capital in a high risk tranche of its structure" and thereby "allocate risk and regard unevenly over a number of investors, thus ensuring some a very safe investment with market return" (Americans for Community Development, 2011). Therefore, unlike the CIC, which caps the rates of return to investment for all investors, L3Cs aim to attract low profit investments from foundations and, by doing so, create the potential to offer market rate investment opportunities for mainstream investors who may or may not be motivated by the social mission.

B Corps

The B Corporation certification launched in 2006 and the associated Benefit Corporation, which codifies the B Corp certification standards into the articles of incorporation, is the brainchild of Jay Coen Gilbert, Bart Houlahan and Andrew Kassoy, founders of B Lab. Certified B Corporations, despite the nomenclature, can take any business form, including C Corporations, S Corporations, limited liability companies and joint partnerships, and therefore have no official tax status in their own right. In April 2010, Maryland became the first state to adopt legislation making certified Benefit Corporations part of official legal statute and a legal option for entrepreneurs, followed by Vermont, Virginia, New Jersey and Hawaii, with several more states in the process of moving legislation forward (New York, Michigan, California, Pennsylvania, North Carolina and Colorado).

The current form of the B Corp certification process requires a minimum score (80 out of 200) on an assessment of social and environmental performance, an annual licensing fee paid to B Lab, and legal changes to the articles of incorporation that institutionalize consideration of stakeholder interests. The B Lab ratings assessment is divided into five categories, the final four all grouped by categories of major stakeholders: accountability, employees, consumers, community and environment. Within each broad category more specific aspects are examined. For example, "accountability" is further broken down into governance, transparency and fair trade (supplier code of conduct); "employees" is further assessed according to compensation and benefits, employee ownership and work environment; "consumers" is examined specifically around the degree to which the company sells beneficial products/services, has beneficial methods of production and provides service to those in need; "community" includes the degree to which the organization is local, diverse and provides direct service; and "environment" further breaks out into questions about corporate offices, transportation/distribution and manufacturing facilities. The certification lasts for two years at which point organizations must reapply. During the certification process, documentation for approximately 20 percent of the survey responses is required and, once certified, B Corporations may be chosen for a random audit in which they will need to provide documentation for all of their responses.

Achieving stakeholder saliency: CICs, L3Cs and B–Corps

Examining these new legal templates through the lens of stakeholder theory, we find that although all three new organizational forms include legal language that provides coverage for directors and managers to act in ways that privilege social or environmental goals over financial performance, legitimizing socially and environmentally oriented stakeholders' claims on the organization, the three approaches of the CIC, the L3C and the B Corp vary in the degree to which they formally empower stakeholders.

CICs

According to Mitchell *et al.* (1997) model for stakeholder salience (those with legitimacy, power and urgency), the evidence reviewed above shows that the CIC models achieve the highest level of saliency for stakeholders by providing both legitimacy for their goals and the power to enforce them (see Table 9.1).

CICs not only require that businesses act in the community interest but also provide stakeholders with the power to hold CICs in accordance to their social goals through their ability to request a review from the regulator. Although the CIC regulations are meant to be "light touch", the regulator has the authority to investigate stakeholder complaints, to change directors of the CIC or to "wind up the company" if the CIC is found to be violating either the community benefit purpose or the asset lock (The Regulator of Community Interest Companies, 2009, 12). Over the 2009–2010 year, nine

Table 9.1 Comparison of CICs, B Corporations and L3Cs

	CIC	B Corporation	L3C
Regulatory environment	Annual reports required to demonstrate community benefit and stakeholder involvement. Regulator endowed with power to change management or close down CIC.	High bar to qualify with documentation requirements, audits and the requirement to reapply for certification every two years.	No gate keeping or auditing mechanisms.
Social goal control elements	Asset locks on transfer of assets. Caps on rates of return for loans or investment.	Shareholders given rights of action to hold directors and managers accountable to social goals.	Social goals stated as predominant in articles of organization.
Legitimacy	√	√	√
Power	√ Ability to request review from the regulator if community interest test violation suspected.	√ Increased indirectly through (1) certification process and (2) new shareholder rights of action to hold directors and managers accountable to social/ environmental goals.	No new powers specified.
Urgency	√ Can use power to request regulator review to establish urgency to claim.	Must construct this through campaign effort.	Must construct this through campaign effort.

Note: Legitimacy, power and urgency are the three elements of stakeholder saliency.

complaints were made to the regulator by stakeholders for reasons such as "conduct of company", "accounting discrepancy", "unfair competition", "community benefit" and "distribution of assets" (ibid., 2010, 13). Of the nine she investigated, five were closed down by her office suggesting that her powers have teeth and that she is not hesitant to use them. In 2010–2011, 13 complaints were filed for misuse of funds, conduct of the company and relations between directors, though this year no action was taken by the regulator (ibid., 2011). Other checks on CICs' adherence to their charitable purposes include annual reports to the regulator on "how they are delivering for the community and how they are involving their stakeholders in their activities" (ibid., 2009, 11).

If a CIC wishes to amend its articles of association, it must pass a special resolution and send a copy of this along with a community interest statement and a plan to inform stakeholders of the alteration to the regulator for approval. The regulator can deny the requested amendments if he or she determines they do not meet the "community interest test" (ibid., 17). In turn, the regulator can push for a change in management or even closure if the CIC is found to be in violation of the community interest test, endowing the stakeholder claim on the social goals with a sense of urgency.

B Corps

B Corporations, as part of the certification process, and Benefit Corporations, as part of the articles of incorporation or governing agreements, are explicitly constituted to allow shareholders to consider broader stakeholder concerns and hold the directors and managers accountable to not only shareholders but also "employees, consumers, the community, and the environment" (B Corporation, 2010). To this end, B Corporations are required to amend their governing documents to "(1) give legal permission and protection to officers and directors to consider all stakeholders, not just shareholders, (2) to create additional rights for shareholders to hold directors and officers accountable to these interests" but, very importantly and explicitly, the final charge is to "(3) limit these expanded rights to shareholders exclusively – non-shareholders are explicitly not empowered with a new right of action" (ibid.).

In B Corporations, stakeholders themselves do not have any new rights of action but socially motivated shareholders may challenge directors or managers on their behalf. In this way, B Corporation models offer a "dependent" form of "expectant saliency" whereby stakeholders have legitimacy and the potential to pursue their goals with urgency but must "rely on the advocacy of other powerful stakeholders", in this case shareholders, to press their case (Mitchell *et al.*, 1997, 877). Benefit corporations, modeled closely on the B Corps certification, go a little further in that they not only require articles of incorporation that establish a commitment to working toward "a material, positive impact on society and the environment" and evaluation by "a third-party standard" such as B Lab, but also require annual reports along the lines of the CIC that report on the progress toward achieving public benefit and some quantification of measurable impact (Chan, 2010). While the regulation regime associated with these requirements will most likely vary from state to state, such requirements for reporting and transparency may provide important leverage for secondary stakeholders to hold social firms accountable in the future.

L3Cs

L3Cs on the other hand, while governed by legal statutes which declare that they must be organized primarily for pursuing charitable or educational purposes and not for the pursuit of profit or accumulation or property, are not subject to ongoing regulation or assessment on whether or not they are meeting these requirements. Further, to the extent that the L3C takes advantage of layered investing (tranching), these foundation stakeholders may end up in a conflictual relationship with non-charitable investors for strategic control of the organization (Kleinberger, 2010). Socially oriented stakeholders, while granted legitimacy in the L3C form, begin from a position of "low saliency" in that they would need to marshal both the power and urgency to press their claims on the organization. Despite their name ("low profit" LLCs), L3Cs do not have ceilings on profit and are subject to varying state level regulation, which preliminary investigations suggest are mild if they exist at all (Cohen, 2009). As Rick Zwetsch (2009), in a guest post on the Social Earth online magazine explains, "Right now, there is no 'low profit' police. No one will be watching over your shoulder deciding how much profit is too much profit. Ultimately, social purpose is your guiding star and if you'll have to answer to anyone, regarding profit, it may be those that that your L3C serves."

Even at the establishment phase, states have not included mechanisms for assessing whether or not the proposed L3C meets a community benefit test (Schmidt, 2010), as was born out early on in Vermont when speculation swirled around the nature of the social purpose imbuing the high end cheesecake L3C business started by a former Pittsburgh steel company.

In summary, while the CIC legal form provides high levels of salience to socially oriented stakeholders, giving them definitive stakeholder status by endowing them with legitimacy, power and urgency, the B Corporation model only increases stakeholders to moderate levels of salience. Although the B Lab certification process explicitly holds businesses accountable as to how well they treat key stakeholders (employee and community) and the degree to which such stakeholders are involved in participatory decision making processes, the B Corporation model explicitly does not endow those stakeholders with direct rights of action or power to press their claims. L3C's offer low levels of stakeholder salience by granting legitimacy but not power or urgency to stakeholders invested in the firm for its social and environmental goals.

Institutionalization of new organizational forms as social movements unfolding in different strategic action fields

Drawing from social movement theory, I next examine the mobilizing structures, political opportunities and framing processes surrounding the establishment of these focal legal forms for social enterprise.

Mobilizing structures

As stated above, mobilizing structures are organizations and personal networks that serve to facilitate collective action by building a resource base and by fostering a collective identity. In the US the L3C and the B Corporation both have active champions with robust web presence aimed at disseminating information about the new legal form, featuring sample legal text developed in consultation with lawyers and which is available to social entrepreneurs for replication.

L3C

To advance field level change, Lang formed a committee called L3C advisors to assist companies considering adopting the L3C form. A website called "Americans for Community Development" which is the "organization for the L3C" compiles all of this legal advice and serves as a one stop shop for passing state legislation by amending the limited liability company code. The site also provides information on the campaign for federal legislation (Americans for Community Development, 2011). The Americans for Community Development (ACD) aims to educate "foundations, attorneys, legislators and policy leaders" about the L3Cs through seminars, workshops, training programs and webinars, all in service of the goal of passing state and federal legislation or, increasingly, to educate the foundation world about the L3C and encourage their support.

Membership to ACD allows you to access listserv discussions in areas of interest. However, to gain access to these working group discussions, membership dues ranging from $300 for individual memberships ($50 for students) to $500 for institutional memberships are required, which restricts participation. As a mobilizing structure, the website and related workshops that provide technical assistance for establishing the right to file as an L3C provides a platform for disseminating information (a key resource) but is less facilitative in harnessing broad base participation or in aiding the construction of a social movement related identity – that is, the "processes by which people are transformed into agents able to challenge the status quo" (Scully and Creed, 2005, 313) to advance the cause. Further, as discussed more fully later in this section, despite robust campaign strategies aimed at educating and disseminating a model for L3C state legislation, so far the movement has been unable to mobilize the key material resource promised by the legal form, namely Foundation PRI.

B Corp

B Lab holds a robust web presence with in-depth information on B Corporations, an overview of the certification process and recommended legal text for necessary changes to by-laws in order to certify organizations as B Corps. However, in addition, B Lab has also worked aggressively to develop an ever expanding set of relationships with key actors in the social business space (including the Yale School of Management, which offers loan reductions to School of Management graduates who go to work for B Corps), and to develop incentives (tax and otherwise) for becoming a B Corp, many of which are preferred pricing options for infrastructure development and capacity building. Further, in addition to mobilizing a growing set of resources available to B Corps, B Lab also works to enhance what scholars refer to as "social identity construction and legitimation" (ibid., 312) through a free advertising campaign featuring specific B Corps and an annual retreat that brings B Corps together for discussions on social business challenges and opportunities.

CICs

Unlike B Corps or L3Cs, which target state law as a key lever in facilitating institutional change, the CIC form was established by an initiative of the New Labour government as an effort of institutional change from above (Davies, 2004). However, as the number of organizations adopting it has grown, the CICs have begun to organize collectively as a group to influence the development of the institutional foundation of this emergent social business field. In the CIC case, rather than focusing collective energy on the establishment of these new legal forms, the initial focus of CIC collective action was on amending the nature of the new institutional rules of the game. Formed in January 2010, the newly formed CIC Association (CIC ASS) grew out of a smaller CIC forum facilitated by the Social Enterprise Coalition to create an online network and further the CIC brand (The Regulator of Community Interest Companies, 2010). In the first year of CIC ASS's existence, they have been most active in lobbying for loosening of the dividend caps to attract more capital (personal communication, CIC ASS director). The CIC forum and CIC ASS have a close working relationship with the CIC Regulator, who, according to the CIC forum minutes posted on the Social Enterprise Coalition's website, attended and made presentations at every CIC forum meeting. Their early efforts have been successful: in its first year in existence, CIC ASS won the adjustments they sought to the dividend cap and allowances for distributable income providing more economic incentive for investors to make loans or buy shares. However, an interview conducted with the CIC ASS director over the summer of 2010 touched on continued branding and legitimacy issues facing CICs as they begin to populate the landscape.

Political opportunities

In considering the political opportunities for institutional change in the broader organizational fields surrounding these new social business forms, it is notable that all three legal forms have emerged in an era of enthusiasm for social entrepreneurship and anti-corporate activism. Throughout the boom economic years of the 1990s, both the US and the UK under President Clinton and Prime Minister Blair embraced a so-called third way to addressing social problems that embraced a social enterprise approach. However, in the UK, unlike the US, the turn to social enterprise was facilitated by government proposals and stewarded by a social enterprise unit within a cabinet level office called the Office of the Third Sector. Outside of government, the Social Enterprise Coalition was formed to "promote the idea and use of social enterprise" (Social Enterprise UK, 2011). In the US, although a grassroots group called the Social Enterprise Alliance has built state level chapters to promote social enterprise and facilitates interaction through an annual conference, there is no cabinet level agency representing their interests, nor a national advocacy organization and few institutional connections to government or policymakers.

Simultaneously, at the global level, a large anti-corporate movement emerged, exploding into full view in Seattle with the now famous teamsters and turtle protests against the World Trade Organization meeting in 1999, and continuing to build through venues like the World Social Forum, a group that since its founding in 2001 holds an annual meeting in a different location around the world where "social movements, networks, NGOs and other civil society organizations opposed to neo-liberalism and a world dominated by capital or by any form of imperialism come together to pursue their thinking, to debate ideas democratically, formulate proposals, share their experiences freely and network for effective action" (World Social Forum, 2011).

Over the 2000s, support for social enterprise in both countries continued to expand beyond initial third way conceptions of market based approaches to social problems. As anti-corporate social movements built awareness and momentum toward another way of doing business, social enterprise organizations increasingly aimed to fulfill that promise. However, comparing the two countries, the social enterprise field has much closer roots to government in the UK and a more developed infrastructure. In fact, just this year the Social Enterprise Coalition changed its name to Social Enterprise UK, a change that they explain on their website is related to the fact that "social enterprise has come into its own and the movement is gaining power, momentum and support. And 'coalition' no longer describes what we do" (Social Enterprise UK, 2011). As the national body for social enterprise in the UK, Social Enterprise UK is now heavily involved in policy work, runs awareness campaigns promoting social enterprise and coordinates many technical training workshops and organizing opportunities for the growing variety of social enterprise forms. In the US, on the other hand, social enterprises are much less embedded in the policy arena and do not yet have a powerful advocacy group as is the case in the UK. These differences provide divergent landscapes of political opportunities for these new social enterprises.

B Corp

It could be argued that the B Lab, of all of the cases, is the most closely aligned with the anti-corporate movement. Jay Coen Gilbert, one of the founders of B Lab, talks of goals of sustainability, inclusion and building a "new kind of corporation" for today's world, a mission that is rooted in a critique of corporate profit maximizing that is unconcerned with social and environmental impacts (Gilbert, 2011). In fact many certified B Corps and newly minted Benefit Corporations are part of this social movement space as well, and their businesses express this in what they do (for example, a focus on clean water or nutritious yogurt) and how they do it (for example, using environmentally friendly production and distribution methods). According to the B Corporation website, as of November 2011, there are 468 B Corporations in 60 industries producing $2.24 billion in revenues. These include well known socially and environmentally oriented companies such as Seventh Generation, Dansko and Numi Organic Tea that capitalize on the consumer markets opened up by organic food and conscious consumption related social movements. Further, B Lab is not only engaged in a campaign to proliferate a new legal framework for governance of socially oriented businesses, but also functions as the certifying body for B Corps and, in that sense, as the field level regulator for the new form. Elisabeth Clemens (2005, 361) noted, in her suburb essay closing the edited volume on social movements and organization theory, that an important aspect of the anti-corporate movement is that "many critical struggles are *about* the rules of the game rather than within these rules". Accordingly, B Lab' has focused on creating new rules of the game through the establishment of a predict-able and rigorous regulatory framework, offering deep synergies with the anti-corporate movement that create numerous networking and coalition building opportunities for their efforts.

L3C

Conversely, the L3C efforts to pass legislation at the state and federal level has met with some resistance. Some in the nonprofit community have expressed concern that the new legal form does not offer enough guarantee of a charitable purpose. The National Association of State Charity Officials have communicated a list of concerns about L3Cs to the Senate Finance Committee, not least questions about "how L3Cs will be monitored to make sure that the profit purpose remains secondary to the charitable purpose" (Elizabeth Grant, Assistant Attorney General in the Oregon Department of Justice, cited in Zouhali-Worrall, 2010).

Although the Council of Foundations is purportedly courting interest for legislation at the federal level (ibid.), a presentation by legal counsel to the structure workshop in Boston, spring 2010, suggested that foundations continue to be wary about making PRIs to newly incorporated L3Cs in the absence of an IRS private ruling recognizing L3Cs as automatically eligible

for PRIs. Federal legislation might reduce a foundation's need for Private
Letter Rulings from the IRS prior to a PRI investment but would most likely
not eliminate any due diligence requirements (Hrywna, 2009). The ACD is
making concerted efforts to educate the foundation community about this
new form, most recently in a day long preconference event at the 2011 fall
meeting for Community Foundations in San Francisco. However, the ambiguity surrounding the regulatory environment for the L3C may create a set
of constraints that may ultimately inhibit the momentum and success of
this new legal form.

CIC

The CIC, from the start, has been supported in its quest for institution-
alization by the broader infrastructure surrounding social enterprise in the
UK. As discussed above, in its early days, the CICs were sponsored by the
Labour Government and initially supported in developing a shared collective identity through the forum set up by the Social Enterprise Coalition.
As the collective identity solidified, and they spun off their own association
(CIC ASS), they focused narrowly on a shared goal: raising the dividend
caps. Once that was secured, CIC ASS turned to concerns about the lack of
brand awareness and the need to promote the CIC model for social business.
In the midst of this early stage of growth and promotion, political power
changed hands and a series of global economic crises emerged. In the 2010
parliamentary elections David Cameron replaced Gordon Brown as prime
minister, ushering in an era of Conservative Party rule and leaving the social
enterprise community unclear as to whether public support would continue
for a field that had grown largely through Labour Party initiatives. However,
the sheer number of field level advocacy and infrastructure organizations
populating the social enterprise space in the UK has continued to facilitate progress on the CIC institutionalization project, even as government
support waivered.

To wit, the 2010–2011 CIC regulator report highlights the regulator's
dual guiding objectives of "creating a wide general awareness of community interest companies" and "building public confidence in CICs through
effective impartial regulation" (The Regulator of Community Interest
Companies, 2011). The brand development work includes workshops or
presentations made to numerous local social enterprise coalition groups
in addition to Social Enterprise UK and key people in the government, a
list that illuminates the highly developed platform for social enterprise
in the UK. The list includes: the Scottish Social Enterprise Coalition,
the Social Enterprise World Forum, the Social Solutions Academy Social
Enterprise Action Day, Social Traders Social Enterprise Trade Fair Cornwall,
Co-Operatives UK, Office of the Third Sector, the Welsh Social Enterprise
Coalition, the Social Enterprise Business Advisors, the Social Enterprise
West Midlands Network Meeting, the Social Firms UK Annual Conference,

Social Firms Wales AGM, among numerous others. From the data available, these efforts appear to have been successful. There are now almost 5,000 CICs operating in the UK, over 1,800 of them converting or incorporating between April 2010 and March 2011 (ibid.).

Frames

Finally, I will assess the three cases according to the framing processes that surround the efforts to establish new legal forms for social enterprise, recognizing that "mobilizing structures and political opportunities are often not sufficient to convince individuals to give of their resources to group efforts" or to advance the cause (King, 2008, 31). Interestingly, the frames associated with the CIC, the L3C and the B Corp are quite different. Frames can be categorized as diagnostic, when they stitch together a narrative of cause and effect, or as prognostic, when they center on a solution to a problematic condition (Snow and Beneford, 1988).

CICs

The diagnostic element of the frame surrounding the development of the CIC model constructs the profit motive itself as a risk to community interest and curtails it through asset locks and rate caps. The prognostic aspect to the frame is one of maintaining community control and to this end these restrictions serve to prevent the productive capacities developed through these businesses from being transferred out of the community through mergers or acquisitions. Thus, CIC commercial activity builds assets that remain anchored in communities, primarily for their benefit. This strong frame of community control provides a focus for socially motivated CIC representatives and the UK government to negotiate over alterations to the rate caps and asset locks over time in such a way that preserves a focus on social goals.

An early issue with the CIC model was that the financial incentives associated with the CIC were so limited that few market based investors were embracing the form, and much effort has been put into adjusting the rate caps to incentivize investors to commit capital and support these emergent social business projects. Therefore, while the stakeholder analysis suggests that CIC social enterprise models most definitively achieve mission control for their organizations, by placing community representatives in key positions of power, and through a consistent, impartial, regulatory regime, such mission related controls either send unclear signals to market actors or are too stringent to attract them, which in the first phase of their development inhibits market investment.

However, aided by a strong infrastructure for social enterprise at the national level and close working relationships with the public sector regulating body, the CIC ASS group successfully adjusted the policy around rate caps to achieve higher returns. The most recent CIC regulator report indicates that this shift seems to have rejuvenated the CIC field, with nearly 2,000 new entrants this year and an upturn in the companies limited by share form, from 25 to 34 percent of all CICs (with a full 57 percent of all conversions to CICs from other forms taking the limited by share form) (The Regulator of Community Interest Companies, 2011). Ironically, a few recent headlines in *The Guardian* and in the blogosphere suggest, in their discussion of the CIC role in proposed National Health Service reform, that it is these higher market rates and their hint of commercial motivation that stoke concerns about privatization of the National Health Service, indicating that the reforms to target more market investment may come at the expense of their social mission-related legitimacy in the eyes of socially minded stakeholders observing CICs in the current reshuffled political landscape (Glaister, 2011; Zetetist, 2011).

By contrast, in L3Cs and in B Corporations, the frame is not about community control over assets and profits but rather one of "doing well by doing good". Further, rather than constructing the profit motive as a potentially corrosive force to be tempered, as is the case with the CIC model, the profit engine is constructed as the primary mechanism for producing social impact (Weber, 2010).

B Corps

In B Corporations, the prognosis is that (i) the current legal structure for business privileges concerns for shareholder profits (thereby restricting the ability of corporations to consider social goals) and (ii) the new legal structure for business legally allows for social goals to take precedence (at times) with incentives for achieving a certain level of environmental and social indicators of performance. The B Lab incentives encourage participation in their certification process by coordinating B Corps discounts, networking and human resource development to further lodge social firms in place and increase the costs of exit. However, much power remains in the hands of shareholders, managers and directors such that it remains to be seen whether B Corps standards actually manifest in a new kind of capitalism.

L3C

Our third case, the L3C, while still in its infancy is already struggling with issues of legitimacy and has become subject to lobbying efforts by charity organizations opposing their institutionalization at the federal level. An analysis based on social movement theory suggests their struggle for legitimacy may be rooted in inconsistent and even contradictory frames. While both the L3C and the B Corporation emphasize the importance of their new social business structures in terms of branding, for L3Cs the brand has virtually no gate keeping or auditing processes in place. Therefore, the L3C model relies on socially motivated managers and investors to participate in these organizations and exercise their influence to keep social goals at the forefront. The dominant frame surrounding the L3C diagnoses the problem as a lack of patient capital for social enterprises and provides the solution of a new legal structure designed specifically to capture Foundation PRI. That said, L3Cs are frequently promoted on the basis of their ability to offer market rate returns to non-charitable investors by using PRIs to absorb a higher portion of risk. Given that in both the L3C and the B Corporation member or shareholder votes (respectively) can undue any statutory obligations to social goals, and (so far) only in the B Corporation has there been a public revoking of a certification status, the lack of clarity in the motivating impulse behind the L3C, combined with a lack of regulation, may explain the initial tepid reception to the legal structure by actors in the broader environment.

Discussion and conclusion

In this chapter I have chronicled the emergence of three new legal forms for socially motivated business enterprises and examined them through the lenses of stakeholder theory and social movement theory. Putting the findings of both the firm level stakeholder saliency analysis together with the field level social movement analysis allows us to explore the interplay between organizational and environmental conditions surrounding the institutionalization of each new form.

Although all three initiatives provide more legitimacy and in some cases power for socially motivated stakeholders, analysis of these new legal forms for social enterprise through the lens of stakeholder theory suggests that the CIC form provides the strongest platform for secondary stakeholders (such as community) to exert control over the direction of the firm. In fact, by including seats for community stakeholders on the board, by requiring annual reports on stakeholder involvement and social benefit impact, and through an active regulatory regime, CICs in many ways reconstruct so-called secondary stakeholders into primary ones. Conversely, in both the L3C and the B Corps models, while social goals are legitimated, enforcing these protections for social goals may still require ongoing efforts by stakeholders to maintain a level of urgency to their claims.

A social movement based analysis sheds light on the divergent contexts in which the efforts to establish and legitimate these three new legal frameworks are unfolding. All three attempt to establish new institutional firm level arrangements for social business to operate within. But, "recognizing that social organization rests on multiple forms of coordination – authoritative rules and relationships, symbolic resonance, embedding in personal ties, and alignment of interests" (Clemens, 2005, 360) the case comparison highlights the complex relationship between the fields and forms that shape these three efforts at institutional change.

In the UK a highly developed infrastructure for social enterprise activity aids the establishment and institutionalization of the CIC form. Under the Labour Party, when social enterprise was strongly associated with a liberal social policy agenda, the strong frame of community control surrounding the CICs aligned well with broad anti-corporate social movements, though the initially low dividend caps inhibited market investment in the new form. As political power changed hands from Labour to Conservative, and the strategic action field changed, market oriented reforms to increase commercial investment in CICs resonated differently as the role of CICs in the National Health Service reform hinted that they may continue to be used as a tool of government, though for a very different agenda.

In the US, the mobilizing structures and political opportunities for social enterprise are less developed at the field level than in the UK. The multilevel analysis highlights the advantages that the B Corp has relative to the L3C, given this landscape. B Lab and the L3C both advance a new legal structure for social business, though B Lab additionally provides the "authoritative rules" governing organizational behavior through the certification process, which provides a "symbolic resonance" with the anti-corporate social movement by framing B Corps as the foundation of a new kind of capitalism, and which has focused the efforts of their mobilizing organization onto both generating resources that create incentives for B Corps participation and on building business networks that are embedded "in personal ties". On the other hand, the L3C suffers from contradictory frames. By advancing both tranching and social purpose dominance as motivating the effort to establish L3Cs, the campaign suffers from the perception of a violation of the "alignment of interests" between social business and anti-corporate movements. The ambiguity surrounding a regulatory regime for L3Cs places them on the wrong side of one of the central anti-corporate social movement frames, whereby a lack of regulation and community input is viewed as fostering corporate misbehavior, and which has generated resistance by those concerned that the L3Cs will be vulnerable to pressures from profit maximizing stakeholders. Further, in a country context without a clear set of rules and regulations governing social enterprise or established working relationships at the national level for advancing these new legal forms, L3Cs may not have the opportunity to make adjustments to the legal framework to address structural tensions in the early phases of development as the CICs did in the UK case.

Given that these organizations are only in the very first stages of legal ratification and adoption, it is yet unclear to what extent these organizational models will be embraced and inhabited. If they are, it is equally unclear how they will behave as they brave the sea of economic and societal forces in new untested organizational models. As these new legal forms establish themselves more fully in the landscape, more research is needed to investigate the extent that socially oriented stakeholders become active to keep social businesses mission directed. Future studies using stakeholder theory in conjunction with social movement theory might explore how collective action varies across stakeholder groups and examine the variance in strategies and tactics used by socially motivated stakeholders across the different organizational models to maintain firm level commitments to social goals.

Note

1. The Charities Act of 2006 expanded the list of acceptable charitable purposes to include: poverty, education, religion, health, community development, arts, culture and science, amateur sport, human rights, environment, relief, animal welfare, armed forces, police and fire, and a catch-all category of similar charitable purposes.

References

Alter, S. K. (2006). "Social Enterprise Models and their Mission and Money Relationships." In A. Nicholls (ed.), *Social Entrepreneurship: New Models of Sustainable Social Change*. New York: Oxford University Press, pp. 205–232.

Americans for Community Development. (2011). www.americansforcommunitydevelopment.org/

B Corporation. (2010). www.bcorporation.net/.

Ball, S. J. (2010). "Social and Education Policy, Social Enterprise, Hybridity and New Discourse Communities." Paper presented at the Social Policy Association Conference, University of Lincoln, UK.

Bode, I., Evers, A., and Schulz, A. (2006). "Work Integration Social Enterprises in Europe: Can Hybridization Be Sustainable?" In M. Nyssens (Ed.), *Social Enterprise: At the Crossroads of Market, Public Policies and Civil Society*. London: Routledge, pp. 237–258.

Chan, E. (2010). Maryland"s Benefit Corporation.

Clemens, E. S. (2005). "Two Kinds of Stuff: The Current Encounter of Social Movements and Organizations". In G. F. Davis, D. Mcadam, W. R. Scott & M. N. Zald (eds), *Social Movements and Organizational Theory*. Cambridge: Cambridge University Press, pp. 351–365.

Cohen, R. (2009). "L3C: Pot of Gold or Space Invader", web log post, www.blueavocado.org/content/l3c-pot-gold-or-space-invader.

Cooney, K., and Williams Shanks, T. (2010). "New Approaches to Old Problems: Market-based Strategies for Poverty Alleviation." *Social Service Review* 84(1): 29–55.

Dart, R. (2004). "The Legitimacy of Social Enterprise." *Nonprofit Management and Leadership*, 14(4), 411–424.

Davies, W. (2004). "How to Tame Capitalism." *New Statesman*, September 13.

Davis, G. F., McAdam, D., Scott, W. R., and Zald, M. N. (eds). (2005). *Social Movements and Organizational Theory*. Cambridge: Cambridge University Press.

Dees, J. G., and Anderson, B. B. (2003). "Blurring Lines between Nonprofit and for-Profit." *Society*, May/June.

Donaldson, T., and Preston, L. E. (1995). "The Stakeholder Theory of the Corporation: Concepts, Evidence and Implications." *Academy of Management Review*, 20(1): 65–91.

Eikenberry, A. M., and Kluver, J. D. (2004). The Marketization of the Nonprofit Sector: Civil Society at Risk? *Public Administration Review*, 64(2): 132–140.

Fligstein, N., and McAdam, D. (2011). "Toward a General Theory of Strategic Action Fields." *Sociological Theory,* 29(1): 1–26.

Foster, W., and Bradach, J. (2005). "Should Nonprofits Seek Profits?" *Harvard Business Review,* 83(February): 92–100.

Freeman, R. E. (1984). *Strategic Management: a Stakeholder Approach.* Boston: Pitman Publishing.

Gilbert, J. C. (2011). "Can I Get a Witness?! The Evolution of Capitalism." *Huffington Post,* September 27. Retrieved from http://www.huffingtonpost.com/jay-coen-gilbert/benefit-corporation-legislation-_b_976650.html

Glaister, D. (2011). "Community Delays Gloucestershire's NHS Community Interest Company." *The Guardian,* October 5.

Hrywna, M. (2009). "The LC3 Status: Groups Explore Structure that Limits Liability for Program-related Investing." *The Non-profit Times,* September 1.

Katz, R. A., and Page, A. (2010). "The Role of Social Enterprise." *Vermont Law Review,* 35: 59–103.

King, B. G. (2008). "a Social Movement Perspective of Stakeholder Collective Action and Influence." *Business and Society,* 47(1): 21–49.

Korosec, R. L., and Berman, E. M. (2006). "Municipal Support for Social Entrepreneurship." *Public Administration Review* (May/June): 448–462.

Kleinberger, D. S. (2010). *A Myth Deconstructed: The "Emperor's New Clothes" on the Low Profit Limited Liability Company.* Legal Studies Research Paper Series Working Paper No. 2010-03. William Mitchell College of Law. Retrieved from http://papers.ssrn.com/sol3/papers.cfm?abstract_id=1554045

Maguire, S., and Phillips, N. (2010). "Theorizing Risk and Organization." Paper presented at the 26th Annual EGOS Conference, Lisbon.

Margolis, J., and Walsh, J. (2003). "Misery Loves Companies: Rethinking Social Initiatives by Businesses." *Administrative Science Quarterly,* 48, 268–305.

Marquis, C., Glynn, M. A., and Davis, G. F. (2007). "Community Isomorphism and Corporate Social Action." *Academy of Management Review,* 32(3): 925–945.

McAdam, D., McCarthy, J. D., and Zald, M. N. (1996). "Introduction: Opportunities, Mobilizing Structures, and Framing Processes Toward a Synthetic Comparative Perspective on Social Movements." In D. McAdam, J. D. McCarthy and M. N. Zald (Eds.), *Comparative Perspectives on Social Movements.* New York: Cambridge University Press.

Mitchell, R. K., Agle, B. R., and Wood, D. J. (1997). "Toward a Theory for Stakeholder Identification and Salience: Defining the Principle of Who and What Really Counts." *Academy of Management Review,* 22(4): 853–886.

Moneybox. (2000). "The Scoop on Ben & Jerry's Sellout." *Slate,* April 12. Retrieved from http://www.slate.com/articles/business/moneybox/2000/04/the_scoop_on_ben_jerrys_sellout.html.

Neck, H., Brush, C., and Allen, E. (2009). "The Landscape of Social Entrepreneurship." *Business Horizons,* 52: 13–19.

Orlistzky, M., Schmidt, F., and Rynes, S. (2003). "Corporate Social and Financial Performance: a Meta-Analysis." *Organization Studies,* 24: 241–265.

Orts, E., and Strudler, A. (2009). "Putting a Stake in Stakeholder Theory." *Journal of Business Ethics,* 88 (Supplement 4): 605–615.

Phillips, R., Freeman, R. E., and Wicks, A. C. (2003). "What Stakeholder Theory Is Not." *Business Ethics Quarterly,* 13(4): 479–502.

Salamon, L. M. (1993). *The Marketization of Welfare: Changing Nonprofit and for-Profit Roles in the American Welfare State.* Baltimore: Johns Hopkins University Press.

Schmidt, E. (2010). "Vermont's Social Hybrid Pioneers: Early Observations and Questions to Ponder." Research Paper no. 10–49, Vermont Law School Legal Studies Research Paper Series. South Royalton, VT.

Scully, M. A., and Creed, W. E. D. (2005). Subverting Our Stories of Subversion. In D. McAdam, J. D. McCarthy, W. R. Scott and M. N. Zald (Eds.), *Social Movement and Organization Theory*. New York: Cambridge University Press, pp. 310–332.

Simmons, J. (2004). "Managing in the Post-Managerialist Era: towards Socially Responsible Coreporate Governance." *Management Decision*, 42(3/4): 601–611.

Snow, D. A., & Benford, R. D. (1988). "Ideology, Frame Resonance, and Participant Mobilization". In B. Klandermans, H. Kriesi, & S. Tarrow (eds), *International Social Movement Research. Vol 1: From Structure on Action: Comparing Social Movement Research across Cultures*. Greenwich, CT: JAI Press, pp. 197–217.

Social Enterprise. (2009). "The LC3: A Complete Backgrounder", http://socialenterpriseblog.com

Social Enterprise UK. (2011). www.socialenterprise.org.uk/.

Spear, R., Cornforth, C., and Aiken, M. (2007). *For Love and Money: Governance and Social Enterprise*. Milton Keynes, UK: Open University.

The Regulator of Community Interest Companies (2009). "Community Interest Companies: Frequently Asked Questions", Department for Business Innovation and Skills. Retrieved from http://www.bis.gov.uk/assets/cicregulator/docs/leaflets/09-1648-community-interest-companies-frequently-asked-questions-leaflet

The Regulator of Community Interest Companies. (2010, July). *Annual Report*. Department for Business Innovation and Skills. Retrieved from http://www.bis.gov.uk/assets/cicregulator/docs/annual-reports/10-p117-community-interest-companies-annual-report-2009-2010.

The Regulator of Community Interest Companies. (2011, September). *Annual Report 2010–2011*. Department for Business Innovation and Skills. Retrieved from http://www.bis.gov.uk/assets/cicregulator/docs/annual-reports/11-p117-community-interest-companies-annual-report-2010-2011

Tuckman, H. P. (1998). "Competition, Commercialization, and the Evolution of Nonprofit Organizational Structures." In B. A. Weisbrod (Ed.), *To Profit or Not to Profit*. New York: Cambridge University Press, pp. 25–45.

Weber, J. (2010). "'Impact Investing' Teeters on the Edge of Explosive Growth." *The New York Times*, October 9, www.nytimes.com/2010/10/10/us/10bcweber.html?_r=1

Weisbrod, B. A. (2004). "The Pitfalls of Profits." *Stanford Social Innovation Review* (Winter): 40–47.

Wheeler, D., and Sillanpää, M. (1998). "Including the Stakeholders: the Business Case." *Long Range Planning*, 31(2): 201–210.

World Social Forum. (2011). http://fsm2011.org/en/wsf-2011.

Young, D. R., and Salamon, L. M. (2002). "Commercialization, Social Ventures, and for-Profit Competition." In L. M. Salamon (Ed.), *The State of Nonprofit America*. Washington, DC: Brookings Institution Press, pp. 423–446.

Zetetist. (2011). "Peninsula Community Health: What Point?" October 5. Retrieved from http://cornishzetetics.blogspot.com/2011/10/peninsula-community-health-what-point.html

Zouhali-Worrall, M. (2010). "For LC3 Companies, Profit Isn't the Point", http://money.cnn.com/2010/02/08/smallbusiness/l3c_low_profit_companies/

Zwetsch, R. (2009). "How-to: An Insider's Look at the LC3 and What it Could Mean for You and Your Social Enterprise." *Social Earth*, www.socialearth.org/how-to-an-insider%E2%80%99s-look-at-the-l3c-and-what-it-could-mean-for-you-and-your-social-enterprise

10
Postscript: The Legitimacy of Social Entrepreneurship: Reflexive Isomorphism in a Pre-paradigmatic Field

*Alex Nicholls**

Introduction

It has become axiomatic in recent years for scholars to make two observations concerning social entrepreneurship: first, that there is no definitive consensus about what the term actually means (Light, 2006, 2008; Perrini, 2006); second, that the research agenda for the field is not yet clearly defined (Nicholls, 2006a, 2006b, 2009; Short *et al.*, 2009). It has also been noted that the community of scholars currently engaging with the subject is small, under-resourced, and somewhat marginalized (Battle Anderson & Dees, 2006). Kuhn (1962) observed that an established academic paradigm attracts legitimacy and resources to a field of action that are largely withheld in a pre-paradigmatic state. Following Kuhn, the current status of social entrepreneurship can be conceptualized as a field that has yet to achieve a paradigmatic consensus and that lacks a "normal science" or clear epistemology. However, despite the apparent constraints of its pre-paradigmatic status, an analysis of social entrepreneurship suggests that emergent patterns of institutionalization can be discerned, each characterized by its own discourses, narrative logics and ideal-type organizational models. Such patterns are characterized here as contests for the control of the legitimating discourses that will determine the final shape of the social entrepreneurial paradigm. This is a particular characteristic of a field that is at a less well-developed stage of legitimacy than the key paradigm-building actors within it.

In an exploratory study, this chapter delineates the construction of social entrepreneurship as an institutional space in terms of the legitimating strategies of the key actors who are driving the processes of paradigm building. Such an analysis suggests that much of this activity reflects a competition for institutional control and paradigmatic dominance as much as a project to support and develop social entrepreneurs. Two new contributions are made here, one theoretical and one empirical.

First, the chapter extends neo-institutional theory in terms of the role played by legitimacy in processes of institutionalization. Using approaches from structuration theory (Giddens, 1984; Nicholls and Cho, 2006), this research explores the microstructures of legitimation in this emergent field and identifies a reflexive relationship between field- and organization-level legitimation strategies in social entrepreneurship. This analysis suggests a new category of organizational isomorphism that is particularly appropriate to emergent fields: reflexive isomorphism.

Second, this chapter carries out a content analysis of the public definitions of social entrepreneurship propagated by eight dominant paradigm-building groups of actors. Following accepted practice for data collection in institutionalist research into organizational legitimacy (e.g. Deephouse, 1996; Singh *et al.*, 1986), two factors are used to identify these actors: their prominence in the existing literature and their level of investment in the field. Categorizing the data reveals distinct clusters of discourses associated with different paradigm-building actors that are used to provide supporting evidence for the chapter's theoretical propositions. Despite the clear influence of the paradigm-building actors on the emerging normative perceptions of social entrepreneurship as a field, no analysis of their public discourses has yet been carried out from an institutional legitimacy perspective.

This research provides three insights with respect to social entrepreneurship that are also relevant to other institutionalization processes in emergent fields more generally. First, the pre-paradigmatic status of a field allows resource-rich actors to leverage power over the legitimating processes that characterize progress toward institutionalization. Second, such actors enact these processes by aligning the key discourses and norms of the field with their own internal logics of action as part of a process of reflexive self-legitimation. Third, there are significant implications of this process for other field actors who lack power or dominance.

The remainder of the chapter proceeds as follows. Next, a Kuhnian analysis of social entrepreneurship is set out to explore its pre-paradigmatic phase of development. This suggests that social entrepreneurship currently represents a fluid institutional space for dominant actors to shape and exploit. After this, the processes by which organizations accrue legitimacy are set out in the context of neo-institutional theory. Particular attention is paid to the microstructures of legitimation in terms of key actors and discourses. This leads to the development of a new construct – reflexive isomorphism – that reflects a structuration (Giddens, 1984) perspective on legitimation in emergent fields. Following this, the dominant actors engaged in the paradigmatic development of social entrepreneurship are identified. A content analysis of these actors' public statements concerning social entrepreneurship reveals three discourses: individualism via the hero entrepreneur; business efficiency; communitarian values and social justice. Returning to legitimacy theory, it is then proposed that the emerging normative discourses and narrative logics of social entrepreneurship represent legitimating material for resource-rich actors. The chapter concludes by delineating a role for scholarly research on social entrepreneurship in terms of its future paradigmatic development.

Social entrepreneurship as pre-paradigm

Kuhn (1962) explored the development of academic fields of study in terms of the conceptual construct of "normal science." Normal science was a function of two elements: "rules," defined as agreed methods and approaches to research, and "paradigms," defined as agreed epistemological systems that set the boundaries for research objects of distinct validity. Normal science was, thus, the application of rules to paradigms. However, Kuhn also observed that this was not a static model and that new paradigms emerge as a consequence of a growing awareness of an anomaly in practice that defied categorization by existing paradigmatic approaches. This recognition is typically characterized by an increase in the empirical and theoretical attention focused on a new field-level phenomenon.

In many accounts, social entrepreneurship has been presented as just such a phenomenon – styled as a new field of practice responding to an increasingly urgent set of global crises with innovation at the systemic level (Osberg and Martin, 2007). However, the development of research into social entrepreneurship to date suggests it is in a pre-paradigmatic phase typified by Kuhn as having deep debates over the legitimate methods, problems and the usefulness and quality of alternative solutions that are appropriate to the new area of study. Thus, social entrepreneurship research has much in common with the "accumulative fragmentalism" noted by Harrison and Leitch (1996) in the establishment of the field of entrepreneurship (Light, 2008; Perrini, 2006).

This has been characterized by a multidisciplinary contest over the epistemology of the field that has failed to set any normative boundaries around the term (Nicholls, 2006a, 2006b; Nicholls and Young, 2008; Peredo and McLean, 2006; Shaw and Carter, 2007; Sullivan Mort *et al.*, 2003; Weerawardena and Sullivan Mort, 2006; see parallels in Aldrich and Baker, 1997, 396). Over the past 10 to 15 years since it first entered mainstream public discourse (e.g., Leadbeater, 1997), social entrepreneurship has been subject to a competing range of definitions, and there still remains a distinct lack of clarity over what it means. Variously, it has been presented as a new model of systemic social change (Bornstein, 2004; Nicholls, 2006b), the solution to state failures in welfare provision (Aiken, 2006; Bovaird, 2006; LeGrand, 2003), a new market opportunity for business (Prahalad, 2005), a model of political transformation and empowerment (Alvord *et al.*, 2004; Yunus, 2008), and a space for new hybrid partnerships (Austin *et al.*, 2006). Furthermore, Perrini

(2006, 6–11) noted that there are "limited" and "extended" definitions of the term: the former positions social entrepreneurship as a new aspect of the not-for-profit world, while the latter discusses it as a wider societal force for change. Similarly, Light (2008) highlighted the apparent tensions between a "big" and "small" tent approach to social entrepreneurship.

The methodologies typical of social entrepreneurship research to date are also clearly pre-paradigmatic in a Kuhnian sense, in that they have often focused on available data – usually in the form of descriptive case studies of the "celebrity" social entrepreneurs identified by other field-building actors – rather than on building new datasets. The lack of a clear epistemology of the field at a societal level presents particular methodological problems since it results in a lack of public datasets (unlike charities, there is no specific legal form for social entrepreneurship) and discourages comparative work. It also has the consequence that innovative research often has to tackle empirical challenges before it can test theory. The effect of these methodological issues has been a polarizing of social entrepreneurship scholarship into either empirical work drawing repeatedly on a small set of the same case examples or theoretical work that lacks empirical support.

With respect to the process of paradigm development, Kuhn suggested that a new paradigm gains status based upon its ability to problem-solve for dominant actors that themselves have influence on relevant institutional structures and logics. Furthermore, Kuhn noted that established paradigms provide sources of legitimacy for such dominant actors, and that this could be a resource strategy. Paradigmatic development is an arena in which power and dominance is expressed often through the deliberative construction of "a dense network of connections" that aims intentionally and systematically to consolidate relevant centers of power and influence to impose the dominance of their views across the institutionalization of the field (Kuhn, 1962, 618). Paradigms are inherently exclusionary, to the point where they may "insulate the community from those socially important problems that are not reducible to puzzle form, because they cannot be stated in terms of the conceptual and instrumental tools the paradigm provides" (ibid., 37).

Building on Kuhn, institutionalist scholars have noted that paradigm development is not a neutral process. In his work on the development of the field of organizational studies, Pfeffer (1993) noted that the observed level of paradigmatic development varies across fields since it is an institutional product dependent on the social structure, culture and power relations that characterize a field (i.e. how it is organized and the factors that create and perpetuate that organization). Moreover, paradigmatic development is often subject to resistance and objection since the successful establishment of a new paradigm can provide status, legitimacy and access to resources to its key actors within a competitive epistemological context (see Abbott, 1988; Lodahl and Gordon, 1972). For example, it has been demonstrated that academic fields with more highly developed paradigms attract more external and internal funding (Lodahl and Gordon, 1973; Pfeffer and Moore, 1980) and have higher peer-reviewed journal acceptance rates (Hargens, 1988). There are also correlations between paradigmatic development and the structure of academic journal editorial boards (Yoels, 1974) and academic departmental governance (e.g., there is more autonomy given to high paradigmatic development fields such as finance: Lodahl and Gordon, 1973). Following the logic of this research into paradigm development, it becomes clear that an analysis of the progression of a field from pre- to post-paradigmatic status can be understood as a contested process of legitimation between different actors, discourses and institutional logics (see parallels in Busenitz *et al.*, 2003). The next section I establishes a theoretical framework to analyze these microstructures of legitimation in social entrepreneurship.

Reflexive isomorphism

This chapter conceives of organizational legitimacy as the consequence of a dynamic interplay between macro level institutional structures and micro-level organizational actors. This approach draws upon two related strands of institutionalist research: first, research into organizational legitimacy that aims to give an account of the processes of legitimation in terms of agency in dynamic settings; second, the institutionalist analyses of the relationship between organizational isomorphism and legitimacy that conceives of legitimation as a process of structuration.

There is a well-established history of theorizing organizational legitimacy in terms of conformance to extra-organizational institutional arrangements and forms (DiMaggio and Powell, 1983, 1991; Dowling and Pfeffer, 1975; Roth and Wittich, 1978). This institutionalist school of thought suggests that individual organizations are subject to resource-based pressures to conform to extant sector- or society-level normative frames of reference in order to survive and prosper (Deephouse, 1996; Oliver, 1997; Pfeffer and Salancik, 1978; Ruef and Scott, 1998; Scott, 1995; Zimmerman and Zeitz, 2002; Zucker, 1977). Institutional theory also acknowledges a cultural dimension in its analysis of the processes of legitimation, noting that organizations also represent theoretical constructs consequent upon, and defined by, existing cultural material and networks of social influence and communication (Carter and Deephouse, 1999; Meyer and Rowan, 1977; Meyer and Scott, 1983; Meyer *et al.*, 1978, 1981; for an overview see Deephouse and Suchman, 2008). Theorists have identified various classifications or types of legitimacy. Aldrich and Fiol (1994) suggested a bifurcation of legitimacy into "sociopolitical" (the process by which key stakeholders deem an organization appropriate) and "cognitive" (the spread of knowledge about a new venture). Scott (1995) and Suchman (1995) focused on the former type and identified a tripartite structure within it characterized as regulative/pragmatic, normative/moral and cognitive legitimacies.

Much of the pioneering institutional research into legitimacy did not consider organizational innovation and the processes of change in institutional systems and presented a largely static model of the structural pressures and macrolevel influences on organizational behavior and form. However, more recent research into organizational innovation and institutional change has acknowledged a more dynamic set of legitimating processes. Stryker (2000) presented legitimacy as the consequence of dynamic political contests between competing institutional logics. Lounsbury (2007) identified three institutional arenas (rhetorical, discursive and technical) within which struggles over what is legitimate and who is authorized to theorize and certify are played out. Other research described the microstructures of legitimation in terms of strategic projects that construct appropriate organizational narratives selectively from an extant "stock" of exogenous cultural norms and myths (Hargrave and Van der Ven, 2006; Lounsbury and Glynn, 2001). This more dynamic perspective acknowledges the interplay between organizations and larger institutional structures as legitimation processes that are constantly in flux (Hybels, 1995).

Congruent with this perspective, another stream of institutionalist research has focused on agency in legitimation processes by exploring the legitimating role and function of various actors and their relationships, including society at large, the media (Baum and Powell, 1995) and specific legitimacy-granting authorities (i.e., the State: Suddaby and Greenwood, 2005). This body of work also examined organizational strategies aimed at influencing legitimacy perceptions, for example by the use of donations, forming cross-organizational management interconnections, obtaining external endorsements (Galaskiewicz, 1985) or using other forms of impression management (Elsbach, 1994; Elsbach and Sutton, 1992). Ashforth and Gibbs (1990) summarized such techniques under two general headings: "substantive" (legitimating strategies based on organizational action) and "symbolic" (legitimating strategies based upon the "essences" of the organization). Suchman (1995) provided the most developed account of the management of organizational legitimacy in a 12-part model of the strategic techniques through which positive legitimacy perceptions are created, maintained and recovered. He explicitly suggested that organizations sometimes gain legitimacy by manipulating rather than conforming to their environments, particularly to support the diffusion and adoption of new models of action. In these cases, organizations actively construct and promote new rationales and logics of social reality. However, Suchman ultimately saw this as an instrumental process aimed at aligning environmental factors with organizational ends: the focus is on shaping existing institutional material to an organization's strategic needs rather than creating a new institutional space as a process of field building per se.

Subsequent work in this theoretical tradition has focused more on the micro level actions that support the strategic management of legitimation processes. Phillips *et al.* (2004) used discourse analysis to explore how the use and creation of texts can shape and determine wider legitimation processes. Drawing on Lukes (1974) and others, such processes were revealed as being inherently political and often coercive expressions of power relationships and structures (for example, in cases of resource scarcity). From this perspective, it is the manipulation of discourses that defines what can be considered as legitimate or illegitimate. These processes reveal dominant actors behaving as "institutional entrepreneurs" who work "to affect the discourses that constitute the institutions or mechanisms of compliance in a particular field in a self-interested way" (Phillips *et al.*, 2004, 648). Such self-interest is often an expression of strategies of self-legitimation as much as an explicit resource-based issue. Phillips *et al.* also noted that new textual material often builds legitimacy by drawing explicitly on other, better established, texts – this is presented as part of a process by which the supremacy of particular discourses is established. Vaara *et al.* (2006) further developed this theme in their analysis of six forms of discourse control within "discursive legitimation" strategies (normalization, authorization, rationalization, moralization and narrativization). This work also noted the close relationship between sources of power and discourse mobilization and propagation. Finally, Kaplan (2008) drew upon social movement theory to propose that cognitive framing is another strategic approach to legitimation that brings in agency at the level of reality construction.

Developing Weberian theory concerning the influence of bureaucracy on organizational forms, DiMaggio and Powell (1983) identified three types of isomorphic pressure that constitute the homogenization processes apparent in highly structured organizational fields. However, in contrast to earlier work that suggested competitive market pressures drove isomorphism, DiMaggio and Powell suggested that competition for organizational legitimacy within structures of institutional norms and power relations was the important causal factor. Coercive isomorphism captured the process by which powerful external actors, such as the state or resource providers, forced organizations toward uniformity. Mimetic isomorphism encouraged organizations to imitate other models to counter the risks of organizational uncertainty in underdeveloped fields. In terms of normative isomorphism, the influence of professional bodies and standards was shown to exert influence. Following Giddens (1984), DiMaggio and Powell suggested that these isomorphic processes represented examples of structuration between organizations and larger institutional forces. However, whilst a clear account is given of the nature of organizational level change, there is much less said about the effects of organizations on the macro level institutional structures with which they interact.

This chapter combines insights from DiMaggio and Powell's work on organizational isomorphism with later institutional theory that examined the patterns of agency in legitimation processes to explore the microstructures within the institutionalization of social entrepreneurship. This approach is used to identify the dominant actors and key discourses that are shaping the field as a paradigm. This research also aims to contribute to a better understanding of the dynamics of agency-structure relationships in institutional legitimation processes, specifically with reference to the power relations between key actors. Although institutional accounts of legitimacy acknowledge the relevance of legitimating actors there is little analysis of their role or function in the larger legitimating process. In a sense, such theorizing has desocialized organizational legitimacy by seeing it as a systemic rather than individualized process (see, for example, Friedland and Alford, 1991).

Social entrepreneurship represents something of a special case with respect to organizational legitimacy since it lacks a well-defined normative logic (within clear epistemological boundaries) against which stakeholder perceptions of action can be compared (Nicholls, 2008, 2010a). In this sense, social entrepreneurs are immune from the conventional isomorphic forces typically identified in start-up or underdeveloped field contexts (Deephouse, 1996; DiMaggio and Powell, 1983; though see Dart, 2004 for a critique of isomorphism in social enterprise). Although this is potentially strategically liberating in the short term, Kuhnian theory suggests that the lack of established institutional patterns and discourses around social entrepreneurship will threaten its overall legitimacy, as a field of action, over time (by undermining its normative mandate to operate) and may be a fatal constraint on resource flows as population ecologists have proved elsewhere (Rao, 1994; Ruef and Scott, 1998). In response to this, a number of paradigm-building actors can be discerned, each of whom is attempting to build a distinct logic of social entrepreneurship that most effectively enhances their own legitimation strategies in a self-reflexive way.

Morgan (2006) suggested that autopoeisis theory – originally developed in studies of closed biological systems (Maturana and Varela, 1973) – could be applied (with caveats) to an analysis of patterns of organizational development. Morgan observed that organizations attempt to achieve a form of self-referential closure with respect to their environments by enacting them as extensions of their own identity. Ultimately, this produced a closed-loop system in which organizations interacted with projections of themselves, mistaking this for institutional material from outside the loop. Morgan also suggested that this type of action should be seen as part of a process of sustaining self-reproduction.

Following Morgan (2006), an analysis of the processes of paradigm building in social entrepreneurship suggests a fourth type of isomorphic pressure that is characterized here as *reflexive isomorphism*. In contrast to the other three forms, this type of isomophic pressure privileges agency over structure by suggesting that dominant organizations can shape the legitimacy of an emergent field to reflect their own institutional logics and norms. Reflexive isomorphism represents a legitimating strategy in which organizations actively engage in processes that align field-level and internal logics to shape emergent institutional fields as closed systems of self-legitimation. It is proposed here that this is a particular characteristic of social entrepreneurship as a field since it currently functions as a closed system characterized by high levels of self-reference and low levels of interaction outside of its own *habitus* (Bourdieu, 1993). In order to explore the patterns of reflexive isomorphism that are currently emerging in social entrepreneurship, the remainder of this chapter first identifies the key paradigm-building actors in this field and then analyzes the discourses, narratives and logics of social entrepreneurship that they are propagating in their public statements. This institutional material serves to reveal the microstructures of legitimation emerging in the field.

Paradigm-building actors

While the landscape of social entrepreneurship is populated with many organizations, there are only a small number that are actively engaged with paradigm building. The latter can be identified by their prominence in the literature and debate around social entrepreneurship and by the resources they have committed to developing the field. Their paradigm-building objectives are often made explicit in statements on websites or are implicit in actions they take such as enacting supporting legislation for social entrepreneurs. Four groups of actors can be discerned:

First, Government has been active in supporting (and shaping) social entrepreneurship, particularly in the United Kingdom via the Office of the Third Sector and, since 2010, the Office of Civil Society (OTS, 2006; Social Enterprise Unit, 2002).
Second, there are Foundations, such as UnLtd (Nicholls, 2006b) and the Skoll Foundation (Lounsbury and Strang, 2009).
Third, there are Fellowship organizations, such as Ashoka (Bornstein, 2004) and the Schwab Foundation for Social Entrepreneurship (Elkington and Hartigan, 2008).
Finally, there are Network organizations (Grenier, 2006): in the United Kingdom, these include the Social Enterprise Alliance, the Community Action Network (CAN) and the Social Enterprise Coalition (SEC: renamed Social Enterprise UK in 2011).

Collectively, these paradigm-building actors have been highly influential in establishing the discourses, narratives and ideal types that characterize the early-stage development of social entrepreneurship. Of course, there are many other influential players active in promoting social entrepreneurship across the globe, many of which are resource providers, for example: Bangladesh Rural Advancement Committee (BRAC) in Asia, Accion in Latin

America and the Jacana Venture Partnership in Africa. However, these actors are typically not focused on paradigm-building issues, but rather direct their efforts toward developing the field of practice by direct interventions and, as a consequence, are excluded from the analysis here.

Government

State investment in social entrepreneurship represents the largest commitment of capital to the field. Such investment typically focuses on capacity development for growing the effectiveness and efficiency of the provision of public goods, often by supporting the social enterprise sector (see Nicholls, 2010c; Nicholls and Pharoah, 2007). In the United Kingdom, state funds already committed to such social investment amounted to more than £750 million by 2010 (Nicholls, 2010c). The UK government also created a new form of incorporation specifically for social enterprises: the Community Interest Company (Nicholls, 2010b). In addition, the Social Enterprise Unit (established in 2000) within the UK government sponsored significant amounts of sector-specific research including a £5 million commitment to a bespoke Third Sector Research Centre at the Universities of Birmingham and Southampton. State expenditure on social investment is far less evident elsewhere in the world, but this is beginning to change in the United States with the establishment of a $50 million (£31 million) Social Innovation Fund within the White House in 2009.

Foundations

An important part of the UK government support for social entrepreneurs is UnLtd, which was set up in 2002 with a £100 million Millennium Commission grant from the UK government. It styles itself as the "Foundation for Social Entrepreneurs" and sets outs its mission as "to support and develop the role of social entrepreneurs as a force for positive change in the United Kingdom." UnLtd is both a grant-giving institution and a consultancy service to social entrepreneurs at different stages of their organizational development. It has four strategic objectives: giving awards, building a fellowship of awardees, carrying out research into the impact of social entrepreneurs on society, and offering consultancy services via its UnLtd Ventures group. By 2009, UnLtd had supported over 5,000 social entrepreneurs. It has awarded approximately £40 million in grants since its inception.

Based in Palo Alto, CA, the Skoll Foundation was founded in 1999 by Jeff Skoll, co-founder and first president of eBay. It is a grant-giving foundation whose mission is "to advance systemic change to benefit communities around the world by investing in, connecting, and celebrating social entrepreneurs." An important element of this mission was the creation of the Skoll Centre for Social Entrepreneurship at the University of Oxford (in 2003), where the annual Skoll World Forum on Social Entrepreneurship is held. By 2009, the foundation had supported 61 Skoll Awardees in Social Entrepreneurship across five continents, providing approximately £120 million in grants.

Fellowship organizations

Ashoka is the largest and most well-established fellowship organization in social entrepreneurship. It was founded by Bill Drayton in 1982 (see Bornstein, 2004, for a comprehensive account of the creation and development of Ashoka). Ashoka's mission is to help "shape a global, entrepreneurial, competitive citizen sector: one that allows social entrepreneurs to thrive and enables the world's citizens to think and act as changemakers." Its key objectives are to support and promote social entrepreneurship and help build a supportive infrastructure for social entrepreneurs. The organization is based in Washington, DC but has a global network of field offices and today has over 2,000 fellows in more than 60 countries. By 2009, Ashoka had invested approximately £220 million in its fellowship.

The Schwab Foundation for Social Entrepreneurship was founded in Geneva in 1998. It grew out of, and is closely linked to, another major institution also created by Klaus Schwab, the World Economic Forum (WEF). Its mission is to provide "unparalleled platforms at the country, regional and global levels that highlight social entrepreneurship as a key element to advance societies and address social problems in an innovative and effective manner." The foundation is not a conventional grant-giving body but rather attempts to build a community of practice and provide access to the WEF for its social entrepreneurs. It is estimated to have invested roughly £4 million directly in social entrepreneurs. In 2010 there were 172 "Schwab Entrepreneurs" across five continents. In 2007, the Foundation embarked on a new project, celebrating a "Social Entrepreneur of the Year" award with key media partners across a number of countries. More recently, the foundation has moved toward closer integration into WEF.

Network builders

Set up in London in 1998, the Community Action Network (CAN) was the vision of three individuals – Andrew Mawson, Adele Blakebrough and Helen Taylor Thompson – all of whom were already proven leaders in innovative community projects. CAN aims to support social entrepreneurs to scale up their activities and maximize their social impact. The CAN does this through practical strategies including providing office space, business support and leveraging social investment. CAN is not a funder itself.

Growing out of the first National Gathering for Social Entrepreneurs held in Colorado in 1998, the Social Enterprise Alliance emerged in 2002 as a partnership between the National Gathering and Seachange, a financial services brokerage organization for social enterprises and funders. The Alliance is a membership network that aims to "build stronger, more effective social enterprises by mobilizing a community of practitioners and investors to advance earned income strategies." The Alliance has a specific focus on not-for-profits that develop earned income strategies, stating that "earned income strategies help to make organizations high-performing. More social benefit can be generated when individual mission-based organizations adopt appropriate earned income strategies as part of their revenue base. Social value can be enhanced when mission-based organizations come together to increase the impact and effectiveness of the field."

Founded in 2000, the Social Enterprise Coalition (SEC) acts as the UK "industry body" for social enterprises. It was originally government-funded and represented one of several policy measures to raise the profile of social enterprise and increase its impact. However, it is not politically aligned and engages with all parties in the UK. The SEC sets out its objectives as the following:

- To promote the benefits of social enterprise through press work, campaigns and events
- To share best practice amongst social enterprises through networks and publications
- To inform the policy agenda working with key decision makers
- To undertake research to expand the social enterprise evidence base

The SEC renamed itself Social Enterprise UK in 2011.

While each of these groups of actors has been engaged in paradigm-building activity, the distribution of resources across them varied significantly. This is reflected in the capital they have invested in the sector and its promotion. The next section considers the different discourses of social entrepreneurship that have been projected by each of these groups of paradigm builders and reflects on the power dynamics across them. Drawing on institutional theory, it is suggested later that these patterns of resource distribution represent important microstructures of power and influence that are promoting particular legitimating discourses in a process of reflexive isomorphism.

Discourses of social entrepreneurship

An analysis of the public statements from the leading paradigm-building actors noted earlier concerning definitions of social entrepreneurship reveals two important dyadic clusters based upon narrative logic and ideal-type organizational models (see Table 10.1). In terms of the narrative logics of social entrepreneurship two sets of discourses can be seen: those that present the hero social entrepreneur as central and those that locate social entrepreneurship in community settings and networks of action. The former is characterized by an individualized focus on key words that capture innate qualities ("leadership," "ambitious," "persistent"), attributes of action ("results-oriented," "pragmatic," "risk-taking") or normative judgments on character ("ethical fiber," "visionary," "passionate"). The former

Table 10.1 Paradigm-building discourses in social entrepreneurship

Discourse cluster	Key words	Source
Narrative logic		
1. Hero entrepreneur	Leadership	Skoll Foundation; Center for Advancement of Social Entrepreneurship (CASE)
	Ambitious	Ashoka; Skoll Foundation
	Persistent	Ashoka; Schwab Foundation; UnLtd
	Opportunistic	Ashoka
	Ethical fiber	Ashoka
	Resourceful	Skoll Foundation; CASE
	Results-oriented	Skoll Foundation; Schwab Foundation; CASE
	Pragmatic	Schwab Foundation
	Visionary	Schwab Foundation; UnLtd
	Passionate	Schwab Foundation; UnLtd
	Risk-taking	Schwab Foundation
2. Community	Community investment	UK Government
	Community cohesion	Community Action Network (CAN)
	Grass-roots driven	CAN
Ideal-type organizational structure		
1. Business-like	Business(-like)	Social Enterprise Alliance (SEA); UK Government; Social Enterprise Coalition (SEC); CASE
	Responsive	UK Government
	Sustainable	Schwab Foundation; Skoll Centre; SEA
	Scale	Ashoka; Schwab Foundation
	Earned income	SEA
	Professional	Schwab Foundation; Skoll Centre
2. Advocacy/social change	Give voice	CAN
	Social value	SEA
	Social justice	SEC

draws on the institutional logic, narratives and myths of commercial entrepreneurship that present successful action as the product of the exceptional individual (Dart, 2004). The latter, in contrast, focuses not on the heroic actor but on localism and bottom-up solutions. This cluster is typified by references to the community and "grass roots" and prioritizes group or network action over individualism. The institutional logic here resonates with the cooperative, communitarian traditions of left-wing politics and ideology and decouples narratives of enterprise from commercial action. This discourse is located within long-standing narratives and rationales of third sector action (Clotfelter, 1992; Evers and Laville, 2004; Salamon and Anheier, 1999).

The second cluster concerns the ideal-type organizational model for social entrepreneurship. In this case, two other sets of opposing institutional logics are evident: those that propose business and commercial models as being central to social entrepreneurship (often associated with notions of sustainability and scale) and those that set social entrepreneurship within a framework of advocacy and social change. The first category presents social entrepreneurship as "social business" and includes key words drawing on the perceived benefits of market-driven organizations ("sustainability," "scale," "professional"). These discourses also suggest that business-like social action is more "responsive" to its social mission and beneficiaries (Blair, 2006). This ideal-type reflects institutional norms concerning the efficiency and effectiveness of commercial organizations in comparison to the state or third sector and draws heavily on the logics of New Public Management and the marketization of the state (LeGrand, 2003; Osbourne and Gaebler, 1992). The second category of key words, on the other hand, builds a discourse of social entrepreneurship based on advocacy and social change. Here, key words include "social value" and "social justice" and ideal-type organizational behavior is characterized as giving beneficiaries voice. Such a discourse draws upon the foundational institutional logics of the third sector and social movements (Davis *et al.*, 2005; Salamon *et al.*, 2003).

This analysis suggests some tensions and conflict across the discourses, narratives and ideal types being presented in the public definitions of social entrepreneurship provided by the main paradigm-building actors. The next section suggests that the clusters can be best understood within microstructures of reflexive isomorphism for specific actors.

Patterns of reflexive isomorphism

Hero entrepreneur narratives

The hero entrepreneur model is given precedence by foundations and fellowship organizations. The dominant internal logic of foundations is to mobilize their resources to bring about change. However, in contrast to traditional philanthropic grant makers that derive their legitimacy from gift giving, the foundations supporting social entrepreneurship draw upon models from private capital that reflect the logics of commercial entrepreneurship. This new "venture" philanthropy is consistent with the normative logics of a number of the successful commercial entrepreneurs – particularly from Silicon Valley – who are currently active in supporting social entrepreneurship. This venture approach legitimates grants as "investments" that demand a maximum "return" on capital. As a consequence, demonstrating effective return on investment becomes the key self-legitimating logic. This leads to a primary focus on success stories (Lounsbury and Strang, 2009) that resonate with existing narratives around commercial entrepreneurs and their achievements. The logic of reflexive isomorphism here is to suggest that social entrepreneurship is legitimated by its hero entrepreneurs and their success stories.

The individual/hero entrepreneur discourse focused on the social entrepreneur itself not only reflects normative notions of the commercial entrepreneur but also lends itself well to marketing activity around building compelling and emotive narratives and myths. The focus on "systemic" change, though never very clearly defined, and going to scale also legitimates a philanthropic model predicated on maximizing return on investment. Presenting social entrepreneurship in this light also satisfies donors who expect more from their money than supporting a welfare service or growing an existing program.

Fellowship organizations have a different internal logic to foundations, based on leveraging social capital around a carefully selected elite. For these actors, demonstrating this leverage effect is their key legitimating factor – a logic borrowed from private capital. As with the foundations engaged with social entrepreneurship, the fellowship organizations also embed the logics of the private sector in their actions, often with explicit connections to important commercial partners such as McKinsey or WEF. Similarly, these organizations exploit the legitimating value of the hero entrepreneur narrative by importing it into the social sphere but also explicitly suggest that such actors gain from a connection to other private-sector actors. The reflexive isomorphism here aims to shape social entrepreneurship as a tightly interconnected elite that shares models and learning within controlled boundaries. The field-shaping role of the paradigm-building actors is quite explicit here since they craft not only the criteria for fellowship but also make the selection decisions.

Foundations and fellowship organizations often use sophisticated marketing communications with which to promulgate their particular legitimating discourses around social entrepreneurship. For example, Participant Productions – an initiative founded by Jeff Skoll in 2004 – has pioneered television and film projects that highlight social entrepreneurs and their work, most notably the "New Heroes" series for Public Broadcasting Service (PBS) in the United States and Al Gore's hit film "*An Inconvenient Truth*." Participant Media aims to use entertainment to bring about social change and also designs campaigns around each of its projects to generate what it calls "lights, camera...social action." Similarly, the Schwab Foundation established key media partners in many countries to promote its hero entrepreneurs and their success stories.

Business model ideal-types

The internal logic of the state is to deliver public goods. In recent years, the public sector has gone through a period of reform that has introduced new management approaches and models based closely on private sector practices. As noted earlier, this model of more responsive and efficient public services delivery – particularly through outsourcing – draws upon the legitimating discourses of New Public Management (Osbourne and Gaebler, 1992;Walsh, 1995) and quasi-markets (LeGrand and Bartlett, 1993), much of which predates the rise of social entrepreneurship by at least ten years. In line with such reforms, states have developed an internal legitimating agenda best understood in terms of notions of increased efficiency, responsiveness and sustainability drawn from business. The dominant model of social entrepreneurship that has attracted government resources has been social enterprise or "businesses trading for a social purpose" (OTS, 2006). These are organizations that explicitly combine social and financial return and apply business models and thinking to achieving their social and environmental aims (Alter, 2006). This ideal-type organizational model has a particular focus on earned income and the use of commercial logics and strategies. In the UK, the government has used its resources both to grow the social enterprise/social business field and to support the establishment of a consistent paradigm of social entrepreneurship based on this model through its use of public policy, more than £750 million of government resources and support of particular public discourses. The effect of this has been striking with more than 55,000 organizations now identified as social enterprises (OTS, 2006). Similarly, more than 50% of UK charity-earned income now comes from the government as contracts rather than grants – introducing business logics into philanthropic contexts (NCVO, 2008). This focus on an ideal-type organizational model drawn from business is also consistent with the Third Way ideology of the New Labour government in the UK that aimed to break down the barriers between the state, the private sector and the third sector (Giddens, 1998, 2000). The reflexive isomorphism here suggests that social entrepreneurship is a field dominated by social purpose businesses, many delivering public welfare contracts.

Community models/social change logics

The pure network organizations demonstrate a dominant internal logic focused on building community voice (Barnes, 1999). This is reflected in logics that aim to legitimate their actions in terms of maximizing community engagement and empowerment. The dominant discourse here is social justice and communitarianism. These organizations closely resemble the conventional structures of the third sector based upon equality and altruism and are self-defined in opposition to models that prioritize individuals or commercial strategies. In this case, reflexive isomorphism suggests that social entrepreneurship shares the cognitive legitimacy of the traditional third sector but with a clearer focus on innovation in goods and services.

The pure network builders have limited capital, do little grant making and lack the dissemination reach of government or marketing power of foundations. As a consequence, they cannot easily propagate their own discourses of social entrepreneurship in opposition to hero entrepreneur narratives and business model ideal-types. Resource constrained actors have two strategies with which to achieve impact. First, they can align their interests with those of more powerful, resource-rich, actors. Thus, while remaining nominally independent of the UK government, the SEC has generally aligned itself with broader policy initiatives as they emerge rather than providing a critical voice against them. Second, they can adopt resistance strategies to counter other trends in the development of the field. Reflecting this, Edwards (2008, 2010) has highlighted the struggle of traditional not-for-profit logics against a new wave of business-driven and business-supported discourses characterized as "philanthrocapitalism."

The analysis earlier suggests two features of the pre-paradigmatic development of social entrepreneurship. First, a small number of actors are shaping the discourses and institutional logics of the field to reflect their own internal logics and to align with their own legitimating norms in a process of reflexive isomorphism (see Table 10.2). Second, this is a process intrinsically connected to power and resource mobilization in which the

Table 10.2 Reflexive isomorphism in social entrepreneurship

Paradigm-building actor	Internal logic	Logic of reflexive isomorphism	Legitimating discourse
Government	Deliver public goods	Maximize efficiency, responsiveness, sustainability (cost–benefit)	Business efficiency
Foundations	Mobilize resources to bring about change	Maximize blended return on investment	Hero entrepreneur
Fellowship organizations	Build social capital	Maximize leverage effects	Hero entrepreneur
Pure network organizations	Build community voice	Maximize engagement and empowerment	Social justice

logics and discourses of those organizations that have access to the greatest resources would be expected to dominate. The four institutional logics of social entrepreneurship described earlier can be reclassified according to how they relate to providers of greater or lesser resources to field-level actors. This suggests that the logics of the hero entrepreneur working within a business (or business-like) setting will come to dominate the paradigmatic development of the field, while the logics of communitarian action linked to social justice and empowerment will become marginalized. Indeed there is already evidence of this (Dart, 2004). The implications of this for practice are profound since, as Kuhn (1962) noted, developed paradigms are, of necessity, exclusionary constructs.

In their account of the development of social entrepreneurship, Lounsbury and Strang (2009) supported this assumption by noting how resource-rich actors are shaping a new institutional logic of social action to address failures in the established bureaucracies of social welfare. This process takes concrete case study examples selectively from the field to use as "discursive fodder" to develop and support new logics that give precedence to institutional myths and narratives drawn from business and accounts of the hero entrepreneur rather than the traditions of structured collective action and solidarity. Of particular importance are success stories as legitimating material for philanthropic activity. Lounsbury and Strang saw this as a characteristically American cultural archetype combining private action and social interest. Yet, as they note, this is a model that prioritizes elites and is far from being grounded in the target communities of social entrepreneurs on the ground (see also Alvord *et al.*, 2004).

Social innovation: Toward an inclusive paradigm?

This chapter has attempted to map the microstructures of institutional legitimation in social entrepreneurship. It has proposed that social entrepreneurship is in a pre-paradigmatic state of development that allows resource-rich actors to shape its legitimation discourses in a self-reflexive way. Moreover, it has suggested that this process is prioritizing two discourses: narratives based on hero entrepreneur success stories and organizational models reflecting ideal-types from commercial business. The former supports internal logics that legitimate new venture philanthropic practices while the latter endorses internal logics that legitimate efficiency and the marketization of the state. A valid objection to the argument presented in this chapter thus far would be that it ignores the paradigm-shaping influence of scholarship itself. Indeed, this could be argued to undermine any Kuhnian analysis. To respond to this, the discussion concludes by acknowledging the role of scholarship in paradigm-building in social entrepreneurship and suggests that academic research may offer a means to resolve some of the tensions between the discourses identified earlier.[1]

The three most influential academic programs on social entrepreneurship are located in the business schools at Harvard, Duke and Oxford. Harvard Business School was the first university to establish a Social Enterprise Initiative (SEI) in 1993. The aim of the initiative was to integrate social enterprise into the MBA curriculum and build a core of cases and research in the subject across its faculty. In 2002, the Center for the Advancement of Social Entrepreneurship (CASE) was established at Duke University by a former Harvard Professor J. Gregory Dees. Finally, the Skoll Centre for Social Entrepreneurship was established with a donation from the Skoll Foundation at the Said Business School, University of Oxford in 2003. In addition to these three academic initiatives, there are two other important research networks within the social entrepreneurial space. The first is the Social Enterprise Knowledge Network (SEKN), a consortium of nine Latin American and Spanish universities linked to Harvard Business School's SEI (see above). The network was formed in 2001 and, since then, has published three books, multiple case studies and a variety of other materials. In line with the dominant logic of the SEI, SEKN has a strong focus on the role of business models in social change. The second network is EMES, a group of nine European universities researching the social economy within the Continent that has been active since 2000. The research group has a particular interest in cooperative models and work integration social enterprises and has published several books (Borzaga and Defourny, 2001; Nyssens, 2006) as well as a range of working papers and other materials.

The work of these pioneers in social entrepreneurship research has produced two different perspectives on the field. First, there is a conceptualization championed by the Harvard Business School SEI that gave precedence to the business logics and hero entrepreneur models already noted earlier. However, an alternative perspective comes from the social innovation tradition that conceptualizes social entrepreneurship as being a process of systemic change rather than a marketization of social goods. The logic of this innovation model is focused at the systems level and argues that changes in social relations represent an important part of addressing market failures in the provision of public and environmental goods (Mulgan, 2007; Nicholls and Murdock, 2011). The model also suggests that this can best be brought about by innovating third sector organizations since they stand independent of the public and private sectors the inherent inertia of whose institutional arrangements are chiefly responsible for the social market failures in the first place. A number of research centers have propagated the innovation model of social entrepreneurship including the EMES research network in Europe, the CASE at Duke University, the Skoll Centre at Oxford University and other influential bodies in the United Kingdom such as The Young Foundation, Demos and National Endowment for Science Technology and the Arts (NESTA). It is also becoming fashionable with policymakers as a solution to reducing welfare costs without reducing entitlements. The social innovation model of social entrepreneurship does not give precedence to any of the four discourses noted above and is agnostic about the role of business. The model also recognizes social innovation as being episodic and dynamic rather than as being epitomized in discrete success stories (Mulgan, 2007).

Of course, scholarship in social entrepreneurship has also been subject to the influence of resource rich providers either as direct or indirect funders or as gatekeepers to case study materials, key social entrepreneurs and other data sources. However, from a Kuhnian perspective, the paradigm of social entrepreneurship can only establish its legitimacy by means of further academic work focused on rigorous theory building and careful empirical testing. Taking a social innovation perspective offers scholars an opportunity to enact their own reflexive isomorphism based on the legitimacy of impartial research. Such work would move social entrepreneurship toward paradigmatic status without prejudicing the terms of research a priori.

Furthermore, a social innovation model of social entrepreneurship offers the opportunity to address one of the most problematic issues arising from the relationship between reflexive isomorphism and resource allocation in the development of the field to date: the relative marginalization of social entrepreneurs, their peers and – critically – their beneficiaries from the processes of legitimation at the discourse level. The marginalization of the legitimating voices of these actors can be seen as a failure of accountability on behalf of the more powerful actors that aim to build the paradigm of social entrepreneurship. Furthermore, over time, this imbalance might be expected to undermine and perhaps even destroy the normative and cognitive legitimacy of social entrepreneurship to a wider audience. While the social innovation construct may offer a space in which scholars can reconcile competing legitimating discourses around social entrepreneurship to build a new paradigm, this process can only lead to the institutionalization of the field in practical terms when the currently dominant actors are prepared to give way to a more pluralistic and grounded debate about the limits, possibilities and values of social entrepreneurship across the world (see further Nicholls and Young, 2008).

Note

*   An earlier version of this chapter was originally published in *Entrepreneurship, Theory and Practice*, 34(4): 611–633 (2010). I also wish to acknowledge and thank the comments on this work provided by Professor Sara Carter and Professor J. Gregory Dees.

1. Paradigm-building actors have also proved to be influential in supporting academic initiatives either through direct funding or though providing access to case material and data leading to the possibility of assimilation or capture of the internal logics of scholarship. Indeed, the assumption that academics are immune to reflexive isomorphism themselves remains unsupported.

References

Abbott, A. (1988). *The System of Professions*. Chicago: University of Chicago Press.

Aiken, M. (2006). "Towards Market or State? Tensions and Opportunities in the Evolutionary Path of Three Types of UK Social Enterprise." In M. Nyssens (ed.), *Towards Market or State? Tensions and Opportunities in the Evolutionary Path of Three UK Social Enterprises*. London: Routledge, pp. 259271.

Aldrich, H. and Baker, T. (1997). "Blinded by the Cities? Has There Been Progress in Entrepreneurship Research?" In D. Sexton and R. Smilor (Eds.), *Entrepreneurship 2000*. Chicago: Upstart Publishing, pp. 377–400.

Aldrich, H. and Fiol, C. (1994). "Fools Rush In? The Institutional Context of Industry Creation." *Academy of Management Review* 19: 645–670.

Alter, K. (2006). *A Social Enterprise Typology*, www.virtueventures.com/typology.php

Alvord, S., Brown, L., and Letts, C. (2004). "Social Entrepreneurship and Societal Transformation: An Exploratory Study." *Journal of Applied Behavioral Science*, 40(3): 260–283.

Ashforth, B. and Gibbs, B. (1990). "The Double Edge of Organizational Legitimation." *Organization Science*, 1, 177–194.

Austin, J., Gutierrez, R., and Ogliastri, E. (2006). *Effective Management of Social Enterprises: Lessons from Business and Civil Society Organizations in Ibero-America*. Cambridge, MA: Harvard University.

Barnes, M. (1999). "Users as Citizens: Collective Action and the Local Governance of Welfare." *Social Policy and Administration*, 33(1), 73–90.

Battle Anderson, B. and Dees, J.G. (2006). "Rhetoric, Reality, and Research: Building a Solid Foundation for the Practice of Social Entrepreneurship." In A. Nicholls (Ed.), *Social Entrepreneurship: New Paradigms of Sustainable Social Change*. Oxford: Oxford University Press, pp. 144–168.

Baum, J. and Powell, W. (1995). "Cultivating An Institutional Ecology of Organizations: Comment on Hannan, Carroll, Dundon, and Torres." *American Sociological Review*, 60: 529–538.

Blair, T. (2006). *OTS (Office of the Third Sector) (2006), Social Enterprise Action Plan: Scaling New Heights*. London: Cabinet Office.

Bornstein, D. (2004). *How to Change the World: Social Entrepreneurs and the Power of New Ideas*. Oxford: Oxford University Press.

Borzaga, C. and Defourny, J. (2001). *The Emergence of Social Enterprise*. New York: Routledge.

Bourdieu, P. (1993). *The Field of Cultural Production: Essays on Art and Literature*. Cambridge: Polity Press.

Bovaird, T. (2006). "Developing New Relationships with the 'Market' in the Procurement of Public Services." *Public Administration*, 84(1): 81–102.

Busenitz, L., Page West, G., Shepherd, D., Nelson, T., Chandler, G., and Zacharakis, A. (2003). "Entrepreneurship Research in Emergence: Past Trends and Future Directions." *Journal of Management*, 29(3): 285–308.

Carter, S. and Deephouse, D. (1999). "'Tough Talk' Or 'Soothing Speech': Managing Reputations for Being Tough and Being Good." *Corporate Reputation Review*, 2: 308–332.

Clotfelter, C. (Ed.). (1992). *Who Benefits from the Nonprofit Sector?* Chicago: University of Chicago Press.

Dart, R. (2004). "The Legitimacy of Social Enterprise." *Nonprofit Management and Leadership*, 14(4), 411–424.

Davis, G., McAdam, D., Scott, W., and Zald, M. (2005). *Social Movements and Organization Theory*. Cambridge: Cambridge University Press.

Deephouse, D. (1996). "Does Isomorphism Legitimate?" *Academy of Management Journal*, 39(4): 1024–1039.

Deephouse, D. and Suchman, M. (2008). "Legitimacy in Organizational Institutionalism." In R. Greenwood, C. Oliver, K. Sahlin, and R. Suddaby (Eds.), *The Sage Handbook of Organizational Institutionalism*. London: Sage, pp. 49–77.

DiMaggio, P. and Powell, W. (1983). "The Iron Cage Revisited: Institutional Isomorphism and Collective Rationality in Organizational Fields." *American Sociological Review*, 48: 147–60.

DiMaggio, P. and Powell, W. (1991). "Introduction." In P. Di Maggio and W. Powell (Eds.), *The New Institutionalism in Organisational Analysis*. Chicago: University of Chicago Press, pp. 1–40.

Dowling, J. and Pfeffer, J. (1975). "Organizational Legitimacy: Social Values and Organizational Behavior." *Pacific Sociological Review*, 18: 122–136.

Edwards, M. (2008). *Just Another Emperor? The Myths and Realities of Philanthrocapitalism*. London: The Young Foundation/Demos.

Edwards, M. (2010). *Small Change: Why Business Won't Save the World*. San Francisco, CA: Berrett-Koehler.

Elkington, J. and Hartigan, P. (2008). *The Power of Unreasonable People*. Cambridge, MA: Harvard Business School Press.

Elsbach, K. (1994). "Managing Organizational Legitimacy in the California Cattle Industry: the Construction and Effectiveness of Verbal Accounts." *Administrative Science Quarterly*, 39: 57–88.

Elsbach, K. and Sutton, R. (1992). "Acquiring Organizational Legitimacy through Illegitimate Actions: a Marriage of Institutional and Impression Management Theories." *Academy of Management Journal*, 35: 699–738.

Evers, A. and Laville, J.-L. (2004). *The Third Sector in Europe*. London: Edward Elgar.

Friedland, R. and Alford, R. (1991). "Bringing Society Back in: Symbols, Practices and Institutional Contradictions." In P. Di Maggio and W. Powell (Eds.), *The New Institutionalism in Organizational Analysis*. Chicago: University of Chicago Press, pp. 232–263.

Galaskiewicz, J. (1985). "Interorganizational Relations." *Annual Review of Sociology*, 11: 281–304.

Giddens, A. (1984). *The Constitution of Society*. Berkeley, CA: University of California Press.

Giddens, A. (1998). *The Third Way*. Cambridge: Polity Press.

Giddens, A. (2000). *The Third Way and Its Critics*. Cambridge: Polity Press.

Grenier, P. (2006). "Social Entrepreneurship: Agency in a Globalizing World." In A. Nicholls (Ed.), *Social Entrepreneurship: New Paradigms of Sustainable Social Change*. Oxford: Oxford University Press, pp. 119–143.

Hargens, L. (1988). "Scholarly Consensus and Journal Rejection Rates." *American Sociological Review*, 53, 139–151.

Hargrave, T. and Van der Ven, A. (2006). "a Collective Action Model of Institutional Innovation." *Academy of Management Review*, 31(4): 864–888.

Harrison, R. and Leitch, C. (1996). "Discipline Emergence in Entrepreneurship: Accumulative Fragmentalism Or Paradigmatic Science." *Entrepreneurship, Innovation and Change*, 5(2): 65–83.

Hybels, R. (1995). "On Legitimacy, Legitimation, and Organizations: a Critical Review and Integrative Theoretical Model." *Best Paper Proceedings of the Academy of Management*, 241–245.

Kaplan, S. (2008). "Framing Contests: Strategy Making Under Uncertainty." *Organization Science*, 19: 729–752.

Kuhn, T. (1962). *The Structure of Scientific Revolutions*. Chicago: University of Chicago Press.

Leadbeater, C. (1997). *The Rise of the Social Entrepreneur*. London: Demos.

LeGrand, J. (2003). *Motivation, Agency, and Public Policy. of Knights and Knaves, Pawns and Queens*. Oxford: Oxford University Press.

LeGrand, J. and Bartlett, W. (Eds.). (1993). *Quasi-Markets and Social Policy*. London: Palgrave Macmillan.

Light, P. (2006). "Reshaping Social Entrepreneurship." *Stanford Social Innovation Review* Fall: 47–51.

Light, P. (2008). *The Search for Social Entrepreneurship*. Washington, DC: Brookings.

Lodahl, J. and Gordon, G. (1972). "The Structure of Scientific Fields and the Functioning of University Graduate Departments." *American Sociological Review*, 37: 57–72.

Lodahl, J. and Gordon, G. (1973). "Differences between Physical and Social Sciences in University Graduate Departments." *Research in Higher Education*, 1: 191–213.

Lounsbury, M. (2007). "a Tale of Two Cities: Competing Logics and Practice Variation in the Professionalizing of Mutual Funds." *Academy of Management Journal*, 50: 289–330.

Lounsbury, M. and Glynn, M.A. (2001). "Cultural Entrepreneurship: Stories, Legitimacy, and the Acquisition of Resources." *Strategic Management Journal*, 22, 545–564.

Lounsbury, M. and Strang, D. (2009). "Social Entrepreneurship. Success Stories and Logic Construction." In D. Hammack and S. Heydemann (Eds.), *Globalization, Philanthropy, and Civil Society*. Bloomington, IN: Indiana University Press, pp. 71–94.

Lukes, S. (1974). *Power: a Radical View*. London: Macmillan.

Maturana, H. and Varela, F. (1973). *Autopoiesis and Cognition: The Realization of the Living*. Dordrecht: Kluwer.

Meyer, J. and Rowan, B. (1977). "Institutionalised Organisations: Formal Structure as Myth and Ceremony." *American Journal of Sociology*, 83: 340–363.

Meyer, J. and Scott, W. (1983). "Centralization and the Legitimacy Problems of Local Government." In J.W. Meyer and W.R. Scott (Eds.), *Organizational Environments: Ritual and Rationality*. London: Sage, pp. 199–215.

Meyer, J., Scott, R., Cole, S., and Intili, J. (1978). "Instructional Dissensus and Institutional Consensus in Schools." In M. Meyer (Ed.), *Environments and Organizations*. San Francisco, CA: Jossey-Bass, pp. 290–305.

Meyer, J., Scott, R., and Deal, T. (1981). "Institutional and Technical Sources of Organizational Structure: Explaining the Structure of Organizations." In H. Stein (Ed.), *Organization and the Human Services*. Philadelphia, PA: Temple University Press, pp. 151–178.

Morgan, G. (2006). *Images of Organization*. London: Sage.

Mulgan, G. (2007). *Social innovation*. Skoll Centre for Social Entrepreneurship, www.sbs.ox.ac.uk/skoll/research/Short+papers/Short+papers.htm

NCVO (National Council of Voluntary Organizations). (2008). *uk Voluntary Sector Almanac 2007*. London: National Council of Voluntary Organizations.

Nicholls, A. (2006a). "Playing the Field: a New Approach to the Meaning of Social Entrepreneurship." *Social Enterprise Journal*, 2(1): 1–5.

Nicholls, A. (2006b). "Introduction: the Meanings of Social Entrepreneurship." In A. Nicholls (Ed.), *Social Entrepreneurship: New Paradigms of Sustainable Social Change*. Oxford: Oxford University Press, pp. 1–36.

Nicholls, A. (2008). "Capturing the Performance of the Socially Entrepreneurial Organisation (seo): An Organisational Legitimacy Approach." In J. Robinson, J. Mair, and K. Hockerts (Eds.), *International Perspectives on Social Entrepreneurship Research*. London: Palgrave Macmillan.

Nicholls, A. (2009). "Learning to Walk: Social Entrepreneurship". *Innovations*: Special Edition Skoll World Forum: 209–222.

Nicholls, A. (2010a). "What Gives Fair Trade Its Right to Operate? Organisational Legitimacy and the Strategic Management of Social Entrepreneurship." In K. Macdonald and S. Marshall (Eds.), *Fair Trade Corporate Accountability and beyond: Experiments in Global Justice Governance Mechanisms*. London: Ashgate, pp. 95–121.

Nicholls, A. (2010b). "Institutionalizing Social Entrepreneurship in Regulatory Space: Reporting and Disclosure by Community Interest Companies." *Accounting, Organizations and Society*, 35: 394–415.

Nicholls, A. (2010c). "The Institutionalization of Social Investment: the Interplay of Investment Logics and Investor Rationalities." *Journal of Social Entrepreneurship*, 1(1): 70–100.

Nicholls, A. and Cho, A. (2006). "Social Entrepreneurship: the Structuration of a Field." In A. Nicholls (Ed.), *Social Entrepreneurship: New Paradigms of Sustainable Social Change*. Oxford: Oxford University Press, pp. 99–118.

Nicholls, A., and Murdock, A. (2011). *Social Innovation*, London: Palgrave Macmillan.

Nicholls, A. and Pharoah, C. (2007). *The Landscape of Social Finance*. Oxford: Skoll Centre for Social Entrepreneurship, www.sbs.ox.ac.uk/centres/skoll/research /Pages/socialfinance.aspx

Nicholls, A. and Young, R. (2008). "Introduction: the Changing Landscape of Social Entrepreneurship." In A. Nicholls (Ed.), *Social Entrepreneurship: New Paradigms of Sustainable Social Change*. Oxford: Oxford University Press: vii–xxiii.

Nyssens, M. (Ed.). (2006). *Social Enterprise*. London: Routledge.

Oliver, C. (1997). "Sustainable Competitive Advantage: Combining Institutional and Resource-Based Views." *Strategic Management Journal*, 18: 697–713.

Osberg, S. and Martin, R. (2007). "Social Entrepreneurship: the Case for Definition." *Stanford Social Innovation Review*, Spring: 28–39.

Osbourne, D. and Gaebler, T. (1992). *Reinventing Government*. Reading, MA: Addison-Wesley.

OTS (Office of the Third Sector). (2006). *Social Enterprise Action Plan: Scaling New Heights*. London: Office of The Third Sector.

Peredo, A. and McLean, M. (2006). "Social Entrepreneurship: a Critical Review of the Concept." *Journal of World Business*, 41: 56–65.

Perrini, F. (Ed.). (2006). *The New Social Entrepreneurship: What Awaits Social Entrepreneurship Ventures?* Cheltenham, UK: Edward Elgar.

Pfeffer, J. (1993). "Barriers to the Advance of Organizational Science: Paradigm Development as a Dependent Variable." *Academy of Management Review*, 18(4): 599–620.

Pfeffer, J. and Moore, W. (1980). "Power in University Budgeting: a Replication and Extension." *Administrative Science Quarterly*, 25: 637–653.

Pfeffer, J. and Salancik, G. (1978). *The External Control of Organizations: a Resource Dependency Perspective*. New York: Harper Row.

Phillips, N., Lawrence, T., and Hardy, C. (2004). "Discourse and Institutions." *Academy of Management Review*, 29: 635–652.

Prahalad, C.K. (2005). *The Fortune at the Bottom of the Pyramid: Eradicating Poverty through Profit*. Philadelphia: University of Pennsylvania, Wharton School Publishing.

Rao, H. (1994). "The Social Construction of Reputation: Certification Contests, Legitimation, and the Survival of Organizations in the American Automobile Industry 1895–1912." *Strategic Management Journal*, 15: 29–44.

Roth, G. and Wittich, C. (Eds.). (1978). *Economy and society*. San Francisco: University of California Press.

Ruef, M. and Scott, W. (1998). "a Multidimensional Model of Organizational Legitimacy: Hospital Survival in Changing Institutional Environments." *Administrative Science Quarterly*, 43, 877–904.

Salamon, L. and Anheier, H. (1999). *The Emerging Sector Revisited*. Baltimore, MD: Johns Hopkins University.

Salamon, L., Anheier, H., List, R., Toepler, S., and Sokolowski, S. (Eds.). (2003). *Global Civil Society: Dimensions of the Nonprofit Sector*. Baltimore, MD: Johns Hopkins University.

Scott, W.R. (1995). *Institutions and Organizations*. San Francisco, CA: Sage.

Shaw, E. and Carter, S. (2007). "Social Entrepreneurship; Theoretical Antecedents and Empirical Analysis of Entrepreneurial Processes and Outcomes." *Journal of Small Business and Enterprise Development*, 14(3): 418–429.

Short, J., Moss, T., and Lumpkin, G. (2009). "Research in Social Entrepreneurship: Past Contributions and Future Opportunities." *Strategic Entrepreneurship Journal*, 3, 161–194.

Singh, J., Tucker, D., and House, R. (1986). "Organizational Legitimacy and the Liability of Newness." *Administrative Science Quarterly*, 31: 171–193.

Social Enterprise Unit. (2002). *Social Enterprise: a Strategy for Success*. London: Department for Trade and Industry.

Stryker, R. (2000). "Legitimacy Processes as Institutional Politics: Implications for Theory and Research in the Sociology of Organizations." *Research in the Sociology of Organizations*, 17: 179–223.

Suchman, M. (1995). "Managing Legitimacy: Strategic and Institutional Approaches." *Academy of Management Review*, 20: 517–610.

Suddaby, R. and Greenwood, R. (2005). "Rhetorical Strategies of Legitimacy." *Administrative Science Quarterly*, 50: 35–67.

Sullivan Mort, G., Weerawardena, J., and Carnegie, K. (2003). "Social Entrepreneurship: towards Conceptualisation." *International Journal of Nonprofit and Voluntary Sector Marketing*, 8(1): 76–88.

Vaara, E., Tienari, J., and Laurila, J. (2006). "Pulp and Paper Fiction: on the Discursive Legitimation of Global Industrial Restructuring." *Organization Studies*, 27: 789–810.

Walsh, K. (1995). *Public Services and Market Mechanisms. Competition, Contracting, and the New Public Management*. London: Palgrave Macmillan.

Weerawardena, J. and Sullivan Mort, G. (2006). "Investigating Social Entrepreneurship: a Multidimensional Model." *Journal of World Business*, 41: 21–35.

Yoels, W. (1974). "The Structure of Scientific Fields and the Allocation of Editorships on Scientific Journals: Some Observations on the Politics of Knowledge." *Sociological Quarterly*, 15: 264–276.

Yunus, M. (2008). *Creating a World without Poverty: Social Business and the Future of Capitalism.* New York: Public Affairs.

Zimmerman, M. and Zeitz, G. (2002). "Beyond Survival: Achieving New Venture Growth by Building Legitimacy." *Academy of Management Review*, 27(3): 414–431.

Zucker, L. (1977). "The Role of Institutionalization in Cultural Persistence." *American Journal of Sociology*, 42: 726–743.

Index